NEW YORK HISTORY

HISTORY

WINTER 2022–2023

The New York State Museum is a program of The University of the State of New York | The State Education Department | Office of Cultural Education

New York History (ISSN 0146-437x) is a peer reviewed journal published two times a year by Cornell University Press in partnership with The New York State Museum. Postage is paid at Ithaca, NY 14850 and additional mailing offices. POSTMASTER: Send all address changes to Cornell University Press, 512 East State Street, Ithaca NY 14850.

New York History is available in print and electronically Project Muse (http://muse.jhu.edu). Cornell University Press does not assume responsibility for statements of fact or opinions made by contributors. Unlicensed distribution of all materials (including figures, tables, and other content) is prohibited. Communications about subscriptions, back issues, reproductions and permissions, and other business matters should be sent to Cornell University Press (nyhjournal@cornell.edu). Digital and print subscriptions, for individuals and institutions, may be ordered via Project Muse (https://www.press.jhu.edu /cart/for-sale?oc=3729). Single print copies and print back issues are available for $20.00 and check should be made out to Cornell University Press. For subscriptions and individual issues, inquiries and orders may be made by email, nyhjournal @cornell.edu, or by mail: *New York History* Journal, Cornell University Press, 512 East State Street, Ithaca NY 14850.

Submitted articles should address, in an original fashion, some aspect of New York State history. Articles that deal with the history of other areas or with general American history must have a direct bearing on New York State history. It is assumed that the article will have some new, previously unexploited material to offer or will present new insights or new interpretations. Editorial communications, including article submissions, should be sent to the Editorial Board via email (NYHJ @nysed.gov) Suggested length is 20-30 double spaced pages (or between 6,000 and 9,000 words), including footnotes. All submitted articles must include a 100-word abstract summarizing the article and providing keywords (no more than 10). Authors must submit articles electronically, with all text in Word and all tables, figures, and images in formats supported by Microsoft Windows. Provision of images in proper resolution (no less than 300 dpi at 5" x 7"), securing requisite permissions, and the payment of any fees associated with images for articles are all the responsibility of the author. *New York History* employs, with some modification, footnote forms suggested in the *Chicago Manual of Style*. More detailed submissions guidelines are to be found on the research and collections page of the New York State Museum: http://www.nysm.nysed.gov/research-collections/state-history/resources/new-york-history-journal

Cover art: *Front*: Workers from Shreve Harmon and Lamb Company building the Empire State Building, 34th Street and Fifth Avenue, 1930. Photograph by Irving Browning. *Back*: Manhattan Skyline and Brooklyn Bridge at night, ca. 1929. Photograph by Irving Browning. Both photographs are courtesy of the New York State Museum, donation in memory of Paul and Gertrude Meistrich and Sue Ben-Dor.

CONTENTS

Volume 103, Number 2

BOOK REVIEWS

LETTER FROM THE EDITORS

Robert Chiles, Devin R. Lander, Jennifer Lemak, and Aaron Noble

One charming yet challenging element of studying New York is the centrality of its history to the broader sweep of American life. This prominence leaves many episodes in New York's past well-known and intensely studied. However, this issue of *New York History* reminds us that innovative methodologies and new documentary evidence ceaselessly open opportunities for fresh insights into the Empire State's rich past—from the social history of New Netherland to mid-twentieth-century design.

In "Dutch *Ladinos/as*?: An Iberian Perspective on the Social and Religious Behavior of New Netherland's Black Population," Jeroen Dewulf adopts a transatlantic perspective on Manhattan's first Black community, revealing that while many of the religious practices of New Netherland's enslaved population appear exceptional in a North American context, numerous elements correspond to patterns found in slave societies of the Iberian world. Considering the diplomatic vicissitudes of the Seven Years' War through the unique lens of epidemiology, John Booss argues in "Fear and Betrayal: Smallpox and the Turning Point of the French and Indian War" that the conflict

actually pivoted on the smallpox epidemic that devastated the tribes in the Pays d'en Haut, elevated Indigenous suspicions of the French, and frayed the crucial Franco-Native alliance by 1758. Reassessing the role of Revolutionary-era committees of safety by analyzing their wartime activities in Westchester County, Dillon Streifeneder argues in "War Comes to Westchester: The Killing of William Lounsbury" that under the stress of British invasion such committees transformed from political organizations into the first war-making institutions of a nascent state

Nineteenth-century New York offers similarly fertile ground for revision. In "Supplanted Sovereignties: Gateways, Commerce, and Dispossession in Postrevolutionary New York," Nolan M. Cool reinterprets Utica's emergence as a commercial center by 1800 as a revealing example of westward-facing commercial ambitions overthrowing a more nuanced, earlier system of diplomacy, accommodation, and Native American sovereignty. Exploring New York's history a half-century later and half a state to the west, Paul C. King's "Roebling's Niagara Railway Suspension Bridge" contextualizes the visually familiar bridges of John A. Roebling through comparison of his methods with those of contemporaries like Charles Ellet Jr., marking Roebling's Niagara triumph as a turning point in his rise to prominence.

This issue's articles also show how new evidence and assiduous, granular analysis can be employed to challenge old assumptions about the lives and experiences of New Yorkers at the grassroots level. Daniel Koch meticulously reconstructs the urban geography of turn-of-the-century Syracuse in "Working-Class Germans in the Salt City: Syracuse, New York, 1860–1916," enriching our understanding of immigrant lives by recovering neglected features of the laboring community that were intentionally ignored in laudatory narratives centered on the success of "model" German immigrants. In "Goodbye Old 1910: Encounters with the Market in the 1910 Diary of a Rural New York Woman," Hamilton Craig explores the diary of Mary Brainard, a farm woman from Wilton, to reveal through her day-to-day reflections how some rural New Yorkers resisted centralizing market forces by relying on existing networks and resources while adapting some traditions to survive in the face of economic change.

Our two features in this issue also offer new angles on recognizable materials. Zachary Deibel's Teach NY feature curates a set of documents on the development of Franklin Delano Roosevelt's New Deal within New York State. The documents are accompanied by a series of analytical prompts that can be used to prepare students for the Regents Exam's civic engagement essay. Jennifer Lemak's Artifact NY feature uses modern flatware as an entry point for exploring the innovative career of the Albany-born artist and industrial designer Marion Weeber and analyzing how her stainless-steel utensils reflect the historic intersection of technology, consumerism, and aesthetics in the twentieth century.

We are pleased to present this issue of *New York History*, which once again reminds us of the diverse opportunities to tell new, vibrant, inclusive, and enlightening stories about our state's past.

Excelsior!
The Editors

JOHN BOOSS

NOLAN M. COOL

HAMILTON CRAIG

John Booss has had a long-standing interest in viruses. With Margaret. M. Esiri he published *Viral Encephalitis in Humans* (1986; and ASM Press, 2003). In *To Catch a Virus*, he examined with Marilyn J. August how viral infections are recognized and diagnosed (ASM Press, 2013). A second edition of this book, with Marie Louise Landry, was published in October 2022. His articles examine the ways in which epidemics among Native Americans have changed history: "Survival of the Pilgrims: A Reevaluation of the Lethal epidemic among the Wampanoag," *Historical Journal of Massachusetts* 47, no. 1 (Winter 2019); and with Melanie J. Norton, "Missionaries, Measles, and Manuscripts: Revisiting the Whitman Tragedy," *Journal of the Medical Library Association* 107, no. 1 (January 2019). Booss is Professor Emeritus at Yale University and former National Program Director, Neurology Service, with the Department of Veterans Affairs.

Nolan M. Cool is Educational Programs Director at Adirondack Architectural Heritage (AARCH), the nonprofit historic preservation organization for New York's Adirondack region. As a public historian, Nolan is passionate about exploring how communities preserve, remember, and use history and historic places to connect past and present. He completed his graduate work in the Public History Program at the University of Massachusetts at Amherst, and he holds an undergraduate degree from Utica College (now Utica University). Nolan's scholarly work focuses largely on the socioeconomic material culture of eighteenth-century New York. Visit https://aarch.org/ to learn more about Adirondack Architectural Heritage's work.

Hamilton Craig is a PhD student in American history at the City University of New York Graduate Center. His research is focused on rural attitudes toward the free market in the nineteenth and twentieth centuries. His article, "Close Community: Rural Working-Class Culture in the 1910 Hudson River Mill Strike," was published in *Tufts Historical Review* 13 (Spring 2021).

ZACHARY DEIBEL

Zachary Deibel is a doctoral candidate in history at Binghamton University, where he studies the history of learning, state formation, and education in eighteenth-century New York. He has taught high school and college history courses for the past ten years, and he is a graduate student intern at *New York History*.

JEROEN DEWULF

Jeroen Dewulf is Queen Beatrix Professor in Dutch Studies in the Department of German at UC Berkeley. He is also director of UC Berkeley's Institute of European Studies and its Center for Portuguese Studies. His most recent book publications include: *The Pinkster King and the King of Kongo* (, 2017) and *From the Kingdom of Kongo to Congo Square* (University of Louisiana at Lafayette Press, 2017). His latest book, *Afro-Atlantic Catholics*, was published in August 2022 by Notre Dame University Press.

PAUL C. KING

Paul C. King, Professor of Architectural Technology at New York City College of Technology, is a licensed architect with degrees in architecture, landscape architecture, and urban design. In demand as a presenter, his research focus is on the early work of John A. Roebling, the most influential American engineer of the nineteenth century. Accepted for publication, his manuscript titled "Roebling: Before the Bridge" focuses on the evolution of Roebling's technical innovations present in his early work and embodied in the design of his final work, the Brooklyn Bridge.

DANIEL KOCH

JENNIFER LEMAK

DILLON STREIFENEDER

Daniel Koch is Headmaster of Loughborough Grammar School, founded in 1495, in Leicestershire, England. He is originally from central New York and studied History and Modern Languages at the State University of New York at Albany before completing his doctoral studies at the University of Oxford. He is the author of *Ralph Waldo Emerson in Europe: Class, Race, and Revolution in the Making of an American Thinker* (I. B. Tauris, 2012). His second book, *Land of the Oneidas*, a history of central New York from its prehistory to the present, will be published by SUNY Press later this year.

Jennifer Lemak is the chief curator of history at the New York State Museum. Prior to this appointment, she served there as senior historian/curator of social history. Major exhibition and publication projects include *Votes for Women: Celebrating New York's Suffrage Centennial* (2017) and *An Irrepressible Conflict: The Empire State in the Civil War* (2012). Lemak is the author of *Southern Life, Northern City: The History of Albany's Rapp Road* (SUNY Press, 2008) and several articles on the Great Migration to Upstate New York.

Dillon Streifeneder is a historian of colonial America and the early American republic. His current project focuses on state formation and governance in New York during the era of the American Revolution. Streifeneder recently completed his PhD in early American history at the Ohio State University.

Dutch *Ladinos/as*?

An Iberian Perspective on the Social and Religious Behavior of New Netherland's Black Population

Jeroen Dewulf

It must have been surprising news for the Dutch admiral Michiel de Ruyter when, during a 1664 campaign near the island of Gorée (in today's Senegal), he was informed that a local African man wished to speak with him about his youth in Zeeland. De Ruyter immediately recognized the man, whom he had met many years ago in his native Flushing (Vlissingen) and with whom he had started his seafaring career as a boatswain's apprentice. Known by the Dutch name Jan Kompany, the man had been enslaved as a child in Africa; he had acquired his freedom upon arriving in Flushing, had learned to speak Dutch, was baptized as a Protestant Christian, and then worked as a sailor on Dutch ships until he decided to return to Africa, where he became an influential viceroy.[1]

Being fluent in Dutch, baptized in the Reformed Church, and familiar with Dutch customs, Kompany was the prototype of a person who, in an Iberian colonial context, was known as a *ladino*, an African who adopted Iberian identity markers and assimilated in accordance with Iberian standards of civilization. While the concept of becoming a *ladino* (male) or *ladina* (female) is considered of key importance to the understanding of slave societies in Iberian colonies, it has rarely been applied to the analysis of colonies outside of Latin America. This is unfortunate considering that the Dutch, English, French, and other Northern Europeans were relative latecomers to the Americas and, despite their anti-Iberian rhetoric, they emulated many Spanish and Portuguese practices.[2] Not by

---

1. Gerard Brandt, *Het leven en bedryf van den heere Michiel de Ruiter, hertog, ridder, &c. l. admiraal generaal van Hollandt en Westvrieslandt* (Amsterdam: Wolfgang, Waasberge, Boom, Van Someren en Goethals, 1687), 6, 313. Unless otherwise noted, all translations are my own.
2. For the case of New Netherland, see Jeroen Dewulf, "Emulating a Portuguese Model: The Slave Policy of the West India Company and the Dutch Reformed Church in Dutch Brazil (1630–1654) and New Netherland (1614–1664) in Comparative Perspective," *Journal of Early American History* 4 (2014): 3–36.

accident, thus, we find references in the Dutch colony of Curaçao to "een ladinsche slaaf" (a *ladino* slave).[3]

The goal of this article is to apply the concept of becoming *ladino/a* to the Black community in New Netherland and to acquire a better understanding of the community's social and religious behavior by analyzing them as people aspiring to be recognized and treated as *ladinos/as*. This methodological approach can be justified with reference to the fact that virtually the entire enslaved population in New Netherland originated from the Iberian Peninsula, Latin America, or a region in Africa with a historically strong Portuguese influence and is likely to have shared (some degree of) familiarity with Iberian customs. There are, thus, good reasons to study the seventeenth-century slave society in New Netherland from a broader, Atlantic perspective.

Portuguese Language

In her influential study *Trabelin' On*, Mechal Sobel studied the Christianization process of North America's Black population in parallel to its acquisition of the English language. She did so by building on Joey Lee Dillard's linguistic research on the history of African American Vernacular English and his identification of three phrases: one in which Black people still communicated in indigenous African languages, one in which they used an African American pidgin English, and a third in which they spoke African American Vernacular English. According to Sobel, the Christianization of North America's Black population followed a similar evolution.[4]

Sobel's decision to study the Christianization process of African Americans in connection to their use of the English language is problematic since it ignores other languages, most notably French and Spanish, and thereby unavoidably presents an Anglocentric perspective that privileges Protestant Christianity. Even if we decide to follow a traditional approach by studying the history of the United States with a focus on the original thirteen states, Sobel's methodology remains questionable. In fact, sources from New Netherland reveal that we make a mistake by assuming that the earliest enslaved Africans to arrive in North America, the so-called charter generations, communicated only in indigenous languages.

For instance, a 1662 court case shows that Resolveert Waldron, a Dutch settler in New Amsterdam, and an enslaved Black man called Mattheu "spoke Portuguese to each other."[5] The same Mattheu was also involved in another case, in which he, together with a certain Swan (probably João or Juan) and Frans (whose original name was Francisco), requested that

---

3. A. F. Paula, ed., *1795: De slavenopstand op Curaçao: Een bronnenuitgave van de originele overheidsdocumenten* (Curaçao: Centraal Historisch Archief, 1974), 65.
4. Mechal Sobel, *Trabelin' On: The Slave Journey to an Afro-Baptist Faith* (Westport, CT: Greenwood Press, 1979), xxiii.
5. Berthold Fernow, ed., *The Records of New Amsterdam from 1653 to 1674*, 7 vols. (New York: Knickerbocker Press, 1897), 4:56–57.

Waldron be their interpreter in court.[6] While the language Waldron had to speak in court is not specified, it is likely to have been Portuguese since he had previously lived in Dutch Brazil.[7]

A similar case is that of the Dutch captain J(oh)an de Vries, who had served at least ten years in Dutch Brazil before coming to New Netherland in 1645. He brought with him a Black female, Elary d'Crioole, who had previously worked at the house of a Portuguese family in São Luís do Maranhão. De Vries later fathered a child with the Brazilian *swartinne* (Black woman) who had accompanied him to North America. The likelihood that de Vries spoke (some) Portuguese may account for his proximity to the Black population. He leased land to several of them and stood up in church as godfather to their children.[8]

The importance of the Portuguese language to the Black community in seventeenth-century North America can also be illustrated with a case from Northampton, Virginia, in which the charter generation consisted mainly of Africans Edmund Scarborough had bought in New Amsterdam.[9] In 1667, a certain Fernando filed a lawsuit in Northampton, claiming that he "was a Christian" and presenting "severall papers in Portugell or some other language which the Court could not understand."[10] The latter are likely to have been *cartas de alforria*, letters that confirmed Fernando's manumission.[11]

The only recorded words of a Black person in New Netherland are unmistakably of

---

6. Fernow, 4:41–42, 56–57.

7. Jasper Dankers and Peter Sluyter, *Journal of a Voyage to New York and a Tour in Several of the American Colonies in 1679–80*, ed. Henry Murphy (Brooklyn, NY: Long Island Historical Society, 1867), 137.

8. Johannes de Laet, *Iaerlyck verhael van de verrichtingen der Geocroyeerde West-Indische Compagnie*, ed. S. P. L'Honoré Naber and J. C. M. Warnsinck, 4 vols. (The Hague: M. Nijhoff, 1931-37), 2:146, 3:209, 4:13; Edmund B. O'Callaghan, Berthold Fernow, and John R. Brodhead, eds., *Documents Relative to the Colonial History of the State of New York*, 15 vols. (Albany, NY: Weed, Parsons & Company, 1853–87), 13:142–43, 152, 273, 328, 330, 338, and 14:52; Thomas Grier Evans, ed., *Records of the Reformed Dutch Church in New Amsterdam and New York: Baptisms from 25 December 1639 to 27 December 1730* (New York: Clearfield Co., 1901), 21–23; Arnold J. F. Van Laer, ed., *New York Historical Manuscripts: Dutch*, Vol. 4, *Council Minutes, 1638–1649* (Baltimore, MD: Genealogical Publishing, 1974), 333; Charles T. Gehring, ed., *Council Minutes, 1652–1654: New York Historical Manuscripts* (Baltimore, MD: Genealogical Publishing, 1983), 129–30; Peter R. Christoph, "The Freedmen of New Amsterdam," in *A Beautiful and Fruitful Place: Selected Rensselaerswijck Seminar Papers*, ed. Nancy A. M. Zeller (New York: New Netherland Publishing, 1991), 129–30; Susanah Shaw Romney, *New Netherland Connections: Intimate Networks and Atlantic Ties in Seventeenth-Century America* (Chapel Hill: University of North Carolina Press, 2014), 215–17.

9. Charles T. Gehring, ed., *Council Minutes, 1655–1656* (Syracuse, NY: Syracuse University Press, 1995), 77; Elizabeth Donnan, ed., *Documents Illustrative of the History of the Slave Trade to America*, 4 vols. (Washington, DC: Carnegie Institute, 1930–35), 3:414–15, 4:49–50; T. H. Breen and Stephen Innes, *"Myne Owne Ground": Race and Freedom on Virginia's Eastern Shore, 1640–1676* (New York: Oxford University Press, 1980), 71.

10. Warren M. Billings, ed., *The Old Dominion in the Seventeenth Century: A Documentary History of Virginia, 1606–1700* (Chapel Hill: University of North Carolina Press, 2007), 200.

11. Jean-Baptiste Du Tertre's seventeenth-century study on the history of the French Antilles reveals that it was not uncommon for Dutch privateers to sell Black people "of free condition" whom they had captured on Iberian vessels. See Jean-Baptiste Du Tertre, *Histoire générale des Antilles habitées par les françois*, 4 vols. (Paris: Thomas Iolly, 1667–1671), 2:494.

Iberian origin. In 1655, Teunis Kraey bought a Black female, who, on their way home, "fell to the ground" and, after shouting the word "*ariba*," lifted herself up again. But "10 to 12 paces farther on," she fell again, "with eyes turning around in her head and white on her mouth," as Kraey described it. When asked what ailed her, "the woman said *more! more!*, while pointing at her breast and legs." She died soon after.[12] The term *more* is most likely the Portuguese third-person singular form *morre* (of *morrer*; to die), whereas *ariba* relates to the Spanish/Portuguese *arriba!* (up!), which may have been spoken by the woman to give herself the courage to stand up again.[13]

These examples reveal the importance to the Black population in New Netherland of Portuguese or, more likely, an Afro-Portuguese pidgin, which raises questions about Sobel's methodology and her decision to begin the history of Black Christianity in North America with eighteenth-century Anglo-Saxon, Protestant missionary work. What the case of New Netherland reveals, instead, is that this history cannot be properly understood without acknowledging the importance of an older layer of Afro-Iberian and Afro-Catholic influences.

There are, indeed, good reasons to question Robert Emmett Curran's assumption that "Catholics themselves were virtually a non-presence" in New Netherland.[14] While the European Catholic population was fairly small, the same cannot be said about the colony's Black community.[15] Documents reveal that all of them had Iberian Catholic baptismal names, or what was known in Portuguese as a *nome de igreja* (a church name). While some also had Iberian surnames, such as Grande, Britto [Brito], Premier/Premero [Primeiro], and Albiecke [Albuquerque], others used surnames that indicated their origin. This was, for instance, the case of Francisco van Capo Verde and Anna van Capoverde, whose surnames indicate that they originated from the Cape Verde Islands; Christoffel Santome and Maria Santomee, whose surnames point to the island of São Tomé; or Susanna Congo and Manuel Congo, whose surnames refer to the Kingdom of Kongo.[16] (The Kongo kingdom was located in the northwestern part of today's Angola and the southwestern part of the modern Democratic Republic of Congo.)

Most enslaved Africans in the Dutch colony had surnames referring to Angola, where

---

12. Fernow, *Records of New Amsterdam*, 1:362–63; Albert Eekhof, *De Hervormde kerk in Noord-Amerika (1624–1664)*, 2 vols. (The Hague: M. Nijhoff, 1913), 2:155.

13. For a more detailed analysis of these sources, see Jeroen Dewulf, "Iberian Linguistic Elements among the Black Population in New Netherland (1614–1664)," *Journal of Pidgin and Creole Languages* 34, no. 1 (2019): 49–82.

14. Robert Emmett Curran, *Papist Devils: Catholics in British America, 1574–1783* (Washington, DC: The Catholic Unιversity of America Press, 2014), 121.

15. On European Catholics in New Netherland, see Jaap Jacobs, *New Netherland: A Dutch Colony in Seventeenth-Century America* (Leiden: Brill, 2005), 311–13.

16. Samuel S. Purple, ed., *Marriages from 1639 to 1801 in the Reformed Dutch Church, New Amsterdam, New York City* (New York: Genealogical and Biographical Society, 1940), 10–30; Evans, *Records of the Reformed Dutch Church*, 10–38.

the main center of Portuguese slave trading operations was located: Luanda. What these names have in common is that they can all be traced back to areas with a strong Iberian influence.

Since these baptismal names were all typically Iberian (and Catholic), it would be wrong to assume that they had been imposed by their (Protestant) Dutch masters. It would also be wrong to think that the Dutch had pressured these Africans to identify with European rather than indigenous names. As John Thornton explained, "Christian names were deep-rooted in Central Africa prior to the Atlantic slave trade."[17] That the identification with an Iberian name was their own choice can also be demonstrated with reference to the seventeenth-century Dutch Cape colony in South Africa, where some of the enslaved originated from parts of Africa with a historically strong Portuguese influence while others came from regions where this influence was insignificant. While the latter are recorded in Dutch documents with indigenous African names, the former are identified with Iberian names.[18] This shows that the use of an Iberian Catholic name by enslaved Africans in New Netherland must have been a voluntary decision, perhaps even a matter of pride.

While it may seem counterintuitive to assume that members of the Black population in New Netherland found pride in using (Afro-)Iberian identity markers, we should not forget that by the time the Dutch appeared as competitors to the Iberians, the latter had dominated the Atlantic realm for over a century and had left a profound cultural mark. As Joseph Miller has argued, enslaved Africans shipped to the Americas from African regions with a historically strong Portuguese presence "must have had a useful familiarity with Portuguese Christianity and used it to find places for themselves without relying on the more 'African' aspects of their origins."[19] Miller, thus, questions the widespread assumption that, upon arrival in America, enslaved Africans identified exclusively with indigenous African customs and adopted European elements only under pressure. Rather, he suggests that some brought to America an African identity that was already influenced by Iberian customs. It is, indeed, questionable whether seventeenth-century people from places such as the Cape Verde Islands or the Kindgom of Kongo considered the Iberian elements that had been introduced in their homelands in the fifteenth century "un-African." We may even suspect that some brought to America a mindset that perceived certain Iberian identity markers, such as a Christian baptism or fluency in an Iberian language, to be signs of modernity or even, to say it with a seventeenth-century expression, they may have identified as *ladinos/as*.

---

17. John Thornton, "Central African Names and African-American Naming Patterns," *William and Mary Quarterly* 50, no. 4 (October 1993): 729.

18. Karel Schoeman, *Early Slavery at the Cape of Good Hope, 1652–1717* (Pretoria: Protea, 2007), 60–61.

19. Joseph C. Miller, "Central Africans during the Era of the Slave Trade, c. 1490s–1850s," *Central Africans and Cultural Transformation in America*, ed. Linda M. Heywood, 21–69 (Cambridge, UK: Cambridge University Press, 2002), 61.

The term *ladino* (or *ladina*)—not to be confused with the Judaeo-Spanish language—has to be understood in connection to the word *boçal* (Portuguese) or *bozal* (Spanish) that was used in reference to an unbaptized, nonacculturated and therefore—from an Iberian perspective—an uncivilized person. Hence the importance of baptism, as a key ritual that initiated a process of assimilation according to Iberian standards, with the goal of becoming a *ladino/a*. The closer one came to this goal, the more opportunities arose to show one's loyalty to the slaveholding elite in exchange for which one could hope to improve one's living conditions or even obtain *alforria*, or manumission (as derived from the Arab /al-furriâ/, freedom).

Being Black in Iberian slave societies was, in fact, not tantamount to being enslaved. A case in point are the Portuguese-controlled African islands of Cape Verde and São Tomé, where the dreadful story of the transatlantic slave trade began. The Portuguese authorities were well aware that the whip alone was insufficient to keep control over the quickly growing African population on these islands and dealt with this challenge by establishing a hierarchy within the Black community that allowed the formation of an elite group of free *ladinos/as*.[20]

Catholic lay brotherhoods (*fraternidades*) or confraternities (*confrarias*) played a key role in the process of becoming *ladino/a*. It was in the context of these mutual-aid and burial societies under Black leadership that newly arrived Africans familiarized themselves with Iberian customs, learned the language, and gradually moved up to a quarter, half, and ultimately, full *ladino/a* status. Outside of urban centers, where priests were scarce, these societies also allowed communities to take matters of faith into their own hands. They typically did so with the help of a lay *sacristão* (sacristan) or *mestre* (teacher), who ensured that people said the right prayers, prepared on time for the upcoming holidays, and executed rituals in accordance with (their understanding of) Catholic doctrine. As an example, there is the case of Seis Cento Lobos, an African whom the Dutch merchant Hendrik Haecxs met in 1646 on the Cape Verdean island of Maio, and who, "due to the absence of a pope[,] served as priest."[21]

Confraternities were also known as *reinados* (kingdoms) since they were typically led by an elected *rei* (king). In 1762, for instance, the Portuguese administrator João Vieira de Andrade complained in a letter to the Crown that "in all neighborhoods of the [Cape Verdean] island [of Santiago] women and men are elected to serve as kings and queens,

20. António Carreira, *Cabo Verde: Formação e extinção de uma sociedade escravocrata (1460–1878)* (Praia: Estudos e Ensaios, 2000), 259–80; David Wheat, *Atlantic Africa and the Spanish Caribbean, 1570–1640* (Chapel Hill: University of North Carolina Press, 2016), 216–52; Philip J. Havik, "Kriol without Creoles: Rethinking Guinea's Afro-Atlantic Connections (Sixteenth to Twentieth Centuries)," in *Cultures of the Lusophone Black Atlantic*, ed. Nancy Priscilla Naro, Roger Sansi-Roca, and David H. Treece (London: Palgrave Macmillan, 2007), 41–74.

21. S. P. L'Honoré Naber, ed., "Het dagboek van Hendrik Haecxs, Lid van den Hoogen Raad van Brazilië (1645–1654)," *Bijdragen en Mededelingen van het Historisch Genootschap* 46 (1925): 167.

who then every Sunday and holiday stage parades with their drums and flutes." Every year, Andrade continued, these societies "have a Mass organized at their kingdom, where they are crowned by a local priest, and in their house, they build an altar, where they worship." Although these rituals were "claimed to be Catholic" by the local population, Andrade advocated for the prohibition of these "scandalous abuses."[22]

While such complaints are recurrent in the eighteenth century, it should be emphasized that Black confraternities enjoyed great prestige in earlier times. At its foundation in 1526, the Black confraternity of Our Lady of the Rosary on the island of São Tomé received authorization from the Crown to purchase the freedom for any enslaved person, male or female, who had proven to be a loyal member, even if against the will of the owner. Equally important is that it was in the context of these societies that Black elites reinterpreted Iberian elements from an African perspective and, thereby, induced a process of African appropriation of the *ladino/a* concept. A reflection of this survives in the name of São Tomé's Luso-African creole language. Since the free *ladino/a* population of São Tomé used a Portuguese-derived language to distinguish itself from enslaved, unbaptized Africans who spoke indigenous languages, it became known as *forro*, the "language of the free." Reflective of the Africanization of the *ladino/a* concept that had occurred in São Tomé, however, is that *forro* was a (Portuguese-based) creole language with clear African features that distinguished it from Standard Portuguese.[23] This Africanization should caution us not to reduce the process of becoming *ladino/a* to mere accommodation to Iberian rule.

Confraternities also accompanied the development of Luso-African communities, known as *Kristons*, that developed in and around Portuguese trading posts in Upper Guinea.[24] In the 1680s, Michel Jajolet de La Courbe observed that *Kristons* spoke a "jargon that resembles somewhat Portuguese" and "bear the names of saints." They wear "a large chaplet around their neck [and] a hat, a shirt, and breeches like the Europeans," and, "although they are black, they nevertheless claim to be white, by which they mean that they are Christians, just like white people."[25]

---

22. Daniel A. Pereira. ed., *Estudos da história de Cabo Verde* (Praia: Alfa-Comunicaçoes, 2005), 337–41.

23. António Brásio, ed., *Monumenta missionária Africana: Primeira série*, 15 vols. (Lisbon: Agência Geral do Ultramar/Academia Portuguesa da História, 1952–88), 1:472–74.

24. George E. Brooks, *Eurafricans in Western Africa: Commerce, Social Status, Gender, and Religious Observance from the Sixteenth to the Eighteenth Century* (Athens: Ohio University Press, 2003), 51–54, 91, 128; Philip J. Havik, *Silences and Soundbites: The Gendered Dynamics of Trade and Brokerage in the Pre-colonial Guinea Bissau Region* (Münster: Lit Verlag, 2004), 45–53, 129–45; Christoph Kohl, *A Creole Nation: National Integration in Guinea-Bissau* (New York: Bergbahn, 2018), 19–30, 50–54; José da Silva Horta, "Evidence for a Luso-African Identity in 'Portuguese' Accounts on 'Guinea of Cape Verde' (Sixteenth-Seventeenth Centuries)," *History in Africa* 27 (2000): 99–130; Peter Mark, "The Evolution of 'Portuguese' Identity: Luso-Africans on the Upper Guinea Coast form the Sixteenth to the Early Nineteenth Century," *Journal of African History* 40, no. 2 (July 1999): 173–91.

25. P. Cultru, ed., *Premier voyage du sieur de la Courbe fait à la coste d'Afrique en 1685* (Paris: E. Champion, 1913), 192–93, 211.

The same occurred in parts of Central Africa with a strong Portuguese influence, most notably in the Kongo region. A 1595 report from the Kongolese ambassador in Lisbon reveals that no fewer than six brotherhoods existed in the kingdom's capital São Salvador—those of Our Lady of the Rosary, the Holy Sacrament, Saint Mary, the Immaculate Conception, the Holy Spirit, and Saint Anthony.[26] Membership was initially the privilege of the kingdom's elite and, therefore, conferred great prestige. Those admitted to one of these confraternities enjoyed royal protection and could in theory not be sold into slavery.[27] Analyzing the social behavior of seventeenth-century Black communities in the American diaspora from the perspective of Africanized *ladinos/as* helps us to understand why the term frequently shows up in reference to maroons, Africans who had escaped from slavery. In 1662, for instance, Bishop Francisco de la Cueva Maldonado reported on a maroon community in Santo Domingo that "was being governed by a community of ladino Negroes," who identified as "Catholics, by placing crosses in front of their houses and praying the Our Father and the Ave Maria."[28] Similarly, sources referring to the inhabitants of Palmares—a community established by Africans who escaped from the plantations when Dutch troops invaded Brazil in 1630—reveal that they had "selected one of the most ladino members of their community, whom they venerate as their priest and who baptizes and marries them."[29] These examples show that it is a misunderstanding to assume that enslaved Africans by definition perceived Christianity as a religion of oppression. While this may have been the case for many, these examples reveal how some Black communities in the American diaspora had embraced their own Africanized version of Christianity to which they held on, even after escaping from slavery.

This same pattern can be observed in Protestant colonies. In the Dutch colony of Curaçao, for instance, the Jesuit Michael Schabel noted in 1705 that virtually all members of the Black community took pride in identifying themselves as Catholic, were eager to have their children baptized with Iberian names, spoke among themselves a form of "broken Spanish" that was known as *habla Cristiano* (to speak like as a Christian), and referred disdainfully to unbaptized newcomers from Africa as *borricos* (asses).[30] This

---

26. Brásio, *Monumenta missionária Africana*, 3:500–504.

27. Brásio, *Monumenta missionária Africana*, 5:605–14; J. Cuvelier and L. Jadin, eds., *L'ancien Congo d'après les archives romaines, 1518–1640* (Brussels: Académie Royale des Sciences Coloniales, 1954), 187; Cécile Fromont, *The Art of Conversion: Christian Visual Culture in the Kingdom of Kongo* (Chapel Hill: University of North Carolina Press, 2014), 202–6; John Thornton, "The Development of an African Catholic Church in the Kingdom of Kongo, 1491–1750," *Journal of African History* 25, no. 2 (1984): 147–67.

28. Carlos Larrazabal Blanco, ed., *Los negros y la esclavitud en Santo Domingo* (Santo Domingo: Julio D. Postigo, 1975), 151.

29. Flávio Gomes, ed., *Mocambos de Palmares: História e fontes (séc. XVI–XIX)* (Rio de Janeiro: 7Letras, 2010), 222.

30. Christine W. M. Schunck, ed., "Michael Joannes Alexius Schabel, S.J., 'Notitia de Coraçao, Bonayre, Oruba' 1705 and 'Diurnum' (1707–1708)," *Archivum Historicum Societatis Iesu* 66 (January 1997): 124–39.

reveals that these people displayed an identity that was shaped by an Africanized *ladino/a* mindset.

A similar situation existed in the Danish Virgin Islands, where Christian Georg Andreas Oldendorp, a missionary worker for the Moravian Church, observed in 1777 that enslaved Africans "who came from Portuguese countries... particularly those from Kongo" used to perform "a kind of baptism." Not only did these people take Christianization into their own hands, they even engaged in missionary work among other Africans. In a manner similar to how priests in Kongo examined "those who were sent to the shore to be sold into slavery" in order to find out "their sins" and, thereupon, "teach, absolve, and baptize them," certain Kongolese provided "a form of baptism to those *bozals* who desire[d] this." Before the baptism could take place, however, "an adult *bozal* had to receive five to six lashes from the baptizer, for the sins he had committed in Africa." Oldendorp also explained that "those *bozals*, who desire[d] this, receive[d] someone who assume[d] the role of father or mother for them." Once admitted to the Afro-Christian community, "there [was] a Negro celebration," after which the baptismal fathers and mothers "adopt those whom they have baptized as their children and look after them as best they can, in particular, when they pass away, because then they provide them with a coffin and burial clothing."[31] The fact that Afro-Catholic Kongolese catered to the needs of newly arrived Africans and organized baptisms and funerals suggests that they operated in the context of mutual-aid and burial societies that, as Jon Sensbachm has noted, have much in common with "black confraternities" in Latin America.[32]

The fact that members of the Black community in the Virgin Islands seem to have established, on their own initiative, mutual-aid and burial societies modeled upon Iberian confraternities is of great interest to New Netherland. In 1999, Graham Hodges's research into the organization of the Black population in this Dutch colony led him to conclude that the "association" Blacks built in order to provide "a supportive model" resembled "the confraternities or brotherhoods found among Kongolese and Angolan blacks living in Brazil."[33] In *The Pinkster King and the King of Kongo*, I further explored this theory by connecting it to references in late-eighteenth and early nineteenth-century Black Pinkster king celebrations in parts of New York that have a Dutch colonial history.[34] This connection between the

31. Christian Georg Andreas Oldendorp, *Historie der caribischen Inseln Sanct Thomas, Sanct Crux und Sanct Jan, insbesondere der dasigen Neger und der Mission der evangelischen Brüder unter denslebe*, ed. Gudrun Meier, Stephan Palmié, Peter Stein, and Horst Ulbricht, 2 vols. (Berlin: VWB, 2000), 1:445–48, 647, 741–43, and 2:758.

32. Jon F. Sensbach, *Rebecca's Revival: Creating Black Christianity in the Atlantic World* (Cambridge, MA: Harvard University Press, 2005), 92–93.

33. Graham Russell Hodges, *Root and Branch: African Americans in New York and East Jersey 1613–1863* (Chapel Hill: The University of North Carolina Press, 1999), 28

34. Jeroen Dewulf, *The Pinkster King and the King of Kongo: The Forgotten History of America's Dutch-Owned Slaves* (Jackson: University Press of Mississippi, 2017), 133–54.

New York Pinkster kings and king election rituals among Afro-Iberian confraternities finds a parallel in the Virgin Islands. While there is no evidence that the societies described by Oldendorp also elected "kings," "queens," and other leadership positions with aristocratic titles—familiar to us from Afro-Catholic confraternities in Africa and Latin America— Thurlow Weed reported in 1845 from the Virgin Islands that "the slaves on each estate elect their queen and princess, with their king and prince." According to the New York publisher and politician, "the free colored people and house slaves form their parties, elect their kings, queens, &c., and dance in like manner."[35] Even after the abolition of slavery in 1848, the Black population in the Virgin Islands preserved an attachment to this tradition. In 1856, for instance, a local newspaper reported on the "absurd exhibition of mock royalty" by a king and queen, who were "richly attired in silk and satins."[36]

These parallels suggest that rituals rooted in African interpretations of originally Portuguese fraternal traditions may have continued to influence Black cultural traditions for many generations, which gives credit to Willem Frijhoff's theory that "the religious practices of Blacks in New Netherland were strongly influenced by Portuguese Catholicism" and that "one can assume that this Catholic heritage survived for a long time."[37]

Dutch *Ladinos/as*?

If, however, enslaved Africans from parts of Africa with a historically strong Portuguese influence remained so attached to African variants of Catholicism and to rituals rooted in Afro-Iberian fraternal practices, one wonders why the Black community in New Netherland was so eager to marry and have its children baptized in the Dutch Reformed Church. Although Dutch Calvinists had strict criteria for baptism, records show that the Reformed Church in New Amsterdam baptized at least fifty-six children of Black families.[38]

This desire is all the more intriguing considering that the Catholic nobility in the Kingdom of Kongo had always resisted Dutch attempts to proselytize. In spite of his political alliance with the Calvinist Dutch, King Garcia II of Kongo made it clear in a 1642 letter to Johan Maurits, the ruler of Dutch Brazil, that he refused to accept Protestant proselytism in his kingdom, stating: "I practice the true Catholic faith."[39] When the Dutch minister Nicolaus Ketel gave him a Calvinist book in Portuguese translation, Garcia allegedly ordered a fire to be lit, and "in the presence of everybody, including the Dutch, he fervently

---

35. Thurlow Weed, *Letters from Europe and the West Indies, 1843–1862* (Albany, NY: Weed, Parsons, 1866), 345.

36. *St. Croix Avis*, January 4, 1856.

37. Willem Frijhoff, *Wegen van Evert Willemsz: Een Hollands weeskind op zoek naar zichzelf 1607-1647* (Nijmegen: SUN, 1995), 774.

38. Jacobs, *New Netherland*, 312–18.

39. "Letter (copy) by Dom Garcia, King of Kongo, Angola et cetera, at the court in Kongo, to Governor-General Johan Maurits van Nassau," May 12, 1642, Archives of the Old/First West India Company, no. 58:211, National Archives, The Hague.

exhorted all the people to stay firm and stable in the Catholic faith, and then impetuously threw the book into the fire."[40]

Not only in Africa, but also in the Americas, we find examples of such Black Catholic zeal. In Barbados, for instance, the French priest Antoine Biet met with a group of six enslaved Africans in 1654, who were all "very good Catholics" and who told him that they were "extremely sorrowed to see themselves sold as slaves on an island of heretics." He also observed that if "some of them received a tinge of the Catholic religion among the Portuguese, they preserve it the best they can, doing their prayers and worshipping God in their hearts."[41] In Dutch Brazil, we find evidence of Catholic militancy turning into physical violence. In 1641, the Reformed Church reported that members of the Black confraternity of Our Lady of the Rosary in the town of Sirinhaém had not only violated Dutch rules by staging "a procession of the idol *Rosário* [i.e., Our Lady of the Rosary]" but also that "good [i.e., Protestant] Christians... who witnessed it and refused to honor [Our Lady]" were "not only treated disrespectfully but at several occasions beaten up."[42]

Such scenes of Black Catholic militancy contrast, however, with the fact that some six hundred Black children were baptized by Reformed ministers in Dutch Brazil. Since the Dutch administration in Brazil tolerated the Catholic Church, their parents had opted for a baptism in the Reformed Church despite the presence of a Catholic alternative.[43] Also in Curaçao, where Spanish missionaries used to come from nearby Venezuela to baptize the children of Black families, a small number of people turned to the Dutch Reformed Church instead. In 1650, Reverend Charles de Rochefort informed the Amsterdam *classis*—the Reformed Church's administrative body—that he had succeeded in baptizing "twelve adult persons, all blacks."[44] The same occurred in the 1640s during the brief Dutch occupation of Luanda, where a handful of African parents reached out to Reverend Ketel with the request that he baptize their children.[45] These examples show that the desire among members of the Black population in New Netherland to have their children baptized in the Reformed Church was not exceptional.

40. Jean-François de Rome, *Brève relation de la fondation de la mission des Frères Mineurs Capucins du Séraphique Père Saint François au Royaume de Congo (1648)*, ed. François Bontinck (Louvain: Nauwelaerts, 1964), 112.

41. Antoine Biet, *Voyage de la France équinoxiale en l'Isle de Cayenne* (Paris: Chez François Clouzier, 1664), 276–77, 292.

42. J. A. Grothe, ed., "Classicale Acta van Brazilië," *Kroniek van het Historisch Genootschap* 29.6, no. 4 (1874): 402.

43. Frans Leonard Schalkwijk, *The Reformed Church in Dutch Brazil, 1630–1654* (Zoetermeer: Boekencentrum, 1998), 151; Leendert Jan Joosse, *Geloof in de Nieuwe Wereld: Ontmoeting met Afrikanen en Indianen 1600–1700* (Kampen: Kok, 2008), 507–8.

44. Hugh Hastings and Edward Tanjore Corwin, eds., *Ecclesiastical Records, State of New York*, 7 vols. (Albany, NY: State Historian, 1901–16), 1:280–81.

45. "Nicolaus Ketel te Luanda" (February 18–March 4, 1642), Archives of the States-General, Part II, no. 5756:145–47, National Archives, The Hague; D. L. Noorlander, *Heaven's Wrath: The Protestant Reformation and the Dutch West India Company in the Atlantic World* (Ithaca: Cornell University Press, 2019), 179–80.

According to Linda Heywood and John Thornton, what mattered most "was the assertion of a Christian identity rather than a sectarian Catholic one."[46] Ira Berlin argues in the same vein: "That the church was Catholic rather than Anglican or Dutch Reformed was less important than that membership knit black people together in bonds of kinship and certified incorporation into the larger community."[47]

We may also reference the importance of material support and a desire to achieve freedom. Ever since the Portuguese had introduced Christianity in Africa, it had come to be associated with the perception that conversion was a first step to becoming a *ladino/a* and thereby improving one's living conditions. The case of Bassie de Neger suggests that members of the Black community in the Reformed Church of New Netherland may have had similar interests. As the Deacons' Accounts from the year 1671 show, Bassie de Neger requested and obtained food and money from the Reformed Church in Rensselaerswyck when he was in financial need. Later, the Church also paid for his coffin and funeral, including the brandy served at the reception that followed.[48] In an Iberian context, such requests would typically have been dealt with by one's confraternity.

The connection between Christian conversion and a desire to improve one's living conditions has been stressed by James Sweet, who has argued that "[enslaved] Central Africans quickly came to understand that Christian practices (however Catholicized or Africanized) were a potential passageway to an improved condition, perhaps even freedom."[49] This implies that the desire of enslaved Africans to join the Protestant community of New Amsterdam may have been intended primarily as a symbolic act to build trust and, later, to capitalize on that trust to demand privileges and, ultimately, manumission. If so, Africans' eagerness to be married and to have their children baptized in the Reformed Church had more to do with tactics than with faith. Such a mindset would also explain why so many enslaved people in New Netherland made a point of identifying themselves as Christian in their petitions for freedom and why Black families frequently asked members of the Dutch community to serve as witnesses for their children's baptisms. One enslaved man, Anthony Ferdinandus, even chose Paulus Heymans, the Dutch overseer of the Company's enslaved Africans, as witness at his son's baptism.[50] Here, again, we see a parallel with Iberian slave

---

46. Linda M. Heywood and John K. Thornton, *Central Africans, Atlantic Creoles, and the Foundation of the Americas, 1585–1660* (Cambridge, UK: Cambridge University Press, 2007), 272.

47. Ira Berlin, *Many Thousands Gone: The First Two Centuries of Slavery in North America* (Cambridge, MA: Belknap Press, 1998), 75–76.

48. Janny Venema, ed., *Deacons' Accounts 1652–1674, First Dutch Reformed Church of Beverwijck/ Albany* (Rockport, ME: Picton Press, 1998), 223–24.

49. James H. Sweet, "African Identity and Slave Resistance in the Portuguese Atlantic," *The Atlantic World and Virginia, 1550–1624*, ed. Peter C. Mancall (Chapel Hill: University of North Carolina Press, 2007), 246.

50. Evans, *Records of the Reformed Dutch Church*, 26. For parallels to English colonies, see Rebecca Anne Goetz, *The Baptism of Early Virginia: How Christianity Created Race* (Baltimore, MD: Johns Hopkins University Press, 2012), 101.

societies. As Gerald Cardoso has shown, once a slaveholder accepted a request to be the godparent of an enslaved child, this would "free the Negro baby at the baptismal font."[51]

The liberal baptismal policy of the Reformed Church in the early decades of New Netherland may, in this way, have contributed to the growth of a free Black community that, by the time the English took over the Dutch colony in 1664, consisted of some seventy-five people.[52] This view is in line with the criticism expressed by New Netherland minister Henricus Selijns to justify a change in the Church's baptismal policy. When writing to the *classis* in 1664, Selijns explained that he and his colleagues had decided to henceforth reject requests by enslaved families to baptize their children "partly because of their lack of knowledge of the faith, and partly because of the material and wrong aim on the part of the aforementioned Negroes who sought nothing else by it than the freeing of their children from material slavery, without pursuing piety and Christian virtues."[53] These words echo a common reproach of *ladinos/as* in Iberian societies, who had the reputation of being opportunists. Indeed, once the memories of slavery had faded, the term acquired a new meaning. In contemporary Spanish and Portuguese, to be *ladino/a* means to be guileful or cunning.

All this suggests that enslaved Africans in New Netherland may have approached Dutch slaveholders with a *ladino/a* mindset and understood conversion to the Reformed Church as a logical step in their transition from Iberian *ladinos/as* into Dutch *ladinos/as*. This theory can be strengthened if we add data from the Virgin Islands to our analysis. The historical presence of the Dutch in the Virgin Islands makes these islands an interesting case for scholars working on the topic of slavery in the Dutch Atlantic. In fact, prior to the Danish, the West India Company had attempted to establish a plantation colony on the island of Saint Thomas in the 1650s. Although this attempt failed and the island was resettled by the Danish in the early 1670s, the Dutch presence was again strengthened when Dutch planters fleeing the island of Saint Eustatius after it was raided by the English in 1666 moved to Saint Thomas. Still, in 1688, no fewer than 60 of the plantations on the island were Dutch-owned, compared to 32 that were English-owned and only 20 that were owned by Danes.[54] This accounts for the fact that not Danish, but Dutch, or rather, a creolized variant of it known as *Negerhollands*, developed into the lingua franca of the Black community on Saint Thomas and remained so until English imposed itself as the dominant language in the early nineteenth century.

---

51. Gerald Cardoso, *Negro Slavery in the Sugar Plantations of Veracruz and Pernambuco, 1550–1680* (Washington, DC: University Press of America, 1983), 140–41.
52. Christoph, "The Freedmen of New Amsterdam," 163–65.
53. A. P. G. Jos van der Linde, ed. and trans., *Old First Dutch Reformed Church of Brooklyn, New York: First Book of Records, 1660–1752*, New York Historical Manuscripts: Dutch (Baltimore, MD: Genealogical Publishing, 1983), 230–31.
54. Cefas van Rossem and Hein van der Voort, eds., *Die Creol Taal: 250 Years of Negerhollands Texts* (Amsterdam: Amsterdam University Press, 1996), 7.

Research by Katherine Gerbner reveals that the enslaved who joined the Dutch Reformed and the Anglican Churches in those early years all tended to stand close to the slaveholding elite in Saint Thomas, either because they had a European father or because they occupied leading positions, such as that of overseer, which "suggests that the most important factor leading to baptism for adults was maintaining a close relationship with a master or mistress."[55] Being allowed to join a Christian church was, thus, perceived as something distinctive, which sealed an alliance with the ruling class and made one part of the island's Black elite. Consequently, when missionaries of the Moravian Church began to reach out to the entire enslaved community on Saint Thomas, they not only faced opposition from slaveholders but also from privileged members of the island's Black community.[56] As Oldendorp confirms, the Moravian Church mainly attracted enslaved people who had been unsuccessful in improving their social position in other ways; whereas "of those slaves who enjoyed the greatest freedom to convert, very few showed interest."[57] Oldendorp also provides examples of how the Black elite on Saint Thomas had been formed. It resulted, for instance, from their participation in the *Marronjagd*, the hunt for runaways, or from membership in the island's Black militia. According to Oldendorp, the Black community had formed "its own company" for which it had chosen "a captain from their own" with the Iberian name [Do]mingo. Whenever the authorities faced a threat, "they were ready to help." In fact, during the 1733–34 uprising by enslaved Africans of the Akan community with roots in West Africa, the planters and colonial authorities were able to count on the assistance of an entirely Black military unit composed of some three hundred men.[58]

Here, too, we find a parallel to New Netherland, where a man called Bastyaen or Bastiaen—a likely Dutch corruption of the Iberian Sebastián/Sebastião—was known as the "Capt. van de Swarten" and "Captyn van de Negers" (Captain of the Black People). Also in New Netherland, it was common practice for the authorities to use loyal Black men for (semi)military operations, from the maintenance of order to participation in wars against Native Americans and in raids to hunt down runaway Africans. A revealing sign of the Dutch authorities' confidence in these men is Petrus Stuyvesant's letter to the Secretary and Council in New Amsterdam, in which he ordered them to "let the free and the Company's Negroes keep good watch on my Bouwery" during his military campaign in the Esopus

55. Katherine Gerbner, *Christian Slavery: Conversion and Race in the Protestant Atlantic World* (Philadelphia: University of Pennsylvania Press, 2018), 79.
56. Gerbner, 138–63. For British colonies in the Caribbean, see Nicholas M. Beasley, *Christian Ritual and the Creation of British Slave Societies, 1650–1780* (Athens: University of Georgia Press, 2009), 74–77.
57. Oldendorp, *Historie der caribischen Inseln*, 2, I:337.
58. Oldendorp, *Historie der caribischen Inseln*, 1:588, 608. See also Albert A. Campbell, "St. Thomas Negroes: A Study in Personality and Culture," *Psychological Monographs* 55, no. 5 (1943): 13; Peter M. Voelz, *Slave and Soldier: The Military Impact of Blacks in the Colonial Americas* (New York: Garland Publishing, 1993), 168–69.

area in 1660.[59] The fact that Bastiaen, the captain of the Black militia, had acquired his freedom and become a landowner confirms that those who provided support to the authorities could expect compensation. Of particular interest is also the religious dimension. Bastiaen married Isabel Kisana van Angola in the Dutch Reformed Church and featured in several cases as baptismal witness for fellow Black families. His son later became a communicant member of the Dutch Reformed Church. Bastiaen's close connection to the Dutch ruling class also explains his presence as witness at the baptism of Captain Jan de Vries's mixed-race son Jan, whose mother was the abovementioned Brazilian woman.[60]

If seen from a *ladino/a* perspective, the decision by the "Black Captain" Bastiaen to feature as baptismal witness in the Reformed Church and to lead a militia that assisted the Dutch are two sides of the same coin. They both reflect a desire to improve one's life in the Dutch slave society by demonstrating loyalty and adopting identity markers of the ruling class in accordance with a *ladino/a* mindset. The fact that Bastiaen's son no longer used the Portuguese name Francisco but the Dutch variant Franciscus may also be interpreted as a sign that the religious transition from Catholicism to Protestantism was accompanied by a linguistic transition from Portuguese to Dutch or, perhaps, a to a New Netherland variant of the Virgin Islands' *Negerhollands*. In good *ladino/a* tradition, Franciscus changed his name again after the English conquered the Dutch colony, this time to Francis.[61] Just how easily *ladinos/as* could switch sides can be illustrated with the example of a "Black ladino from Kongo," whom the Capuchin Juan de Santiago encountered on a Dutch ship that, in the mid-seventeenth century, was captured by the Portuguese near the African island of Príncipe. It turned out that this man, who had been baptized as Catholic in Kongo, had at one point been captured by the Dutch and taken to Amsterdam, where he converted to Protestantism and started to work as a sailor on Dutch ships. Now, captured again—this time by the Portuguese—he reconverted to Catholicism.[62]

This attitude can easily be misunderstood as a sign that, to Africans, Christian conversion remained meaningless, similar to what was claimed by the Dutch Olfert Dapper, who in 1668 argued that Kongolese Christianity was merely "a sham," since "many who call themselves Christians don't act like that, except when Europeans are present because then it is in their interest to pretend to be Christian."[63]

---

59. O'Callaghan, Fernow, and Brodhead, *Documents Relative to the Colonial History*, 13:152.
60. Van Laer, *New York Historical Manuscripts*, 4:96; Evans, *Records of the Reformed Dutch Church*, 17–19; Charles T. Gehring, ed., *New York Historical Manuscripts: Dutch,* vols. GG, HH & II, *Land Papers* (Baltimore, MD: Genealogical Publishing , 1980), 56; Christoph, "The Freedmen of New Amsterdam," 159; Frijhoff, *Wegen van Evert Willemsz*, 769; Romney, *New Netherland Connections*, 215–17.
61. Purple, *Marriages from 1639 to 1801*, 14, 71.
62. F. Leite de Faria, "Fr. João de Santiago e a sua relação sobre os Capuchinhos no Congo," *Portugal em África* 59 (1953): 323.
63. Olfert Dapper, *Naukeurige beschrijvinge der Afrikaensche gewesten* (Amsterdam: Jacob van Meurs, 1668), 588.

Such stereotypical opinions about Black Christianity are contradicted, however, by scenes Schabel and Oldendorp witnessed among the enslaved in Curaçao and the Virgin Islands. A legitimate question, therefore, is whether Africans who identified as Catholic upon arrival in the Americas but who then converted to a Protestant church had the genuine intention of leaving their entire Afro-Iberian, Afro-Catholic heritage behind. Here, the case of the Black community in seventeenth-century Amsterdam is of interest, since its African roots (in Cape Verde, São Tomé, Kongo, and Angola) are virtually the same as those of the Black community in New Netherland. Research by Mark Ponte reveals that these men and women shared familiarity with Iberian culture and language, which even fostered bonds between them and indigenous peoples from Portuguese possessions in Asia (such as Goa and Malacca). While most marriages within this nonwhite community took place in the Dutch Reformed Church, which, as Ponte points out, was a precondition to receiving financial benefits, most of their children were baptized in the Catholic house church Moyses (the later Moses and Aaron Church).[64] The latter was a clandestine church, since the public display of Catholic services was not tolerated in Amsterdam. What occurred in seventeenth-century Amsterdam, thus, renders credibility to Frijhoff's theory that the decision by the Reformed Church in New Netherland to adopt a stricter baptismal policy in the 1660s resulted from disappointment over the ongoing attachment among Black converts to Afro-Iberian, Catholic traditions.[65]

While lack of evidence makes it difficult to assess the veractiy of this observation, it is not inconceivable that what members of the Black community who approached the Reformed Church in New Netherland cared about was the administration of the sacraments, not unlike Catholics in isolated parts of Africa who would, at best, see a priest once a year and who otherwise took the organization of all forms of spiritual and social aid into their own hands. This would imply that their *ladino/a* attitude vis-à-vis Christianity was only characterized by opportunism in relation to Europeans, while, among themselves, they held a sincere desire to maintain a Christian congregation according to African norms and values.

Building on Patricia Bonomi's plea to erase "the artificial line between pre– and post– Great Awakening black Christianity," one could hypothesize that, in New Netherland, we find the earliest signs of an attitude that was to characterize the relation between African Americans and Christianity in the centuries to come, in the sense that there was a strong interest in this religion, but only insofar as it allowed autonomy of the congregation.[66] As John W. Catron points out, "One of the key reasons for the evangelicals' success among

---

64. Mark Ponte, "'Al de swarten die hier ter stede comen': Een Afro-Atlantische gemeenschap in zeventiende-eeuws Amsterdam," *Low Countries Journal of Social and Economic History* 15, no. 4 (2010): 33–62.

65. Frijhoff, *Wegen van Evert Willemsz*, 779.

66. Patricia U. Bonomi, "'Swarms of Negroes Comeing about My Door': Black Christianity in Early Dutch and English North America," *Journal of American History* 103, no. 1 (June 2016): 58.

people of African descent arose from their willingness to allow blacks to preach to their fellows and to have real power within their churches."[67]

To begin the history of African American Christianity not with white missionaries in eightieth-century America but rather with seventeenth-century Black congregations who self-organized into brotherhoods also sheds new light on the abundance of parallels between fraternities and the nation's earliest Black evangelical churches. As Franklin Frazier argues in his classic study *The Negro Church in America* (1964), a singular feature of these churches is precisely the combination of spirituality with forms of social and material support. Recent research by John Giggie confirms that the nation's earliest African American evangelical churches "appropriate[ed] many of the institutional resources and rituals of black fraternal culture."[68]

This suggests that the genesis of Black evangelical churches in North America should not be reduced to a mixture of European Protestant with indigenous African elements, as has traditionally been assumed. Rather, a third source of influence might be added, that of brotherhood practices rooted in seventeenth-century Afro-Iberian/Catholic fraternal traditions.[69] This would imply that the fate of charter generations in New Netherland and other parts of North America represented much more than a fascinating though ultimately inconsequential chapter in the history of African American identity formation. Rather, it shows that these communities may have had a crucial influence on the way African American identity was to develop in later centuries.

---

67. John W. Catron, *Embracing Protestantism: Black Identities in the Atlantic World* (Gainesville: University Press of Florida, 2016), 82, 151.

68. John M. Giggie, "For God and Lodge: Black Fraternal Orders and the Evolution of African American Religion in the Postbellum South," in *The Struggle for Equality: Essays on Sectional Conflict, the Civil War, and the Long Reconstruction*, ed. Orville Vernon Burton, Jerald Podair, and Jennifer L. Weber (Charlottesville: University of Virginia Press, 2011), 200.

69. Some sections of this chapter summarize findings I previously presented in my book *Afro-Atlantic Catholics: America's First Black Christians* (Notre Dame, IN: Notre Dame University Press, 2022) and are updated here with new data.

Fear and Betrayal

Smallpox and the Turning Point of the French and Indian War

John Booss

The Indians fear nothing so much as this disease....

—Louis Antoine de Bougainville, *Adventures in the Wilderness*

It is in the nature of great events, as Francis Parkman has said, to obscure the great events that came before them.[1] The American Revolution has greatly eclipsed the French and Indian War in the popular imagination and in scholarly attention; yet, it has been called "The War That Made America."[2] In this article, I examine the French and Indian War in which the two great colonizing powers, France and England, grappled for control of the North American continent.[3] For Indigenous peoples, the conflict threatened their lands, their way

---

Epigraph source: Louis Antoine de Bougainville, *Adventures in the Wilderness: The American Journals of Louis Antoine de Bougainville, 1756–1760*, ed. and trans. Edward P. Hamilton (Norman: University of Oklahoma Press, 1964), 8.

1. Francis Parkman, *Montcalm and Wolfe* (1884; repr., New York: Crowell-Collier, 1962), 13.

2. Fred Anderson, *The War That Made America: A Short History of the French and Indian War.* (New York: Viking Penguin, 2005).

3. Concerning the naming of the war. The term used here "The French and Indian War" reflects the perspective of the British colonies and ran from 1754 to 1760. The thesis of this article is specific to the conflct in North America. The most commonly used term from the perspective of the French and British empires has been "The Seven Years' War." It reflects the span of years between the declarations of war by the combatants in 1756 to the settlement in the Treaty of Paris in 1763. The conflict was global in nature and has been called the first world war. Paul Kelton has argued that since the Cherokees "fought against and negotiated with multiple Native and non-Native actors," they helped determine the outcome of the "important imperial struggle." Hence, he reasons that the term French and Indian War is antiquated. Paul Kelton, "The British and Indian War: Cherokee Power and the Fate of Empire in North America," *William and Mary Quarterly* 69, no.4. (October 2012): 763–792, 791. Guy Fregault has referred to the war as "The War of Conquest" that changed the nature of life living under French rule to that under British rule. Guy Fregault, *Canada: The War of the Conquest*, trans. Margaret G. Cameron (New York: Oxford University Press, 1969), xii. The war from the perspective of the indigenous peoples on whose ground it was being fought identified the combatants, the French

of life, and their very existence. In 1758 the Moravian minister Christian Post was told by Delaware Indian leaders that "you and the French contrived the war, to waste the Indians between you; and that you and the French intend to divide the land between you."[4]

The focus here is on the role of an outbreak of smallpox in the turning of the tide, or in marking the turning point from French and Indian victories to English dominance and ultimate triumph. I examine a smallpox outbreak among the Native allies of the French between August 1757 and the start of 1758. As suggested by my use of "turning point," the war can be split into two periods: the first, in which the French and their Indian allies predominated, from 1754 to 1757; and the second, in which the British predominated and ultimately prevailed, from 1758 to 1760. A major cause of the turn of the tide was the infection by smallpox of Indians from the upper Great Lakes region (Pays d'en Haut) following the siege of Fort William Henry on Lake George in August 1757. The infection was carried by the Indians back to their home villages and caused a massive outbreak and, subsequently, devastating mortality. The consequent refusal of the Indians of the Pays d'en Haut to join the French in their campaign of 1758 ensued.

The role of smallpox in the participation by Amerindian allies of the French has been studied by D. Peter MacLeod.[5] He examined reports of the annual number of Indians serving with the French and determined that smallpox was critical to decisions about whether the Indians would participate in the annual campaigns. He noted that the fluctuations of the numbers of Indian warriors were "of limited significance to the outcome of the war." His concern was the "political independence and freedom of action of the Indians."[6] I examine the refusal of the Indians from the Pays d'en Haut to participate in the campaign of 1758 as a consequence of the smallpox epidemic in their villages, which had resulted from exposure during the campaign for Fort William Henry in 1757. Modifying MacLeod's conclusion, I contend that their refusal, subsequent to the outbreak of smallpox, was a critical component in the turning point of the war. The explicit connection between smallpox brought from the campaign for Fort William Henry and the turning point of the war does not appear to have been previously developed in detail.

In contrast to the highly focused role of a smallpox outbreak in the French and Indian War, historians have recorded the massive effects of smallpox on other conflicts in the New

---

and English war. See Colin Calloway, *First Peoples: A Documentary Survey of American Indian History*, 4th ed. (Boston: Bedford/St. Martin's, 2012), 172 The most descriptive title would be "The War for North America, 1754 to 1760."

4. Jeffrey Ostler, "'To Extirpate the Indians': An Indigenous Consciousness of Genocide in the Ohio Valley and Lower Great Lakes, 1750s–1810." *William and Mary Quarterly* 72, no. 4 (October 2015): 587–622, 595.

5. D. Peter MacLeod, "Microbes and Muskets: Smallpox and Participation of the Amerindian Allies of New France in the Seven Years' War," *Ethnohistory* 39, no.1 (Winter 1992): 42–64.

6. MacLeod, 55.

World. Smallpox epidemics played a major role in bringing down the Aztec and Inca cultures in Mexico and Peru, respectively.[7]

The role of smallpox in the defeat of the Aztec empire by the Spaniards and Indigenous allies in 1519–21 at Tenochtitlan was so dramatic that William H. McNeil began his epochal book *Plagues and Peoples* with that "extraordinary story."[8] He later stated, "Clearly if smallpox had not come when it did, the Spanish victory could not have been achieved in Mexico."[9] Alfred W. Crosby opened his 1967 paper titled "Conquistador y Pestilencia: The First New World Pandemic and the Fall of the Great Indian Empires" with the assertion, "The most sensational military conflicts in all history are probably those of the Spanish conquistadores over the Aztec and Incan empires. Cortes and Pizarro toppled the highest civilizations of the New World in a few months each." The epidemic "sapped the endurance of Tenochtitlan to survive the Spanish attack."[10] In Panama too, "Of all the killers operating in early Panama, however, smallpox was undoubtedly the most deadly to the Indians."[11] Of this New World epidemic, Henry F. Dobyns has written, "The Andean natives shared with those of Mexico and Central America the devastation of the first New World smallpox epidemic, in all likelihood the most severe single loss of aboriginal population that ever occurred."[12]

Warfare in eighteenth-century North America was often complicated by epidemics of smallpox. For example, the Anglo Cherokee War of 1759–61, a distinct conflict within the French and Indian War, was highly destructive of the Cherokees. Jeffrey Ostler cites data that the population dropped from nine thousand in 1745 to seven thousand in the mid-1760s.[13] Paul Kelton reports that Jeffery Amherst oversaw a scorched-earth campaign that facilitated the spread of smallpox because the Natives were deprived of sustenance, and a mass of refugees "curtailed them from taking effective measures to inhibit infections." It was human agency that facilitated Indigenous infection.[14] In another example, at the start of the American Revolution, the colonists attempted to take Quebec. The attempt was routed in large part by a self-sustaining outbreak of smallpox. In a gripping account, Elizabeth A. Fenn describes the abject misery and decimation caused by smallpox among the colonial troops in their retreat from the Plains of Abraham to Lake George.[15]

---

7. Alfred Crosby, "Conquistador y Pestilencia: The First New World Epidemic and the Fall of the Great Indian Empires," *Hispanic American Historical Review* 47, no 3. (August 1967): 321–27; William McNeil, *Plagues and Peoples* (Garden City: Anchor Press/Doubleday, 1976), 369.
8. McNeil, *Plagues and Peoples*, 1
9. McNeil, 207.
10. Crosby, "Conquistador y Pestilencia," 330.
11. Crosby, 331.
12. Henry F. Dobyns, "An Outline of Andean Epidemic History to 1720," *Bulletin of the History of Medicine* 37 (November 1963): 514.
13. Jeffrey Ostler, *Surviving Genocide: Native Nations and the United States from the American Revolution to Bleeding Kansas* (New Haven: Yale University Press, 2019), 34.
14. Paul Kelton, *Cherokee Medicine, Colonial Germs* (Norman: University of Oklahoma Press, 2015), 105.
15. Elizabeth A. Fenn, *Pox Americana: The Great Smallpox Epidemic of 1775–82* (New York: Hill and Wang, 2001), 62–79.

TABLE 1. CHRONOLOGY OF KEY EVENTS OF THE FRENCH AND INDIAN WAR, 1754–1760

START OF THE WAR IN NORTH AMERICA

1754	FORT NECESSITY, THE LOSS AND HUMILIATION OF GEORGE WASHINGTON

PHASE OF FRENCH DOMINANCE, 1754–1757

1755	DEFEAT OF GENERAL BRADDOCK AT THE MONONGAHELA RIVER BATTLE OF LAKE GEORGE, CONSTRUCTION OF FORT WILLIAM HENRY ACADIAN EXPULSION
1756	FORT OSWEGO TAKEN BY FRENCH UNDER GENERAL MONTCALM FRENCH AND BRITISH EACH DECLARE WAR, THE GLOBAL SEVEN YEARS' WAR BEGINS
1757	FRENCH UNDER MONTCALM TAKE FORT WILLIAM HENRY BY SIEGE, FOLLOWED BY MASSACRE; INDIANS ARE INFECTED WITH SMALLPOX MONTCALM CANNOT PROCEED TO FORT EDWARD NOR ON TO ALBANY

TURNING POINT

1757–1758	INDIANS BRING SMALLPOX BACK TO PAYS D'EN HAUT VILLAGE POPULATIONS VIRTUALLY WIPED OUT INDIANS OF PAYS D'EN HAUT REFUSE TO PARTICIPATE IN CAMPAIGN OF 1758 UNDER MONTCALM

PHASE OF BRITISH DOMINANCE AND VICTORY, 1758–1760

1758	BRITISH CAPTURE LOUISBOURG BRITISH CAPTURE OF FORTS OSWEGO, FRONTENAC, AND DUQUESNE MONTCALM REBUFFS BRITISH ATTACK ON FORT CARILLON (TICONDEROGA)
1759	BRITISH TAKE FORTS NIAGARA, TICONDEROGA, AND CROWN POINT QUEBEC FALLS TO COORDINATED BRITISH SIEGE

END OF THE WAR IN NORTH AMERICA

1760	MONTREAL FALLS TO THE BRITISH AND ARTICLES OF CAPITULATION SIGNED

Smallpox played a focused and crucial role in the turning point in the French and Indian War. The military events of the war are presented chronologically in table 1.

The French and Indian War started with a dispute over the control of the Ohio Valley in 1754. French Canada viewed control over the Ohio Valley as necessary to maintain communications between and the safety of Montreal and New Orleans, its widely separated colonial centers. British colonies on the East Coast eyed the Ohio Valley as a fertile region for expansion beyond the Appalachian Mountain chain and for land sales. George Washington had been sent on a military expedition by Governor Dinwiddie of Virginia in response to French incursions in the area. En route to the forks of the Ohio River, where the Allegheny and Monongahela Rivers join to form the Ohio River, Washington's force, including some

Seneca warriors, encountered a small French unit. On first contact, a young French ensign named Jumonville was killed. A larger force led by Jumonville's brother subsequently forced Washington to surrender at Fort Necessity.[16]

While the surrender at Fort Necessity in 1754 would mark the beginning of the French and Indian War, the French and English and their colonies in North America had been at each other's throats for decades. The wars on the North American continent were reflections of European conflicts. King William's War, 1689–97, was the colonial arm of the War of the League of Augsburg.[17] Queen Anne's War in North America was part of the 1701–13 War of Spanish Succession in Europe. The Treaty of Utrecht, which ended that war, included provisions that gave the British Newfoundland and part of Nova Scotia. The third war on the North American continent, preceding the French and Indian War, was King George's War, which was part of the European War of the Austrian Succession, 1744–1748. That conflict was ended by the Treaty of Aix-la-Chapelle in 1748, which returned Louisburg, a key strategic site for the entrance to the St. Lawrence River, to the French. Most importantly, the treaty left ambiguous the control of the interior of the continent. In conflicts between the French and the British, Indians would play major roles, with the majority siding with the French. Slightly more than half a decade would pass after the Treaty of Aix-la-Chapelle before war boiled over again. This time the start would focus on lands of the Ohio Valley.[18]

With one important exception, the war can be seen as playing out along a few waterways radiating from the hub of Quebec/Montreal. Key to defense of the hub were the Gulf of St. Lawrence and the St. Lawrence River. As the British navy gained superiority, it provided the means to block the resupply of New France via the St. Lawrence River. And with the support of the British navy, the river also became the path from which to launch ground attacks on Montreal and Quebec. The Gulf of St. Lawrence was the site of important naval installations: Louisbourg and Halifax. The lower Great Lakes, Lakes Ontario and Erie, and Forts Frontenac, Oswego, and Niagara extended the St. Lawrence waterway. The upper Great Lakes, Huron, Michigan, and Superior, subtending the high country, or the Pays d'en Haut, were connected to the hub of Quebec/Montreal either through the lower Great Lakes or through the French and Ottawa Rivers.

The Montreal to Albany waterway through the Richelieu River, Lake Champlain, and

---

16. Fred Anderson, *Crucible of War: The Seven Years' War and the Fate of Empire in British North America, 1754–1766* (New York: Vintage Books, 2001), 50–65.

17. It is not the intent of this paragraph to describe in detail the three wars of France and England that preceded the French and Indian War. Rather, the intent is to put them into context. A succinct text is the introduction to Ronald J. Dale, *The Fall of New France: How the French Lost a North American Empire, 1754–1763* (Toronto: James Lorimer, 2004), 7–12. A useful chronology appears in William M. Fowler Jr., *Empires at War: The French and Indian War and the Struggle for North America, 1754–1763* (New York, Walker & Company, 2005), xxi-xxv.

18. For this and the next three paragraphs see map 9 in H. H. Tanner, J. Peterson, R.J. Surtees and cartography by M. Pinther, *Atlas of Great Lakes Indian History* (Norman: University of Oklahoma Press, 1987), 40–41.

Lake George (Lac Sacrament), and then portage to the Hudson River also played a major role in this story. Several critical forts and locations were laid out along that route: Ile-aux-Noix, Fort St. Frederic (Crown Point), Fort Carillon (Ticonderoga), Fort William Henry, and Fort Edward (Fort Lyman). It was the campaign for Fort William Henry that led to the acquisition of smallpox by the Indians of the Pays d'en Haut. It is at the southernmost tip of Lake George, now the site of Lake George Village. Had General Montcalm started his campaign earlier in the season and had he been able to hold his forces together, not losing the Indians, who felt betrayed, and the Canadians to the harvest, he might have marched on to take Fort Edward at the Great Carrying Place on the Hudson. He could then likely have moved unopposed to the capital of Albany. How different the war might have been had he taken Albany, with its direct access to New York City via the Hudson River, to western New York State via the Mohawk River, and to its land routes to western New England. Ironically, had the Indians continued with Montcalm on to Fort Edward and Albany, they would likely have come down with smallpox, weakening the fighting force.

The one exception to the Montreal/Quebec hub and spoke model was the site at the forks of the Ohio River, the juncture of the Allegheny and Monongahela Rivers. The forks served as a hub, too, with a water route west and ultimately south to New Orleans via the Mississippi River. The land route from the east to the forks was painfully constructed by Gen. Edward Braddock in his spectacularly unsuccessful attempt to reach Fort Duquesne, which guarded the forks. Fort Duquesne would become Fort Pitt when it fell into British hands.

The French and Indian defeat of Braddock at the Monongahela River on July 9, 1755, was astonishing and representative of French and Indian dominance during the first phase of the war. It demonstrated the lethal effectiveness of guerrilla style fighting used by the Indians against numerically superior fighting forces that were highly trained in formal battle lines and siege warfare. The French and Indian force arrayed against Braddock was heavily weighted with warriors from the Pays d'en Haut.[19] The image of the inexorable march of a massive war machine of 1,500 soldiers, heavy artillery, supply wagons, animals for slaughter, and camp followers under the courageous if implacable and inflexible General Braddock is likely one the British were happy to project. Cutting its way through the frontier forest, its goal was the relatively small and undermanned French fort at the Monongahela River. On the day prior to battle, the fort's commander, Picaudy de Contrecour, and the leader of a relief force, Capt. Lienard de Beaujeu, decided to go out and meet the enemy with a mixed detachment. That detachment consisted of 72 marines, 146 Canadians, and 637 Indians.[20] Although other tribes were represented, the French allied Indians were mainly "from the north and west—Ottawas, Mississaguas, Wyandots, Potawatomis—lured

---

19. Michael A. McDonnell, *Masters of Empire: Great Lakes Indians and the Making of America* (1969; repr., New York: Hill and Wang, 2015), 169
20. Fregault, *Canada*, 95.

Figure 1. "Defeat of General Braddock, 9th July 1755." Wood engraving, 1836. COURTESY OF THE LIBRARY OF CONGRESS, PRINTS AND PHOTOGRAPHS DIVISION, LC-USZ62-63135.

by the prospect of captives and booty."[21] After a first engagement, the advance troops of the British fell back into the main body, causing chaos. Their circumstances were impossible. As described by Guy Fregault, "A narrow road bordered on both sides by dense forests led up from the shores of the Monongahela to the higher ground where the two forces had met."[22] Indians and Canadians were deployed in the forest on both sides of the narrow road. They "were free to fire on a vulnerable mass—defenseless, disorganized, blind. In the slaughter 'whole ranks fell at once.'"[23] Braddock was killed. His documents, including the British plans for the war, were captured. The defeat was shattering. The British beat a hasty retreat, leaving or destroying heavy equipment and artillery. The retreat, ultimately to Philadelphia, and the road painfully built through the forests and over difficult terrain left the frontier open to bloody raids by Indians. The attackers included the Potawatomi and their allies.[24] Thus the Indians of the upper Great Lakes region made major contributions to the defeat of Braddock and to the fearful sequelae of frontier raids. In contrast, the

---

21. Anderson, *Crucible of War*, 99.
22. Anderson, *Crucible of War*, 95.
23. Fregault, *Canada*, 96.
24. Russell D. Edmonds, *The Potawatomis: Keepers of the Fire* (Norman: University of Oklahoma Press, 1978), 51.

Indians' later withdrawal of support for the French in the campaign of 1758 would be crucial. It followed the smallpox epidemic that swept through their villages in the Pays d'en Haut and which was carried there from the campaign for Fort William Henry. Their withdrawal would be a major component in the turning point of the war in favor of the British.

The year 1756 was one of continuations and beginnings. The continuing assaults on the frontier by Indians, often supported by French and Canadians, seemingly without military opposition, terrified British colonials. It was also the year in which the European combatants engaged in the war on a formal basis, declaring war on each other. But significant appointments constituted crucial beginnings. The Marquis de Montcalm, a highly experienced French military man, was dispatched to New France to direct military operations. William Pitt was appointed as British Secretary of State. Pitt would pour the necessary resources into the North American conflict, which in combination with other factors (see table 2) would ultimately wrest control of the continent from the French.

The site where the Oswego River flows into Lake Ontario had been a thorn in the side of the French since 1727, when British traders had set up a trading post there. The French had had a lucrative trade in furs brought by the Indians from points west to be traded at Montreal. The British traders' post at Oswego diverted some of that trade to the Oswego and Mohawk Rivers, sending the furs to Albany instead of to Montreal.[25] The post ultimately became a British garrison. That challenged French control of Lake Ontario, with Fort Frontenac at the origin of the St. Lawrence River on its the eastern end and Fort Niagara at its western end. Hence, the ways west and south and their associated trade routes were jeopardized. Fort Oswego was thus an important target for Canada's Governor Vaudreuil at the start of the French and Indian War.[26] The siege in August 1756 was carried out by General Montcalm, newly arrived from France. Fort Oswego consisted of three forts that were poorly designed and hard to defend. The British surrendered after a brief siege, and hundreds were taken prisoner. The French left the fort in ruins. According to Francis Parkman, the victory " . . . was the greatest that the French arms had yet achieved in America." With it, "France had conquered the undisputed command of Lake Ontario, and her communications with the west were safe."[27] Of the British, Francis Jennings wrote, "The whole episode is a mind-boggling story of asininity and worse."[28] But the greatest impact was on the Indian tribes who professed greater support for the French after their decisive victory.

The year 1756 strengthened the Indians' commitment to the war. It was a time of raiding the frontiers in the wake of Braddock's devastating defeat the previous year. As a measure of their closeness with Canadians, "many of the Potawatomis brought their families to

---

25. Fowler, *Empires at War*, 7.

26. Parkman, *Montcalm and Wolfe*, 236–37.

27. Parkman, 241.

28. Francis Jennings, *Empire of Fortune* (New York: W.W. Norton, 1988), 293.

Montreal to live with the Canadians while the warriors raided against the British."[29] Indian enthusiasm for aiding the French against the British was considerably enhanced by Montcalm's taking of Oswego (Chouegen). According to Pierre Pouchot, "they underst[ood] very well the advantage of adhering to the stronger side."[30] Pouchot, who had served as the engineer for Montcalm at the taking of Fort Oswego, recorded that "the capture of Chouegen had a very great influence on all the Indian nations.... One might say that since the operation, they increased their loyalty to & friendship for the French...for although some of them are genuinely fond of us, they only like Europeans in relation to their own self interest."[31] The likelihood of spoils of war was a great motivator. The spoils included "loot," prisoners, and scalps.[32] Prisoners were taken for the purpose of ritual torture or, exactly the opposite, to be adopted, replacing lost family members. These latter prisoners were treated with great support and affection. According to Louis Antoine de Bougainville, scalps "are their trophies, their obelisks, their arches of triumph; the monuments which attest to other tribes and consign to posterity the valor, the exploits of the warriors and the glory of the cabin."[33]

Reaching the principal theater of war for 1757, the Lake Champlain–Lake George valley, would be difficult for the Indians of the high country. Although experienced canoeists, they would have to paddle hundreds of miles to Montreal and then start down the Montreal to Albany route. And unfortunately, at the time, there was an ongoing smallpox epidemic in Canada and in the areas through which and to which the Indians would have to travel. John Joseph Heagerty has noted that the smallpox epidemic in Canada in 1755, which continued on into 1756 and 1757, was so widespread that 1755 became known as "the year of the great smallpox epidemic."[34] In his review of smallpox in the colonies, John Duffy reported that the 1755 Canadian epidemic had moved into New York.[35] It was observed that when smallpox arrived in Albany, it "frightened the provincial troops more than the appearance of Montcalm himself would have done."[36] According to Ian K. Steele, "Some

---

29. Edmonds, *The Potawatomis*, 52.
30. Pierre Pouchot, *Memoirs on the Late War in North America between France and England*, trans. Michael Cardy, ed. Brian L. Dunnigan (Youngstown, NY: Old Fort Niagara Publications, 1994), 105.
31. Pouchot, *Memoirs on the Late War*, 105.
32. These were the "essential symbols of martial success for the Indians" per Ian K. Steele, *Betrayals: Fort William Henry and the "Massacre"* (New York: Oxford University Press, 1990), 184.
33. Louis Antoine de Bougainville, *Adventures in the Wilderness: The American Journals of Louis Antoine de Bougainville, 1756–1760*, ed. and trans. Edward P. Hamilton (Norman: University of Oklahoma Press, 1964), 242. James Axtell and William C. Sturtevant have reviewed the history of scalping, including in Europe and pre-Columbian America, prior to its use in post-contact conflict. See James Axtell and William C. Sturtevant, "The Unkindest Cut, or Who Invented Scalping?," *William and Mary Quarterly* 37, no.3 (July 1980): 451–72.
34. John Joseph Heagerty, *Four Centuries of Medical History in Canada and a Sketch of the Medical History of Newfoundland*, Vol. 1 (Toronto: MacMillan, 1928), 40.
35. Reported in John Duffy, *Epidemics in Colonial America* (Baton Rouge: Louisiana State University Press, 1953), 86–87.
36. Duffy, 88.

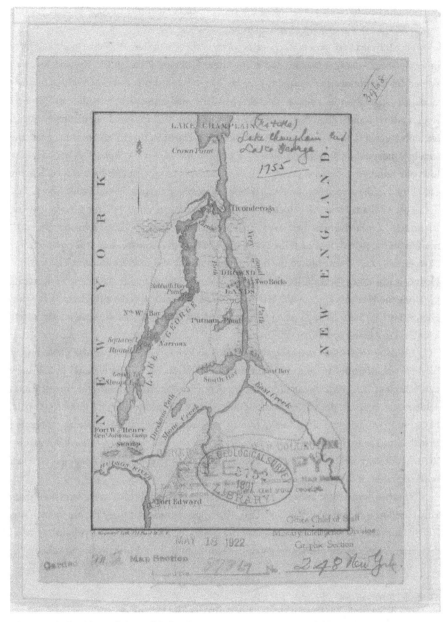

Figure 2. Lake Champlain and Lake George, 1755. COURTESY OF THE NATIONAL ARCHIVES.

warriors turned back after hearing of the prevalence of smallpox in New France, yet one thousand warriors arrived in Montreal in July 1757.[37]

Fort Edward was some sixteen miles south of the site of Fort William Henry and forty miles north of Albany. It was located at the Great Carrying Place on the Hudson River, so named for the portage site around the rapids.[38] Fort Edward was associated with a military smallpox hospital on an adjacent island. The island was subsequently named after Robert Rogers whose Rangers had their base on the island from 1757 to 1759. The smallpox hospital was constructed in the summer of 1757. According to David Starbuck, "As far as I can tell, the smallpox hospital on Roger's Island was in continuous use for a couple of years, having at least one hundred patients at times."[39] Hence, it would appear that smallpox was sufficiently established in the area at that time that a military smallpox hospital would be kept busy.

Fort William Henry was located at the southernmost point of Lake George, or Lac Sacrament. An earthworks fort, it was built at the insistence of William Johnson, the commander of the British Forces at the Battle of Lake George. Construction was completed in November 1755.[40] It constituted the northernmost point of British fortifications at the time. Hence, it was a key location for the defense of the British colonies. The New York colony lay along the Hudson River, with New York City to the south and New England to the east. Hence, Fort William Henry was a crucial target for a French invasion sweeping down the Montreal to Albany corridor.

Utilizing that water corridor, Rigaud de Vaudreuil, the brother of the Governor of New France, Marquis de Vaudreuil, launched an attack on Fort William Henry in February and March of 1757. Without artillery, the French were unable to capture the fort. Rigaud's soldiers succeeded in destroying outbuildings containing war equipment, numerous boats, barks and two galleys.[41] The destruction of the boats at Fort William Henry prevented British attacks on French forts farther north on the Lake George–Lake Champlain–Richelieu River corridor that season. Montcalm would organize a massive attack on the fort in the summer of that year.

The two forces that assaulted Fort William Henry in July 1757 were launched from Fort Carillon by Montcalm.[42] A land-based detachment of about three thousand men was led by Chevalier de Levis, and a waterborne flotilla of 3,842 men was led by Montcalm; this latter force was supplemented by more than eight hundred Indians in 150 canoes.[43] A

---

37. Steele, *Betrayals*, 80.
38. David R. Starbuck, *The Great Warpath: British Military Sites from Albany to Crown Point* (Hanover, NH: University Press of New England, 1999), 54, 83.
39. Starbuck, 65.
40. Steele, *Betrayals*, 62.
41. Fregault, *Canada*, 151.
42. Steele, *Betrayals*, 93–94.
43. In organizing Montcalm's forces at Fort Carillion prior to setting out, there were 979 Indians from the high country and Middle West, and 820 mission Indians. They represented thirty-three nations in all. Anderson, *Crucible of War*, 188–89.

remarkable feature of the flotilla was the transport of carriage-mounted guns and mortars. These were carried by "pontoons," which were two bateaux fastened together. Artillery was to be the fundamental component of the siege of Fort William Henry. The land and water-borne contingents met up at Ganaouske Bay, present-day Bolton, New York. The two forces then moved on to set up the siege works to assault Fort William Henry.[44]

After the strategic establishment of the siege works, the siege itself was of a relatively brief duration. The French artillery simply overwhelmed the fort. The fort was led by the heroic Lt. Col. George Monro. He had hoped for military assistance from the commander of Fort Edward, Gen. Daniel Webb. That help was not to materialize as General Webb was fearful of leaving Fort Edward vulnerable to attack by Montcalm and thence leaving the route to Albany open. On August 9, after Fort William Henry's defenses were virtually depleted and the French guns had been moved into deadly firing distance, a discussion of surrender was agreed upon. Montcalm, impressed by the courage shown in the defense of the fort, offered terms of an honorable surrender, and Monro accepted. The surrender included the parole of the British forces to Fort Edward with colors flying and the retention of unloaded arms and personal belongings.[45]

The Indians were enraged by these terms of surrender.[46] A French attempt to escort the British to Fort Edward at night was considered and rejected, but it nonetheless further infuriated the Indians. According to Steele, "They resented the European conspiracy, which had defrauded them of their share of the loot in the fort and now, apparently, plotted to trick them out of the timely search for spoils of war out of the encampment as well."[47] The following morning, August 10, brought mayhem. The Indians attacked the column of British prisoners who had lined up to be marched to Fort Edward, plundering, killing, and scalping them, and taking many prisoners. Ultimately order was restored but not before Montcalm's attempt for an honorable surrender had been destroyed. Scalps had been taken and the Indians headed off to Montreal with prisoners who would be ransomed or kept. The aftermath of the surrender at Fort William Henry would go down as a massacre. The honor of the French military in North America was badly damaged for failing to protect their British prisoners.[48] Years later, Capt. Jonathan Carver,[49] a volunteer who had fought at Fort William Henry, described the chaos and his escape from the melee. "But whatever

---

44. Steele, *Betrayals*, 94.

45. Steele, *Betrayals*, 110. The term quoted by Steele is "brave and honorable defense."

46. According to Crouch these peoples included the Anishinabeg of the Great Lakes and the Iroquois, Abenakis, Nipissings, and Hurons of the St. Lawrence reserves. Christian Ayne Crouch, *Nobility Lost: French and Canadian Martial Cultures, Indians, and the End of New France* (Ithaca, NY: Cornell University Press, 2014), 87.

47. Crouch, *Nobility Lost*, 113.

48. Anderson, *Crucible of War*, 185-201.

49. Jonathan Carver's "eyewitness" account of the killings at Fort William Henry was called by Steele the most influential at the time they were published in London during the American Revolution (Steele, *Betrayals*, 157–58). Carver would be castigated as an unreliable witness. Yet Steele would write that Carver "could not forget his own harrowing experience" (158).

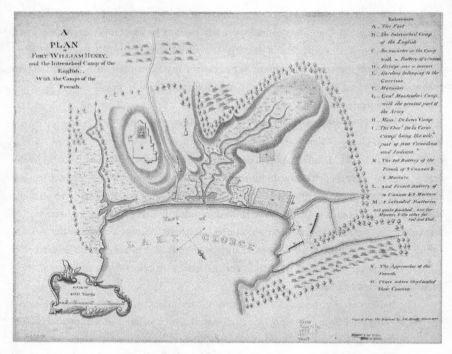

Figure 3. A Plan of Fort William Henry, and the Intrenched Camp of the English—with the Camps of the French, 1763. Courtesy of the Library of Congress.

was the cause from which it arose, the consequences of it were dreadful, and not to be paralleled in modern history."[50]

For the Indians two consequences unfolded. First, Indian allies of the French felt betrayed, and many would not fight for Montcalm again. They had spent up to twelve weeks canoeing hundreds of miles to reach Montreal, had faithfully participated in the campaign to capture Fort William Henry, and yet were denied the spoils of war.[51] Second, devastatingly, dreaded smallpox had (unknowingly) been transmitted to them in the campaign for Fort William Henry. And they carried it back to the high country of the Great Lakes. "The western Indians would discover too late that the English and provincials at William Henry were suffering from the smallpox, and thus the captives, scalps, and clothing they brought back carried the seeds of a great epidemic, which would devastate their homelands."[52] One must recognize, too, that the Indians themselves would maintain chains of infection. Pouchot would report that some of the Indians, seeing freshly dug graves, exhumed them,

50. Capt. J [as given] Carver, "A Detail of the Massacre of the English, by the French Indians, at Ft. William Henry, in America, in 1757," *Arminian Magazine* 17 (January 1794): 33–38, 35.
51. McDonnell, *Masters of Empire*, 36.
52. Anderson, *Crucible of War*, 199.

counter to usual behavior, for their scalps. Some of those victims had died from small-pox, which then spread among the Indians. Of the Potawatomi nation he wrote, "One of the bravest & most faithful to the French cause was almost wiped out by the epidemic."[53] Deaths were accelerated by the practice of plunging into water: "Whilst their blood was in the state of fermentation, and nature was striving to throw out the peccant matter, they checked her operations by plunging into the water: the consequence was, that they died by hundreds."[54]

The question of where exactly the Indians of the Pays d'en Haut were infected during the campaign for Fort William Henry has been raised by Gregory Evans Dowd in his 2015 book *Groundless*.[55] "Did they acquire smallpox precisely through their siege of Fort William Henry or more pointedly in the course of the post-surrender mayhem on August 9 and 10?"[56] On his examination of the evidence he concludes, "The point remains that we do not know how many, if any, of the sick attacked after the surrender had the dreaded disease."[57] But that the western Great Lakes were decimated by smallpox is not contested. "Ottawas, Ojibwes, and Potawatomis suffered, and they would not again contribute such large numbers to French campaigns."[58]

The incubation period, that is, the time between exposure to the smallpox virus and the appearance of symptoms of disease, was between twelve and fourteen days.[59] The disease was highly contagious.[60] There would have been many cycles of infection, amplification of the infection, and expansion of the number of Indians infected as the Indians paddled their way home. Hence, it is surprising that the first mention of smallpox among the Indians returning home was not until November 12 in a letter from Fort Niagara.[61] The disease also killed colonist troops later as redeemed prisoners and parolees.[62]

The trip from Montreal back to the Indians' villages in the Pays d'en Haut, was described by McDonnell as "seven hundred miles or so from Montreal to Michilimackinac along the Ottawa River."[63] The straits of Michilimackinac lie between the Great Lakes of Huron and Michigan. They are connected to a "vast interconnected system of waterways

---

53. Pouchot, *Memoirs on the Late War*, 121.
54. Carver, "A Detail of the Massacre of the English," 37.
55. Gregory E. Dowd, *Groundless: Rumors, Legends, and Hoaxes on the Early American Frontier* (Baltimore, MD: Johns Hopkins University Press, 2015), 391.
56. Dowd, *Groundless*, 51.
57. Dowd, *Groundless*, 53.
58. Dowd, *Groundless*, 50.
59. A. B. Christie, *Infectious Diseases: Epidemiology and Clinical Practice*, 3rd ed. (Edinburgh: Churchill Livingstone, 1980), 231. See also the helpful table on communicability, time after infection, symptoms and pathogenesis in Fenn, *Pox Americana*, 19.
60. The past tense is used as smallpox was eliminated worldwide in 1979 by the WHO Global Eradication Program. See John Booss and Marie L. Landry with Marilyn J. August, *To Catch a Virus*, 2nd ed. (Washington, DC: ASM Press, 2023), 51.
61. Dowd, *Groundless*, 56.
62. Steele, *Betrayal*, 138, 143.
63. McDonnell, *Masters of Empire*, 54.

PLATE XI.

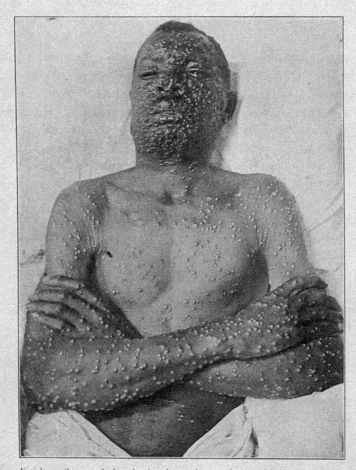

Variola on the seventh day, showing the usual preponderance of lesions on the face, hands, and wrists (courtesy of Dr. J. F. Schamberg).

Figure 4. Smallpox lesions, 1968. COURTESY OF THE CENTERS FOR DISEASE CONTROL, PUBLIC HEALTH IMAGES LIBRARY.

which could take a savvy paddler just about anywhere on the continent and beyond."[64] To modern experience, the trip was a remarkable feat: traversing the Ottawa River, the French River, and Lake Huron "requiring thirty or more portages."[65] Other routes were also taken. Some Indians stopped off at Fort Detroit at the western end of Lake Erie on the way home to their villages.[66] Not surprisingly, given the multiple cycles of infection that would have been possible, McDonnell noted, "Some reportedly died on their way home from the campaign. Others lived long enough to bring it [smallpox] back to their villages."[67] Of relevance to acquired immunity, Steele notes that the Indians from the Pays d'en Haut, on returning home, found that "were bringing with them a devastating epidemic of smallpox." In contrast, "The mission Indians had also been exposed to smallpox regularly for generations, so their acquired resistance and survivors' immunities lessened the ravages of the disease in their communities."[68]

The strategic consequence to the French of the immediate departure of the Indians after the siege and massacre at Fort William Henry was highly significant. Without the Indians' scouting and fighting prowess Montcalm would be unable to march on to take Fort Edward and then continue on to Albany—had he even planned to do so. Other factors intervened as well. Many Canadians had to return home to harvest their crops. The harvest of 1756 had been poor, and the 1757 harvest would also turn out badly. In Pouchot's estimation, "The capture of Ft. William Henry filled the province of New York with consternation. It is certain that, had M. de Montcalm been able to keep the Indians, he could have dominated the entire region, including the capital, as it was entirely defenseless."[69] It is highly unlikely that Montcalm had envisioned pushing on to Fort Edward. If so, he surely would not have paroled the British prisoners to that British fort.

Bougainville would write that there were several issues mitigating against marching on to Fort Edward (Fort Lydius). "In regard to the enterprise against Fort Lydius, invincible obstacles prevented us from thinking of it, the lack of munitions, and provisions, the difficulty of a portage of six leagues without oxen or horses, with an army worn out by fatigue and bad food, the departure of all the Indians of the Far West who have five hundred leagues to go over lakes and rivers which freeze and prevent them remaining longer, the flight of almost all of the domesticated Indians, the necessity of sending back the Canadians for the harvests already ripe, sixteen hundred men assembled at the fort whose capture they [Canadian critics] think so easy, these are the reasons which stopped the further advance of the King's army."[70]

---

64. McDonnell, *Masters of Empire*, 21.
65. McDonnell, *Masters of Empire*, 36
66. Tanner, *Atlas of Great Lakes Indian History*, Map 9, 41–42; and Map 23, 127.
67. McDonnell, *Masters of Empire*, 188. The Odawa accounts are quoted on 189.
68. Steele, *Betrayals*, 132.
69. Pouchot, *Memoirs on the Late War*, 121.
70. Bougainville, *Adventures in the Wilderness*, 171.

Had Montcalm's army been able to start the campaign six weeks earlier, Bougainville noted "… the difficulties outlined above would not have existed, and I dare say that today we would have had Fort Lydius."[71] That turn of events would have set the stage for a very different campaign of 1758. If Montcalm had been able to continue on, taking Fort Edward and then Albany, it is by no means certain that a shift to British dominance in the war the following year would have occurred at that time.

Montcalm, it was felt by the Indians, had treated them badly. For this observation, Bougainville refers to letters from Vaudreuil to Montcalm. Vaudreuil cautioned that "the colony owes its safety to the Indians, that these tribes require much gentleness and complaisance, that they complain in open council that he [Montcalm] has treated them harshly and [they] will no longer return to war in the region as long as he commands there."[72] That complaint by the Indians amplified the decision of the high country Indians to withdraw from the campaign of 1758 because of the devastation wrought by smallpox. While the behavior of Montcalm toward the Indians was surely a strong detriment, it would not have physically impaired the Indians' capacity to mount a campaign. In contrast, the very severe depletion of the warrior forces by the smallpox epidemic in 1757–58 would have physically prevented the Indians from the Pays d'en Haut from mounting a campaign in 1758.

The Indians blamed the French for inviting them into the arena where they were infected with the smallpox. MacLeod notes, "It quickly became apparent that Franco-Amerindian harmony in the pays d'en haut was going to be one of the casualties of the epidemic."[73] In May 1758, Bougainville commented, "Finally [the relations of] all these nations [with us] are on the decline. What is the cause of it? The great loss they have suffered from the smallpox, the bad medicine the French have thrown to them, the great greed of the commanders of the posts and their ignorance of Indian customs?"[74] Anderson summarizes the outcome: "No Warriors from the pays d'en haut would help Montcalm again, and even the converts from the St. Lawrence missions would become reluctant to take up the hatchet."[75] The experience of the epidemic was so severe that "Potawatomis, Ojibwe, and Ottawa in the Great Lakes area voiced allegations of genocide in the wake of the 1757–1758 smallpox epidemic that ravaged their communities."[76]

There are no written contemporary records from the Indigenous peoples themselves of the effects smallpox epidemic of 1757–58. There is written history taken from the oral history of the Indians, and there is a transcript of testimony of a former colonist prisoner. D. Peter MacLeod has reviewed the historiography of the Great Lakes area and found that the oral history of the seventeenth and eighteenth centuries was preserved in printed

71. Bougainville, *Adventures in the Wilderness*, 172.
72. Bougainville, *Adventures in the Wilderness*, 259–60.
73. MacLeod, "Microbes and Muskets," 50.
74. Bougainville, *Adventures in the Wilderness*, 204.
75. Anderson, *Crucible of War*, 199.
76. Ostler, "'To Extirpate the Indians,'" 591.

fashion in the nineteenth century.[77] Andrew J. Blackbird, born an Ottawa, was able to publish the history of his tribe in 1887.[78] He noted that the Ottawa "were greatly reduced in numbers from what they were in former times on account of the smallpox which they brought from Montreal during the French war with Great Britain." He describes how they brought home self contained tin boxes within the last of which were "mouldy particles," after which smallpox broke out. The graphic description followed: "Lodge after lodge was totally vacated—nothing but dead bodies lying here and there in their lodges—entire families being swept off with the ravages of this terrible disease." In addition, Elizabeth A. Fenn reports on the exceptional, near contemporary, manuscript giving the testimony of Cornelius Van Slyke to William Johnson. Van Slyke had been held prisoner by the Chippewa and the Potawatomis for four years. He said that the Indians "believed that the great Number they lost of their people at & returning from Lake George in 1757 was owing to ye. English poisoning the Rum, & giving them the Small Pox, for which they owe them an everlasting ill will."[79]

Considering the fighting forces of the French, the siege and surrender of the British at Fort William Henry ended up as something of a pyrrhic victory. The Indians from the Pays d'en Haut, disgusted with Montcalm and the smallpox epidemic in their villages, resolved not to fight further for the French. The violent aftermath of the siege of Fort William Henry further widened the gap between the Natives, the Canadian marines, and the French officers from the metropole. Adhering to European standards of honor, according to Christiane Crouch, junior French officers considered the behavior of the Indians degenerate. And "for the first time, the poor behavior of the marines" came under scrutiny.[80] For their part, Natives, too, "began to believe that something was not right with their European allies. They had ceased to behave as they should. Gifts became contested, siege assaults were expected and French leaders interacted awkwardly with or neglected female delegates, young men, and orators."[81] Thus, divisions and tensions emerged in the heterogeneous fighting forces that had hitherto functioned effectively together.

In the campaigns of 1758, the British forces dominated with victories at Louisbourg, Fort Duquesne, Fort Frontenac, and Oswego. There was the notable exception of General Montcalm's holding of Fort Carillon (Ticonderoga), due in large measure to the death of the British Brigadier-General Howe. The British sweep of victories continued in 1759 at

77. D. Peter MacLeod, "The Anishinabeg Point of View: The History of the Great Lakes Region to 1800 in Nineteenth-Century Mississauga, Odawa, and Ojibwa Historiography." *Canadian Historical Review* 73, no. 2 (June 1992):194–210, 195.

78. Andrew J. Blackbird, *History of the Ottawa and Chippewa Indians of Michigan: A Grammar of Their Language, and Personal and Family History of the Author* (Ypsilanti, MI: Ypsilantian Job Printing House, 1887), 9–10.

79. Elizabeth A. Fenn, "Biological Warfare in Eighteenth-Century North America: Beyond Jeffery Amherst," *Journal of American History* 86, no. 4 (March 2000) : 1552–80, 1566n26.

80. Crouch, *Nobility Lost*, 88.

81. Crouch, *Nobility Lost*, 91.

Fort Niagara, Fort Ticonderoga, and Crown Point. Crucially, in a highly complex and co-ordinated ground and naval siege, the British took Quebec. The victory was highlighted by General James Wolfe's daring climb to the Plains of Abraham and by the subsequent deaths of both Wolfe and Montcalm.[82] The year 1760 saw the end of the war in North America with the surrender of Montreal and the articles of capitulation. These specified that Canadians would retain their language, the Roman Catholic religion, and their civil law. Furthermore, they retained their properties and their rights in trade.[83] There was some expectation that in a future treaty concluding the international Seven Years' War, that Canada would revert to the French empire. That did not happen. The war and the 1760 capitulation would be deemed "the most important event in Canadian history."[84]

With the benefit of hindsight, it is apparent that the tides of war had shifted and that a turning point had occurred following the siege of Fort William Henry in the late summer of 1757. From the loss by George Washington at Fort Necessity in 1754, which opened the war in North America, to the French victory at Fort William Henry in 1757, the British had suffered loss after loss. Most dramatic was the devastating loss by General Braddock in the forests of Pennsylvania, which had been characterized by the Indians and Canadians attacking the British in a forest guerrilla–style ambush.

Yet, following the French victory at the siege of Fort William Henry, fortunes turned. Historians have identified the transition from the August 1757 siege and massacre at Fort William Henry to the campaigns of 1758 as the turning point in the war. In his laudatory review of Ian Steele's book, *Betrayals*, Fred Anderson writes that Steele's "account provides more than enough evidence to support" the conclusion that the siege at Fort William Henry was the "strategic turning point of the war." He observes that the French had "forfeited the Indian support that they needed to defend Canada."[85] In his own masterpiece, *Crucible of War*, Anderson labels the years 1756–1757 as the "Nadir," and the year 1758 as the "Turning Point."[86] He specifically links the smallpox brought from the Fort William Henry campaign, the epidemic in the homelands of the Indians of the Pays d'en Haut, and the Indians' determination not to assist Montcalm again.[87]

Ian Steele's focus was that the Indians felt betrayed by their allies, the French, because of what they saw as collusion with their enemies, the British. Yet he juxtaposes smallpox and betrayals in his comment on why the Indians would not return to battle for the French: "what they saw as the subsequent collusion with the enemy after the siege. The returning Indians had fewer prisoners or scalps to display than their success warranted, and they

---

82. Anderson, *Crucible of War*, 344–68.
83. Dale, *The Fall of New France*, 77.
84. Fregault, *Canada*, ix.
85. Frank Anderson, review of *Betrayals: Fort William Henry and the "Massacre,"* by Ian K. Steele, *Journal of American History* 78, no. 2 (September 1991): 639–40.
86. Anderson, *Crucible of War*, x.
87. Anderson, *Crucible of War*, 199.

had little remaining plunder. Before long they also discovered that they were bringing with them a devastating epidemic of smallpox. They did not return in comparable numbers to help New France again."[88]

In addition to the scouting and fighting capacities of the Pais d'en Haut Natives lost to the French forces, another significant element in the turning point of the war was the mounting cost to the French ministry. The Indian participation in the 1757 campaign at Fort William Henry and their losses due to smallpox were substantial. Governor Vaudreuil had already heard from the French authorities about the "excessive expenditure" for the colony. Then there were another million livres in costs to cover the losses of Indians who had succumbed to smallpox.[89] The greatly enhanced British resources and personnel were major factors in the decisive victories in the campaign of 1758. But as McDonnell explains, "the loss of their native allies at such a critical moment was at least as heavy a blow. Their absence contributed substantially to the inability of the French to defend themselves at this critical turning point."[90] MacLeod's data shows a rebound of Indigenous participation with the French in 1759. Yet it was to no avail, the war was essentially lost at that point, "Finally in 1759, the presence of thousands of Amerindian warriors in the field did not save the French."[91]

A specific tactical example of the effect of the absence of Native support, ironically, is in the one significant French victory in the campaign of 1758, the holding of Fort Carillon (Fort Ticonderoga) by Montcalm. Writing of his inability to pursue the British after their failed assault, Montcalm said, "What a day for France! If I had had two hundred Indians to send out at the head of a thousand picked men under Chevalier de Levis, not many would have escaped."[92]

Richard White, comparing the events with those in the preceding King George's War (1744–1748), summarizes, "Once more smallpox epidemics ravaged the Indians. Once more warriors became disgruntled and alienated, and once more the alliance began to fall apart in the *pays d'en haut*."[93] Thus, smallpox was at the root of a dissolution of the diplomatic alliance.

Taken together, the financial, tactical, military, and diplomatic evidence supports the critical role that the smallpox decimation of the Native peoples of the Pays d'en Haut played in their withdrawal from the conflict and in the turning point of the war.

Parkman, in his foundational *Montcalm and Wolfe*, closes the chapter on Fort William

---

88. Steele, *Betrayals*, 131-132.
89. McDonnell, *Masters of Empire*, 194. The French correspondence is cited on 363n66.
90. McDonnell, *Masters of Empire*, 194. The French correspondence is cited on 363n67.
91. MacLeod, "Microbes and Muskets," 55.
92. Rueben Gold Thwaites, *France in America, 1497–1763* (New York: Harper & Brothers, 1905), 233. The recipient, Doreil, is noted in text. Of interest: the running chapter head is "Turning Point."
93. Richard White, *The Middle Ground: Indians, Empires, and Republics in the Great Lakes Region, 1650–1815* (Cambridge, UK: Cambridge University Press, 2011), 246.

Henry with a melancholic passage: "The din of ten thousand combatants, the rage, the terror, the agony, were gone; and no living thing was left but the wolves that gathered from the mountains to feast on the dead."[94] That melancholy would dramatically change for the British in the following year; their fortunes soared in 1758. A significant part of the turnaround was the absence of Indians from the Pays d'en Haut who had been markedly depleted by smallpox and were now unwilling to fight for the French.

For centuries, smallpox had inspired great fear, as described by the British historian Thomas Babington Macaulay in his *History of England,* "turning the babe into a changeling at which the mother shuddered, and making the eyes and cheeks of the betrothed maiden objects of horror to the lover."[95] A scourge for centuries, smallpox would be defeated by an English country physician. Edward Jenner applied the simple but revolutionary principle of gaining immunity through the inoculation of a related benign virus, cowpox. The advance rested on the commonplace observation that milkmaids who had had cowpox appeared to be protected from getting smallpox. He published his stunning results in 1798, at the close of the century in which Britain had wrested control of the North American continent from the French and in which the Americans won their independence from the British.[96] How different would have been the course of the French and Indian War had the combatants, particularly the Indians, been vaccinated. Ironically, less than half a century later, vaccination was demonstrated to a "grand embassy" of Indians by President Thomas Jefferson in Washington, DC, in the winter of 1801–2. Jefferson had them vaccinated, explained that they would be protected from the disease, and gave them the vaccination matter with instructions on its use.[97]

The great loss of Indigenous life on contact with Europeans and their diseases, as for example in Mexico and in the Pays d'en Haut, has provoked prolonged historical thought. Almost a decade after he published "Conquistador and Pestilencia" describing the fall of the Aztecs to the Spaniards and smallpox, Alfred Crosby laid out a universalizing concept for "aboriginal decline in the Americas"[98] He defined "virgin soil epidemics" as "those in which populations at risk have had no previous contact with the diseases that strike them and are therefore immunologically almost defenseless."[99] That is, these populations had had no previous opportunity to develop acquired immunity with which to protect themselves. Speaking to the issue as to whether the Indians had some genetic weakness, he wrote: "The scientific community inclines toward the view that Native Americans have

94. Parkman, *Montcalm and Wolfe,* 298.
95. Quoted in Logan Clendening, *Sourcebook of Medical History* (New York: Dover, 1960), 292.
96. Edward Jenner, *An Inquiry into the Causes and Effects of the Variolae Vaccinae* (London: Sampson Low, 1798).
97. E. Wagner Stearn and Allen E. Stearn, *The Effect of Smallpox on the Destiny of the Amerindian* (Boston: Bruce Humphries, 1945), 56–57.
98. Alfred W. Crosby, "Virgin Soil Epidemics as a Factor in the Aboriginal Depopulation in America," *William and Mary Quarterly,* 33, no. 2 (April 1976): 289–99.
99. Crosby, "Virgin Soil Epidemics," 289.

no special susceptibility to Old World diseases that cannot be attributed to environmental influences, and probably never did."[100] Furthermore, "The genetic weakness hypothesis may have some validity, but it is unproven and probably unprovable."[101] The role of acquired immunity is emphasized. "Infants are normally protected against infectious diseases common in the area of their birth by antibodies passed on to them before birth by their immunologically experienced mothers. ... This first line of defense does not exist in virgin soil epidemics."[102] Thus the crucial role of acquired immunity in virgin soil epidemics was demonstrated, and the genetic weakness hypothesis was said to be "a weak reed to lean upon.[103]

Yet, the virgin soil thesis is only part of the story in explaining the multiple destructive effects of colonialism on a subjected people. Scholars such as David Jones and Paul Kelton have focused on the pernicious colonial roles of violence, malnutrition, slave labor, social disruption, and displacement. Jones takes issue with writers like Jared Diamond, whom he says favor immunological determinism. Jones argues that theories of immunological determinism "can still assuage European guilt over American Indian depopulation." He concludes that "virgin soil epidemics may be nothing more unique than the familiar forces of poverty, malnutrition, environmental stress, dislocation and social disparity."[104] In a later writing Jones comments on two styles of explanation, one biological and deterministic, the other social and contingent.[105]

Paul Kelton starts his landmark *Cherokee Medicine, Colonial Germs* by writing that he wishes that he did not have to write the book, "that a world existed for our indigenous ancestors in which colonial violence and germs did not exist." His intent is to honor their legacy "by setting the record straight and telling their story of survival."[106] Although he offers alternatives to Crosby's virgin soil thesis, he is gracious in noting that "this book would not have been possible without his pioneering efforts." He also acknowledges Crosby's "efforts to bring to light the ordeal that indigenous peoples faced after 1492."[107] Kelton comes down on the side of human agency: "Rather than genetics and even the universal

---

100. Crosby, "Virgin Soil Epidemics," 291.
101. Crosby, "Virgin Soil Epidemics," 292
102. Crosby, "Virgin Soil Epidemics," 294.
103. Crosby, "Virgin Soil Epidemics," 294.
104. David S. Jones, "Virgin Soils Revisited," *William and Mary Quarterly* 60, no. 4 (October 2003): 703–42. Jones was candid in acknowledging that his perspective was shaped by an awareness of social factors, skepticism about "increasingly detailed genetic information", and the tendency "to blame victims to avoid responsibility for disparities in health status" (742n125).
105. David S. Jones, "Death, Uncertainty, and Rhetoric," in *Beyond Germs: Native Depopulation in North America*, eds. Catherine M. Cameron, Paul Kelton, and Alan C. Swedlund (Tucson: University of Arizona Press, 2015), 16–49. While drawn to the contingent (40), he noted that one of the choices for scholars is to acknowledge "that the determinists and the contingents have both produced powerful arguments and detailed case studies." (42).
106. Paul Kelton, *Cherokee Medicine, Colonial Germs*, xiii.
107. Kelton, *Cherokee Medicine, Colonial Germs*, xiii.

TABLE II. FACTORS IN THE DEFEAT OF THE FRENCH BY THE BRITISH IN THE FRENCH AND INDIAN WAR

PRIME MINISTER WILLIAM PITT'S COMMITMENT TO THE BRITISH CAUSE IN NORTH AMERICA
DOMINANCE OF BRITISH NAVY
BRITISH MILITARY STRATEGY IN THE LAST YEARS OF THE CONFLICT
NUMERICAL SUPERIORITY OF BRITISH COLONISTS
SIEGE WARFARE OF BRITISH
LOSS OF SUPPORT OF FRENCH ALLIED INDIANS FROM PAYS D'EN HAUT BECAUSE OF SMALLPOX
FAILED CANADIAN HARVESTS IN 1757 AND 1758
FINANCIAL CONSTRAINTS ON THE FRENCH GOVERNMENT AND CANADIAN CORRUPTION

absence of acquired immunity to smallpox that characterized Indigenous societies before 1518, human agency played a determinative and unmistakable role in shaping the contours of death and survival of indigenous peoples during their long struggle with colonialism."[108]

With Tai Edwards, Kelton comments that "Native depopulation occurred within the larger historical context in which the choices and actions of colonizers mattered."[109] They argue that recent scholarship should "finally destroy the false dichotomy of germs or genocide that still pervades religious, political, and educational contexts."[110]

Human agency played a crucial role in the spread of smallpox to the Indians from the Pays d'en Haut in 1757. They had paddled hundreds of miles to participate in the battle for Fort William Henry between two dominant European colonizers and had become infected. That infection with smallpox was brought back to their homeland, and it decimated their tribes. The destruction of tribal villages created a pivotal point in the conflict. It resulted in the withdrawal of the Indians of the Pays d'en Haut from the campaign of 1758, the year the tides of war turned. It has been the task of this article to establish the role of smallpox as a crucial factor in that turning point of the war.

---

108. Kelton, *Cherokee Medicine, Colonial Germs*, 20.
109. Tai S. Edwards and Paul Kelton, "Germs, Genocides, and America's Indigenous Peoples," *Journal of American History* 107, no. 1 (June 2020): 75.
110. Edwards and Kelton, "Germs, Genocides, and America's Indigenous Peoples," 76.

Acknowledgments: I thank Professor Stephen K. Amerman of the Department of History at the Southern Connecticut State University for advice and for a critical reading of the manuscript. I thank Frank Bia, Professor Emeritus of Infectious Diseases at the Yale University School of Medicine for his helpful discussions and critical reading of the manuscript. Professor Paul Kelton of SUNY Stony Brook provided a close critical reading and offered numerous crucial suggestions for which I am grateful. Two anonymous readers for *New York History* helped to further refine the manuscript. Mistakes of fact, omission, or interpretation remain my responsibility.

Supplanted Sovereignties

Gateways, Commerce, and Dispossession in Postrevolutionary New York

Nolan M. Cool

Traveling slowly along the muddy, loamy road west from German Flats toward Old Fort Schuyler in the heat of early June 1791, an inquisitive Scottish physician, Alexander Coventry, "found the road grow worse the further I went...mostly level." Within three miles of Old Fort Schuyler, he explained, there were "several new improvements" along the road, populated "seeming[ly] by Germans." Coventry drew attention to a "Capt. [Stephen] Potter and family well, living in a neat log house, and himself [busy] planting corn," thus reflecting farming's continued prominence across the postcolonial countryside. The physician highlighted the settlement's landscape, observing, "An old log house stands where Old Fort Schuyler used to be." Coventry thereby reveals that a developing, culturally entangled borderland village was gradually swallowing the colonial post.[1]

In his 1791 travels, future New York jurist and scholar James Kent mirrored Coventry's conclusion, commenting that "where old Fort Schuyler stood...now there is no vestige."[2] Riding westward, Kent writes that nearby "White's Town is the center of the population and is amazingly increasing."[3] Stopping at Oriskany, a former Oneida village, Kent explains that about "a dozen log houses" stand at this newly engulfed American settlement, as the "Oriskies [Oneida villagers] went off to the westward this spring, their lands being purchased by us." Traversing the well-worn road through Whitestown, Coventry captures the overarching sentiment of the period's travelers, traders, farmers, and settlers gazing at New York's expanding borders, asserting that "this when cleared will be a most beautiful

---

1. Alexander Coventry, *Memoirs of an Emigrant: The Journal of Alexander Coventry, M.D. in Scotland, the United States and Canada During the Period 1783-1831* (Albany, NY: Typescript Prepared by the Albany Institute History and Art and New York State Library, 1978), 546–47.
2. John T. Horton, "The Mohawk Valley in 1791," *New York History* 22, no. 2 (April 1941): 208, 211.
3. Coventry, *Memoirs of an Emigrant*, 547, 549.

country."[4] Coventry represents a landed, white, slaveholding elite—a handful of people who came to erode the diplomacy, reciprocity, and security promised to settlers and Indians alike in New York's borderlands.[5] The picture Coventry paints and the language that he and others like him employed asserts a cosmopolitan, white settler-colonial empire that would soon dominate New York's countryside.

Old Fort Schuyler (present-day Utica), a growing postrevolutionary village in Central New York, constituted a pivotal gateway to early American settler-colonial expansion toward the Great Lakes even before the Erie Canal opened as a crucial corridor funneling people, commerce, and Anglo-American imperialism toward the continental interior in the 1820s. Old Fort Schuyler served to channel the organized development of Central and Western New York, and by extension, an evolving, agrarian-industrial economy toward the North American interior. Here, state officials and encroaching communities perfected the business of Indian removal and explicitly aimed to replace the economy of the Haudenosaunee (or Six Nations) with an American industrial economy fueling continued settler-colonial expansion.[6] The echo of the ax reverberated as settlers downed trees and brush along the border of Indian country, and land acquisition and commercial dominance became the preeminent tools of American settler-colonial projects and territorial expansion.

American settlers like Coventry and Peter Smith, a storeowner and major regional land magnate, favored a vision of log houses, towns, newly established farmsteads, and communities dotting the landscape alongside an increasing number of brick and limestone mansions in growing city-towns that would replace upstate New York's dense forests and small, isolated trading posts. The history of communities like Old Fort Schuyler, which stood between east and west, constitute a foundational framework of how federal, state, and private interests made postwar towns into commercial outposts from which Americans launched colonization efforts to transform the borders of Indian country.

During the 1780s and 1790s, geography, demographic growth, and commercial development converged in New York State to steer settler-colonial expansion westward to the Great Lakes and, by extension, to control the coveted American interior. Old Fort Schuyler's merchants, settlers, and land-hungry speculators like Peter Smith molded the post's economy into a major staging ground for the development of New York's borderlands. Former and newly acquainted neighbors from New England and throughout the Northeast

---

4. Coventry, *Memoirs of an Emigrant*, 549.
5. Alexander Coventry to Charles C. Brodhead, October 7, 1804, in Brodhead Family Papers, 1795–1848, Oneida County History Center, Utica, NY. This document refers to an enslaved man who, Coventry explains, he jailed in Herkimer, NY, because of his several attempts to escape bondage.
6. The Mohawk, Oneida, Onondaga, Cayuga, Seneca, and later, Tuscarora, make up Haudenosaunee Confederacy, or "People of the Long House."

exchanged rum, cloth, sundries, scarce American currency, and land. Geographically at the eastern end of the Mohawk Valley, the village and its economy directed migration and coordinated expansion into what the contemporaries of the nineteenth century labeled a "gateway to the west." This borderland was long a landscape of cross-cultural, interdependent accommodation and commercial and military reciprocity during the seventeenth and eighteenth centuries; yet, these earlier accommodations began to erode under the pressures exerted by settler-colonial networks that relied on deception and forced assimilation of the once-powerful Haudenosaunee. Land, a vital source of sovereignty, food, comfort, and security to the Indigenous peoples, became a bargaining chip of survival in the early Republic. State and private interests needed Old Fort Schuyler to succeed commercially to ensure continuing development projects in Western New York, to enforce the legally codified removal of the Oneida and neighboring tribes, and to steward the American market to and from the disputed continental interior. Indian removal served as an extension of the market's reach into the borderlands. In a cash poor space with a high land-to-labor ratio, Haudenosaunee land became the commodity linking together a network of market-connected moneyed men, farmer-settlers, state officials, Native American agents caught up in this political economy, and others aiming to keep settlement and development churning through the Mohawk River corridor.

Old Fort Schuyler serves as a microcosm and reveals the important role that borderland communities played in the nation's early economic trajectory and evolution as a settler-colonial project. Surrounding Old Fort Schuyler, several satellite communities developed in Whitestown, a large swath of increasingly populated territory west of the village and bordering Oneida Indian lands. Much of the historiography related to New York's territorial and commercial expansion focuses on land development schemes in Western New York, Native American dispossession, and the Erie Canal; but these studies seldom explore the impact many smaller, culturally entangled market-oriented communities had on the state's early commercial development.[7] The village and surrounding communities provided

---

7. Regarding late eighteenth-century Native American dispossession and postrevolutionary Indian affairs, the most useful studies include Karim M. Tiro's exhaustive study of the Oneida Nation in *The People of the Standing Stone: The Oneida Nation from the Revolution through the Era of Removal* (Amherst: University of Massachusetts Press, 2011), and Lawrence Hauptman's *Conspiracy of Interests: Iroquois Dispossession and the Rise of New York State* (Syracuse, NY: Syracuse University Press, 1999). Detailed studies of settlement, migration, and settler colonial expansion in post-Revolutionary Upstate New York include Charles E. Brooks's *Frontier Settlement and Market Revolution* (Ithaca, NY: Cornell University Press, 1996), William Wyckoff's *The Developer's Frontier: The Making of the Western New York Landscape* (New Haven, CT: Yale University Press, 1988), and although dated, David Maldwyn Ellis's *Landlords and Farmers in the Hudson-Mohawk Region, 1790–1850* (Ithaca, NY: Cornell University Press, 1946). Alan Taylor's *The Divided Ground: Indians, Settlers, and the Northern Borderland of the American Revolution* (New York: Knopf, 2006) offers the best guide for understanding the cross-cultural nuances of the transformation of Indian relations in postwar New York, and Taylor's Pulitzer Prize–winning book *William Cooper's Town: Power and Persuasion on the Frontier of the Early American Republic* (New York: Vintage, 1995) presents a useful guide for exploring a place-based approach to understanding

a nexus for commercial maturation, which simultaneously eroded Native American sovereignty and economy. Ultimately, a prolonged push by local and state officials for large-scale internal improvement projects seeded the region's prominence in state-sponsored canal-building. Settlers and speculators increasingly poured onto new Western New York farms and into developing towns and villages like Old Fort Schuyler. Welcomed by New York State, these populations aided the spread of state-sponsored economic control over an expanding western borderland that connected the Great Lakes and the Atlantic world. Furthermore, the area's geographic centrality to the United States' early industrial gaze westward laid the groundwork for a political economy that gradually traded coexistence, diplomacy, and reciprocity for socioeconomic and territorial control.[8] In 1798, the post was officially incorporated as the village of Utica. By 1800, its transformation from a small outpost into a gateway of mixed agrarian and industrial commerce marked Central New York's transition from a culturally entangled borderland to a base for a new era of national expansion toward the continental interior.

Entangled Borders in Pre- and Postwar New York

Before increasing numbers of settlers, farmers, speculators, and merchants targeted Old Fort Schuyler as a developing postwar commercial gateway, the post had served as a military stopover at a major fording point along New York's Mohawk River. The site had fallen into disuse soon after the French and Indian War, and the borderland with Indian country increasingly attracted farmer-settlers, who edged in on Haudenosaunee territory. Throughout most of the seventeenth and the first three-quarters of the eighteenth centuries, Haudenosaunee nations maintained a reasonably cordial coexistence with their English, Dutch, Scots, and German neighbors. Six Nations diplomats attempted neutrality during the lead-up to and during the American Revolutionary War once tensions between Great Britain and its American colonies exploded in the 1770s. Near the site of Old Fort Schuyler and Fort Stanwix (present-day Rome), Oneida women and men sold and occasionally bartered extracted resources like furs and animal pelts with their neighbors for

---

Upstate New York as an important socioeconomic and cultural crossroads of the early Republic. Charles Sellers's seminal book, *The Market Revolution: Jacksonian American, 1815–1846* (New York: Oxford University Press, 1991), highlights the convergence of urban and countryside economic spheres. Helpful journal articles include Anthony Wonderley's "'Good Peter's Narrative of Several Transactions respecting Indian Land': An Oneida View of Dispossession, 1785–1788," *New York History* 84, no. 3 (Summer 2003): 237–73; and Barbara Graymont's "New York State Indian Policy After the Revolution," *New York History* 78, no. 4 (October 1997): 374–410.

8. Tiro, *People of the Standing Stone*, xii–xiv, 65–66, 108; Brooks, *Frontier Settlement and Market Revolution*, 4, 9, 22, 33; Wyckoff, *Developer's Frontier*, 2, 9–15, 101; Sellers, *Market Revolution*, 4–8, 18–20; David L. Preston, *The Texture of Contact: European and Indian Settler Communities on the Frontiers of Iroquoia, 1667–1783* (Lincoln: University of Nebraska Press, 2009), 267–68; David J. Silverman, *Red Brethren: The Brothertown and Stockbridge Indians and the Problem of Race in Early America* (Ithaca, NY: Cornell University Press, 2010), 150–53.

tools, subsistence equipment, clothing, iron implements, tin and brass kettles, and other Euro-American commodities that were becoming increasingly important to their changing lifestyle. Acknowledging this economic relationship during the war, Continental Army Gen. Philip Schuyler opened a trading post for the Oneida as a means to earn their wartime support. Local trade networks and diplomacy between Central New York's settlers and Haudenosaunee residents resulted in an American-Oneida alliance during the war. However, continued conflict between the United States and Great Britain prompted Gen. George Washington's 1779 order for American soldiers to raid and raze uncooperative Six Nations villages. Continental Army soldiers burned Western New York's maize and vegetable crops during what became known as the Sullivan Campaign. Such an attack on food, supplies, and lands tended by women, who were societal guides and political power brokers among the Haudenosaunee, established the American precedent of effectively removing any uncooperative Native American neighbors. By the war's end, the Haudenosaunee numbered roughly six thousand.[9]

Despite a coexistence based in reciprocity in New York's borderlands in the decades prior, westward-facing settler colonialism quickly bled into the minds of statesmen and settlers in New York after the American Revolutionary War ended. In a January 1784 address to Governor George Clinton, the State Assembly reflected on the postwar situation in New York. Alongside encouraging economic recovery and establishing educational centers, the Assembly promoted "the speedy settlement of the uncultivated Territory of the State."[10] As their brazen assumption of completely open western borders echoed throughout the corridors of city hall in New York City, the Assembly expressly ignored their Native neighbors and former wartime allies. In reality, the Oneida and other Native Americans had remained steadfast and rebuilt their villages in Central New York following the war.

Postwar New York's new and old borderland residents thus found themselves in a complex, historically entangled region adjacent to Indian country, where they initially continued a cordial coexistence with Haudenosaunee neighbors. Despite federal checks on state land purchases from Native American nations, Governor Clinton felt that New York

9. David L. Preston, "'We intend to live our lifetime together as brothers': Palatine and Iroquois Communities in the Mohawk Valley," *New York History* 89 no. 2 (Spring 2008): 188–89; David Levinson, "An Explanation for the Oneida-Colonist Alliance in the American Revolution," *Ethnohistory* 23, no. 3 (Summer, 1976): 280, 284; Tiro, *People of the Standing Stone*, 10, 55, 193; Barbara Graymont, *The Iroquois in the American Revolution* (Syracuse, NY: Syracuse University Press, 1992), 112, 163–64; Maeve Kane, "'She Did Not Open Her Mouth Further': Haudenosaunee Women as Military and Political Targets during and after the American Revolution," in *Women in the American Revolution: Gender, Politics, and the Domestic World*, ed. Barbara B. Oberg (Charlottesville: University of Virginia Press, 2019), 90–91; Alan Taylor, "The Divided Ground: Upper Canada, New York, and the Iroquois Six Nations, 1783–1815," *Journal of the Early Republic* 22, no. 1 (Spring 2002): 57–58.
10. New York State, *Journal of the Assembly of the State of New York at Their Seventh Session ... January 1784* (Albany, NY: Samuel and John Loudon, Printers to the State, 1784), 17. Several bound Assembly journals can be found at the New York State Archives in Albany.

State held exclusive rights to deal with the remaining Six Nations in Central and Western New York. As a means of securing their executive position in New York's Indian affairs, officials commissioned the state militia for the "protection of the north-western frontiers, to defend settlers" and to contain the "depredations of the Indians and to prevent unwarrantable intrusions."[11]

While Congress appointed federal Indian commissioners in March 1784, the remaining Six Nations peoples banked on a more reciprocal alliance with New York State that summer. In a conference with federal officials at Fort Stanwix that year, the state's Haudenosaunee representatives resolved to "promote Trade and Commerce and renew that former Friendship and Compact anciently made" with New Yorkers. The state also found land grants to meet their debt to Revolutionary War veterans and former militia. At Fort Stanwix, New York State representatives reaffirmed Oneida protections from private land speculators. But that October, federal officials warned the Oneida that deals with New York State remained legally invalid while state officials repeatedly assured Native representatives of their support for Indigenous sovereignty. The federally sanctioned 1784 Treaty of Fort Stanwix weakly reaffirmed Oneida and Tuscarora sovereignty, yet it forced other British-allied Haudenosaunee nations who had been removed to Canada or who were refugees on the Niagara River to surrender claims to swaths of Western New York land and all but one parcel of Allegheny land in Pennsylvania.[12] However, throughout the 1780s, treaties came to represent little more than forced land cessions, or as one historian argues, treaties constituted the "legal arm of dispossession" favoring Euro-American officials who both wrote and interpreted them to Native peoples. Throughout the remainder or the decade, New York State and private actors gradually acquired, leased, or sold ancestral Haudenosaunee lands and defied federal orders by entering into the business of Indian land acquisition and subsequent dispossession. For the Oneida, these pressures arrived at their borders later in the decade.[13]

Economic recovery in the late 1780s spurred merchants and speculators to expand

---

11. New York State and Franklin B. Hough, *Laws of the State of New York: Passed at the Sessions of the Legislature Held in the Years, 1777–1801*, 4 vols. (Albany, NY: Weed, Parsons, 1886), 2:153, 721; Barbara Graymont, "New York State Indian Policy after the Revolution," *New York History* 78, no. 4 (October 1997), 379.

12. New York State and Franklin B. Hough, *Proceedings of the Commissioners of Indian Affairs, Appointed by Law for the Extinguishment of Indian Titles in the State of New York*, 2 vols. (Albany, NY: Joel Munsell, 1861), 1:49; Michael Leroy Oberg, *Peacemakers: The Iroquois, the United States, and the Treaty of Canandaigua, 1794* (New York: Oxford University Press, 2016), 2, 29–33; Graymont, "New York State Indian Policy after the Revolution," 380–82, 384–88.

13. Oberg, *Peacemakers*, 3–4, 31–34, 41; Graymont, "New York State Indian Policy after the Revolution," 391; Mary Jo Kline, "The 'New' New York: An Expanding State in the New Nation," in *New Opportunities in a New Nation: The Development of New York after the Revolution*, ed. Manfred Jonas and Robert V. Wells (Schenectady, NY: Union College, 1982), 15. At a June 1785 meeting at Fort Herkimer, the Oneida ceded a huge swath of tribal land along the Chenango and Unadilla Rivers, for which they received a meager $11,500 and American goods in exchange.

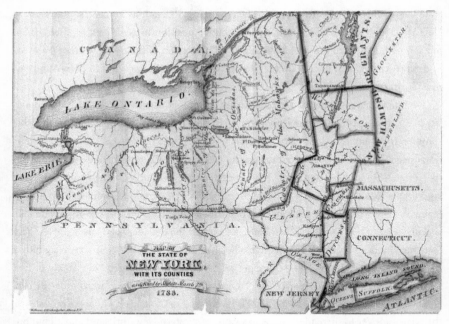

Figure 1. This 1788 map of New York State illustrates county lines and the borders of Haudenosaunee territory. Old Fort Schuyler sat between Fort Dayton (present-day Herkimer, NY) and Fort Schuyler (Stanwix). COURTESY OF THE NEW YORK STATE ARCHIVES, SERIES A0448-79, "RECORDED INDIAN TREATIES AND DEEDS, 1703–1871," VOL. 1, P. 1.

their bids to exploit Western New York. While farmers and settlers exported surplus grain, timber, potash, and other goods from land clearance to commercial centers like Albany and New York City, land values steadily rose and New Englanders bypassed the Hudson Valley's landed estates for the newly cleared lots in New York's borderlands farther west.[14] John Langston and other speculators formed the Genesee Company of Adventurers, a private interest group targeting lands in Western New York. Circumventing both state and federal laws prohibiting land purchases from the Six Nations, speculators like Langston and John Livingston organized 999-year leases with the Oneida. Living mostly on a parcel of unceded land near the south side of Oneida Lake, the Oneida rented the majority of their lands by 1788.[15]

During the late 1780s, Central New York served as a major staging ground for the initiation of more widespread development and settler-colonial expansion along New York's western borderlands. While white settlers and businessmen increasingly pressured their

---

14. Sellers, *Market Revolution*, 14–15; Ellis, *Landlords and Farmers*, 76; Reeve Huston, *Land and Freedom: Rural Society, Popular Protest, and Party Politics in Antebellum New York* (New York: Oxford University Press, 2000), 14.

15. Tiro, *People of the Standing Stone*, 76–77; Wonderley, "'Good Peter's Narrative of Several Transactions respecting Indian Land,'" 255–56; Oberg, *Peacemakers*, 35–36.

Six Nations neighbors to exchange land as a commodity, New York land speculators grew bolder in the acquisition of Haudenosaunee land as the state government idly supported private interests. Old Fort Schuyler steadily developed as these land speculators and expansionists aimed to create commercial "city-towns" that bolstered development efforts even farther west. In late 1788, New Englanders Nathaniel Gorham and Oliver Phelps proposed plans to commercialize Western New York's Genesee Country. The pair purchased a two-million-acre patent of unceded Haudenosaunee territory to develop its lands, establish settler-colonial communities, and drive local economies. Phelps and Gorham improved the muddy, underdeveloped roads west of Whitestown and Fort Stanwix, thereby connecting the Mohawk Valley to the Genesee River valley. In the spring of 1789, the two businessmen planned to build even larger communities than Old Fort Schuyler, starting with Canandaigua, the state's westernmost village during the period. While their partnership ended in 1791, Phelps and Gorham had laid the groundwork for a pivot westward that depended on Old Fort Schuyler and Whitestown. These interwoven communities constituted a major stopover for migrating settlers, a hub for the provision of goods and services, and a conduit to Atlantic markets at the head of the Mohawk River.[16]

In 1792, the Dutch-banker-formed Holland Land Company purchased roughly 3.3 million acres of land and organized the most aggressive and transformative development scheme on territory bordering the Great Lakes. Although the Holland Land Purchase did not formally open until 1800, its planning and promotion brought company agents to the region to actively entice settlers to leave their old plots for new opportunities in New York's land-rich backcountry. These development schemes later plotted an orderly set of lots and townships, but they also required more extensive road networks to connect Central New York, where many company agents operated, to the growing western sector. This project demanded capital investment, expert marketing, and the building of major village centers to facilitate the migration of farmers westward to develop this land and send backcountry goods back to eastern markets. Success in these ventures demanded investment in a network of "city-towns," like what Old Fort Schuyler gradually transformed into, and needed entrepreneurs acting in concert with financial funders, local and state officials, and farmers alike. Although the countryside market generated scarce cash, surplus products needed an outlet, and state officials and metropolitan merchants alike preferred these goods flowing to and from its financial center in New York City instead of to rival British wholesalers in Montreal. These same dynamics of government-sponsored development came to define a growing divide between agrarian producers and market capitalists in the borderlands.[17]

---

16. William H. Siles, "Pioneering in the Genesee Country: Entrepreneurial Strategy and the Concept of a Central Place," in Jonas and Wells, *New Opportunities in a New Nation*, 37, 49–53, 62, 65; Wyckoff, *Developer's Frontier*, 16.

17. Brooks, *Frontier Development and Market Revolution*, 4–10; Wyckoff, *Developer's Frontier*, 9, 13–4, 65. Wyckoff details several of these and additional traits for what he labeled a "developer's frontier."

However divisive, this movement remained firmly unified in the business of removing Indians.

New York's borderlands had evolved from a backwater into a corridor for the state's settler-colonial expansion westward, all funneled through the small, but centrally located Old Fort Schuyler. The decade not only brought new opportunities for entrepreneurs to try their luck in the countryside but also brought together a loose coalition of developers, moneymen, merchants, tenant farmers, few freeholders, and settler families moving westward for land and the promise of a new national autonomy in the expanding United States. Many even settled at Old Fort Schuyler upon their arrival.[18] Fast-moving development placed New York's upstate Native peoples squarely in the way of where countryside and distant market economies converged.

(Dis)possessing the Borderlands

Demographic growth and political action framed an expansionist agenda in New York throughout the 1790s. Increasingly families collected their children and spouses and trekked the long miles west into the state's borderlands. Approximately 340,120 New Yorkers appear in the 1790 federal census, and just under two thousand called Whitestown home.[19] Politically, New York's Federalists sponsored a strong central government for bolstering commercial and industrial expansion nationally, while Democratic-Republicans favored free and open commerce.[20] Where rural and city political economies converged, the state's elites favored territorial expansion. New York State officials and statesman largely supported a Federalist agenda, as upstate businessmen maneuvered economically and politically to promote state-sponsored infrastructural improvements including turnpikes, canals, and stable transportation networks through Central New York and out to Western New York. By 1790, the state possessed roughly $75 million in "unsold public lands," leading land speculators and state officials to collaborate with each other in the integration of new markets and territories along the nation's expanding western borders.[21]

A well-dressed, young, mobile, ambitious, and aggressively shrewd twenty-one-year-old salesman, Peter Smith, operated as a key figure in Old Fort Schuyler's development as a growing preindustrial village and launch point for New York's expansion. Trained as

18. New York State, *Journal of the Assembly of the State of New York at Their Twelfth Session… December 1788*, 33–34, 83; New York State and Hough, *Laws of the State of New York… 1777–1801*, 4 vols. (Albany, 1887), 3:356–58.

19. David Maldwyn Ellis, "Rise of the Empire State, 1790–1820," *New York History* 56, no. 1 (January 1975): 6; David Maldwyn Ellis, "Whitestown: From Yankee Outpost to Cradle of Reform," *New York History* 65, no. 1 (January 1984): 36.

20. Carol Sheriff, *The Artificial River: The Erie Canal and the Paradox of Progress, 1817–1862* (New York: Hill and Wang, 1996), 15.

21. Brian Philips Murphy, *Building the Empire State: Political Economy in the Early Republic* (Philadelphia: University of Pennsylvania Press, 2015), 6, 56–57.

a businessman in New York City, Smith had trekked north to Albany and hopped on a stagecoach into the Mohawk Valley in autumn 1788.[22] He briefly settled and opened a store at Canajoharie (present-day Little Falls), near the site of a former Mohawk village east of German Flats.[23] In 1789, he moved from Canajoharie to Old Fort Schuyler. By June, Smith opened a new store, and eagerly supplied the migrants edging closer to New York's western borders. He quickly became a leading storeowner and regional commodity provider. A calculating merchant, he greeted customers with piercing eyes.[24] Prior to his arrival in the Mohawk Valley, Smith had formed a business partnership with New York City merchant John Jacob Astor. Smith pursued the pair's interests in the fur trade through scattered agents and Haudenosaunee neighbors in Central New York. In November 1789, one local man purchased flour at Smith's Old Fort Schuyler store, paying with "2 Bear Skins Sold in N. York," presumably through Astor.[25]

Smith emerged as a major player in Old Fort Schuyler's commercial and demographic growth. Between June and July 1789, both newly arrived and established settlers visited Smith's store in Old Fort Schuyler. As a major countryside supplier of families moving west from New England, eastern New York, and Pennsylvania, Smith soon eclipsed other businessman in Central New York, and he no doubt hedged his bets on cashing in as a well-connected goods broker. Customers also visited his store from the growing village and nearby farming communities in German Flats and Whitestown.[26] Additionally, Smith built

22. Michael Kammen, "'The Promised Sunshine of the Future': Reflections on Economic Growth and Social Change in Post-Revolutionary New York," in Jonas and Wells, *New Opportunities in a New Nation*, 140. Albany businessman Elkanah Watson operated a stagecoach from Albany to Schenectady during the late 1780s.

23. Peter Smith, Canajoharie Day Book, 1788–1792, pp. 1–2, 8–12, Box 16, Peter Smith Papers, 1763–1850, Special Collections Research Center, Syracuse University Libraries, Syracuse, New York, hereafter cited as PSP-SUL. German women including "Gertraut Harkimer," "Widow H. Harkimer," and "Widow Leah Schuyler" provided ginseng to Smith for a short period, while many Oneida customers paid with cash and deer skins, beaver pelts, and a variety of animal hides; Peter Smith, Old Fort Schuyler Indian Blotter, 1788–1802, p. 1-3, Box 8, PSP-SUL. Page numbers cease after "5" in Smith's Indian Blotter. Smith retained his connections to New York City's merchant importers and sold, and occasionally bartered, rum, tobacco, sugar, silks, fabrics, blankets, buttons, shoes, coats, and other clothing to predominantly German and Oneida.

24. Taylor, *The Divided Ground*, 228; Moses M. Bagg, *Pioneers of Utica* (Utica, NY: Curtis and Childs, 1877), 17–18. While Bagg's work ranges in accuracy, a portrait at the Madison County Historical Society corroborates his description of Smith.

25. Smith, Canajoharie Day Book, 1788–1792, pp. 13, 26, 69; Smith, Old Fort Schuyler Indian Blotter, 1788–1802, p. 1; Peter Smith, Old Fort Schuyler Blotter A, 1789–1791, p. 2, Box 6, Oversize 1,PSP-SUL; Norman K. Dann, *Practical Dreamer: Gerrit Smith and the Crusade for Social Reform* (Hamilton, NY: Log Cabin Books, 2009), 17; Lester Grovesnor Wells, "Indian Personal Name Entries in Peter Smith's Indian Blotter," *New York History* 28, no. 4 (October 1947): 466, https://www.jstor.org/stable/23147932.

26. Smith, Old Fort Schuyler Blotter A, 1789–1791, pp. 1, 5, 11–12, 38, 91. Other Whitestown, German Flats, and Old Fort Schuyler locals appearing in Smith's store ledgers and the 1790 census included New Hartford founder Jedediah Sanger, Clinton's Ebenezer Butler, Old Fort Schuyler storeowner John Post, as well as settlers John Cunningham, John Bellinger, Sylvanus Morey,

a sizable network of Oneida, Tuscarora, Stockbridge, Cayuga, Onondaga, and Brothertown customers between the summer of 1789 and early 1790s. American farmers, tenants, traders, and laborers extracted potash and pearl ash from New York's thinning forests, furs and animal hides, wheat, and increasingly, currency. In exchange, both American and Haude-nosaunee customers purchased or traded for pork, beef, bread, rum, tea, knives, flints, gunpowder, linens, silk, calico, and other imported fabrics, clothing, and attire at Smith's thriving store.[27]

As the depressed national economy recovered in the new decade, Peter Smith's extensive business relationships connected Old Fort Schuyler to New York City, and broader transatlantic markets to the Mohawk Valley, which remained a major route connecting East Coast entrepôts to people and goods headed to and from the interior. Smith operated similarly to his successful counterpart to the south, William Cooper. Although not as ideally placed geographically to facilitate streams of westward settlers, Cooperstown, Cooper's village founded in 1786, flourished, sustained by the young entrepreneur's merchant connections in New York City, Albany, and Philadelphia.[28] Like Cooper, Peter Smith contributed to the burgeoning economic stability at Old Fort Schuyler through his position as a successful storeowner attracting clients for his growing land speculation interests. Settling down in 1792 with his wife, Elizabeth Livingston, and their two children, Smith carved out a life and successful business enterprise in New York's developing countryside.[29] His business records not only illustrate his willingness to personally monopolize and remove obstacles to his business interests but also reveal Old Fort Schuyler's centrality as a pivot point for the state to extend its growing population and markets westward, closer to land and resources sought in the continental interior. With Smith's and the village's increasing prosperity, New York's unique upstate geography and waterways cemented the region as a major national space for growth opportunities in commercial industrial development, community settlement, and settler-colonial expansion as well as for competitive land speculation and Indigenous dispossession.

Streams of migrants flooded New York State, helping borderland posts like Old Fort Schuyler to prosper. Smith's business picked up a year after his arrival at Old Fort Schuyler, capitalizing on Central and Western New York's demographic growth. On January 25, 1790, Smith paid German Flats's Peter S. Deygert for "bringing a Load from Albany," while on March 4, Adam Bellinger paid Smith with "a Trip to OFS [Old Fort Schuyler] with ye Sleigh." That May, Smith ramped up his dealings with white settlers arriving at developing western posts, but he also engaged Haudenosaunee customers. Onondaga settler Hezekiah

---

Samuel Rust and his wife, and Jacob Christman George Staples, James Sherman, Bezelial Willy, Richard Damuth, Adam Starring, Johannes Helmer, and Peter B. Deygert.

27. Smith, Old Fort Schuyler Indian Blotter, 1788–1802; Smith, Old Fort Schuyler Blotter A, 1789–1791, pp. 6–8, 74, 79, 91.
28. Taylor, *William Cooper's Town*, 8, 107–9.
29. Dann, *Practical Dreamer*, 17; Ellis, "Whitestown," 37.

Olcott purchased hats, pipes, tobacco, and "374 yds Durant" fabric. An early settler in the distant western post "Canadasago" (the former Seneca village of Kanadaseaga, later Geneva), trader James Latta paid Smith for cotton, peas, and pork.[30] New York's government aided networked merchants like Smith with investments in transportation and infrastructural improvements along the Hudson and Mohawk Rivers.[31]

A June 26, 1790, letter from Geneva settler John Bortle Jr. to Peter Smith illustrates the Old Fort Schuyler merchant's deep business connections and his coordination of the state's growing westward-facing commerce. Scrawling on then fresh parchment with thick ink, Bortle writes, "I have just Received the goods which you was pleased to Send by the boat," continuing "I promis'd Myself that You would Send the Articles that you know will answer for the Indian Trade." However, Bortle complains that he finds Smith's prices "Morally impossible" and too expensive to work with. Bortle's scattered and increasingly dispossessed Haudenosaunee neighbors in Western New York sought cheaper goods, corn, and rum. In exchange, Bortle received furs, which he sent along to Smith, writing "I Send you the furrs & Skins I have Taken in."[32] Smith relied on middlemen like Bortle to reach New York's western borders, and he cemented himself as a centralized storeowner catering to the region's culturally diverse customers. As Old Fort Schuyler served as a hub in the nexus of settler-colonial expansion westward, merchants and settlers remained involved in business with the Six Nations, who—due to land and economic pressures—increasingly sought to obtain Euro-American goods.

No longer as profitable for Central New York's businessmen following the War for Independence, the fur trade survived as a sporadic holdover from New York's colonial economy. Smith's longtime connection to New York City merchant John Jacob Astor generated a partnership targeting the state's fur trade in the early 1790s. A well-dressed German immigrant with deep eyes, a rounded face, and a thick accent, Astor became an immensely successful and wealthy businessman, entrepreneur, merchant importer, and New York City real estate speculator. From Manhattan, Astor aimed to profit from exporting furs across the Atlantic to fashion markets in European entrepôts like London and Amsterdam. In a November 2, 1790, letter, he asked Smith to "Buy as much furrs as you Can," but not to send "Any mor Bade furrs" unless obtained at a lower price. Astor's requests illustrate the fragility of the fur market. Attempting to corner the market for their partnership, Astor scribbled "you may be Sure that no Person has this information from me in & about your Countrey."[33] In March 1791, Smith faced increased competition in the exchange of pelts from his

---

30. Smith, Canajoharie Day Book, pp. 36, 64.
31. New York State, *Journal of the House and the Assembly of the State of New York at Their Fourteenth Session...January 1791* (Albany, NY: Francis Childs and John Swaine, Printers to the State, 1791), 74.
32. John Bortle Jr. to Peter Smith, June 26, 1790, Peter Smith Papers, 1788–1820, Oneida County History Center, Utica, NY, hereafter cited as PSP-OCHC.
33. John Jacob Astor to Peter Smith, November 2, 1790, PSP-OCHC.

migrant neighbors. Astor explained "I am Sawry to See the new Englandmen get so menny furrs which you was to have had." Ever the autonomous entrepreneur, Smith resisted Astor's suggestions, including the New York City merchant's proposal that he establish a store "at or about Canada Sago [Geneva]." Smith turned down Astor's recommendation and the promise of cheaper imported goods for use in the Indian trade.[34] Instead, he remained in his power position at Old Fort Schuyler while retaining connections to peltry suppliers from Western New York and the Great Lakes through intermediaries like Geneva trader James Latta.[35]

In the early part of the decade, profitable industrial activity increasingly took root in Old Fort Schuyler and the surrounding communities in Whitestown. In 1791, newly arrived migrant families busied themselves at mills, sawing lumber and gathering potash to sell to neighbors and merchants.[36] Extracting ashes required very little labor and paid for its transportation costs, making it profitable to rural farmers. While families congregated around Peter Smith's store and Old Fort Schuyler's community, Archibald and Elias Kane exploited Whitestown's centrality and increased settlement, operating a store and "pot or pearl ashworks: perhaps the largest in the State." Whitestown evolved into a center for selling pearl and potashes.[37] In 1791, James Kent explained that the Kanes maintained the "best pearl-ash manufactory in the state at White's Town," and supply "chiefly the petty traders away in the Genesee country" farther west.[38] Moneyed men who were connected to Atlantic markets, like Smith and Cooperstown's William Cooper, capitalized on the increase of countryside ash producers.[39] A 1790s transplant from Connecticut to Whitestown, Elijah Risley quickly followed suit. "I send you here fore Barels of perl ash & have more I Shall bring as quick as I Can git them" wrote Risley to Peter Smith in October 1791.[40] Cleared forests bordering the Great Lakes meant greater profits for Central New York market operatives.

While rural businessmen largely aimed to establish themselves in hubs like Old Fort

---

34. John Jacob Astor to Peter Smith, March 16, 1791, PSP-OCHC.
35. Peter Smith, Old Fort Schuyler Blotter C, 1792–1793, p. 277, Box 7, PSP-SUL.
36. Account Book, 1765-1792, Wetmore Family Papers, 1765–1792, pp. 82, 99, Oneida County History Center, Utica, NY. The Wetmore family migrated from Middlefield, Connecticut to Whitestown, where they operated a sawmill.
37. Coventry, *Memoirs of an Emigrant*, 548; Brooks, *Frontier Settlement and Market Revolution*, 62–65; Wyckoff, Developer's Frontier, 15; Ellis, *Landlords and Farmers*, 89, 113; Ellis, "Rise of the Empire State," 13. Following the Revolution, demand for ashes rose dramatically. Even before the conflict, New York merchants exported 1,782 tons in 1770. The state remained Britain's biggest supplier of ashes for soap, dyes, glass, saltpeter, and pharmaceutical manufacturing. Settlers gathered ashes from deforested properties, after the clearing of trees, and moved the product for $3.00 to $6.00 per acre's yield.
38. Horton, "The Mohawk Valley in 1791," 211.
39. Alan Taylor, "The Great Change Begins: Settling the Forest of Central New York," *New York History* 76, no. 3 (July 1995): 280–82; and Taylor, *William Cooper's Town*, 95, 108–10. Taylor meticulously outlines the process to create salable ashes. Ash factories like the one near Kane's store boiled hardwood ashes to produce a fine residue known as potash. Baking potash further in heated kilns created a finer product called pearl ash.
40. Elijah Risley to Peter Smith, 6 October 1791, Box 1, PSP-SUL.

Schuyler, merchants attached themselves to land speculation and migration. An August 1, 1791, broadside illustrated that available lands required migrant and local farmers to settle them and to build new communities in Central and Western New York. With this broadside, New England farm owner and eventual Whitestown migrant Jedediah Sanger, Montgomery County representative Michael Myers, and speculator John I. Morgan aimed to profit from selling parcels from 71,500 acres of land "adjoining settlements in *Whitestown* and *Clinton*" that New York State "lately surveyed" eight miles from the Mohawk River.[41] In December 1792, Sanger individually acquired 50,000 acres bordering Whitestown, in Herkimer County, from New York City speculator James A. Stewart for £984.[42] Increasingly, migrating New York and New England settlers made the journey through Old Fort Schuyler and Whitestown to newly opened land. In April 1792, Central New York's rapid demographic growth prompted the state to formally divide Whitestown and organize several new townships.[43] Peter Smith capitalized on government action to accommodate the ballooning population. On October 17, 1792, German Flats and Assembly representative Michael Myers requested four thousand shingles "for the [Herkimer County] court haus."[44] As a major importer, Smith's Old Fort Schuyler store remained ideally located to support and empower these newly organizing communities amid demographic change, commercial expansion, and westward migration.

In the early 1790s, New York officials and private businessmen devoted greater resources and attention to developing and expanding the state's interior infrastructure, thereby aiding access for its new settler population. Central New York's unique geography directed settlers westward, toward newly "opened" territories and dictated the state's infrastructural plans through the Mohawk Valley, a natural and solitary gap in the Appalachian Mountain chain. To improve long-term inland navigation and accommodate demographic, commercial, and agricultural growth, the state chartered and incorporated the Western Inland Lock Navigation Company in 1792.[45] Albany patrician Philip Schuyler and canal promoter, traveler, and banker Elkanah Watson directed the interior canal projects, while

41. "LANDS For Sale," August 1, 1791, broadside (BRO1177), New York State Archives, New York State Library.
42. Deed of Sale, from James A. Stewart and Wife Sarah to Jedediah Sanger, December 1, 1792 (Recorded April 21, 1794), Herkimer County, NY, in Land Title Papers II, 1703–1813, Oneida County History Center, Utica, NY. This land eventually became Sangerfield in Central New York. Note that the pound remined popular currency in the countryside, even after passage of the 1792 Mint Act. See Michael Guiry and Sally M. Schultz, Sally, "The Changing Nature of Mid-Hudson Valley Business during the Dawn of the Industrial Era (1783–1835): Evidence from Early American Newspaper Advertising," *Hudson River Valley Review* 26, no. 2 (Spring 2010): 7–10.
43. New York State and Hough, *Laws of the State of New York*, 3:356–58.
44. Michael Myers to Peter Smith, 17 October 1792, Box 1, PSP-SUL.
45. Nathan Miller, "Private Enterprise in Inland Navigation: The Mohawk River Route Prior to the Erie Canal," *New York History* 31, no. 4 (October 1950): 398, 404–5, 408; Nathan Miller, *The Enterprise of a Free People: Aspects of Economic Development in New York State during the Canal Period, 1792–1838* (Ithaca, NY: Cornell University Press, 1962), 21; Hauptman, *Conspiracy of Interests*, 36–37.

connected statesmen, merchants, and speculators with vested interests in Western New York land financially backed them.[46] Traveling between Old Fort Schuyler and Schenectady at the project's outset, Yale College president Timothy Dwight remarked that "merchants along its [Mohawk River] banks often choose to transport their commodities . . . in wagons," along rough, muddy, and worn dirt roads. Additionally, Dwight referenced a major problem for the Western Inland Lock Navigation Company —"oppressive" tolls.[47] While an unpredictable local labor market of low-grade mechanics, high costs and tolls, delays, and stock drops plagued the company during its construction undertakings, its canalizing efforts cut traveling costs between Albany and Niagara in half. Merchant exporters transporting salt, wheat, furs, lumber, pearl ash, and other commodities to New York City and European markets largely profited from the project, thereby cementing the route's continued popularity in the wake of state-sponsored settler colonialism.[48]

While white settlers cleared and cultivated deforested swaths of land in Central and Western New York, the Oneida struggled to maintain autonomy amid the steady American push west. By 1791, Central New York remained home to approximately 590 Oneida and roughly 80 Tuscarora, many of whom faced land loss and an increase in disease. Their land holdings dropped substantially from over five million acres in 1784 to only seven hundred eighty acres in 1792.[49] In his fiery testimony from that year, Oneida chief and orator Good Peter (Agwerondongwas) addressed the state's role in increasing dispossession and external pressures on the nation. Reflecting on numerous treaties signed between the United States and the Oneida during the 1780s, he explained, "We then thought we should be the sole proprietors of our own land, and that our disposal should be optional with us." He continued "Our brother New York has every thing springing up in abundance from the ground we leased to him whereby the wealth of its people is greatly increased. He [New York neighbors] is rising up—and I am sinking down."[50] In this summation, Good Peter emphatically proclaimed that tribal sovereignty and territorial autonomy declined in the face of American expansion, dispossession, and increased colonization of Oneida lands.

From Old Fort Schuyler, Peter Smith privately maneuvered to simultaneously support and erode Oneida sovereignty. Between December 1790 and December 1791, Oneida representative Peter Otsiquette, or "French Peter," trekked from Kanonwalohale, a central

46. Ronald E. Shaw, *Erie Water West: A History of the Erie Canal, 1792–1854* (Lexington: University of Kentucky Press, 1966), 15–16.

47. Miller, *Enterprise of a Free People*, 23.

48. Miller, "Private Enterprise in Inland Navigation," 401–3; Hauptman, *Conspiracy of Interests*, 83–84.

49. Tiro, *People of the Standing Stone*, 40, 57; Wonderley, "'Good Peter's Narrative of Several Transactions respecting Indian Land,'" 242; Taylor, "The Divided Ground," 63; Hauptman, *Conspiracy of Interests*, 27; Shaw, *Erie Water West*, 18.

50. Wonderley, "'Good Peter's Narrative of Several Transactions respecting Indian Land,'" 239, 242, 271–72.

Oneida village, to Smith's store. Uniquely, Otsiquette served as the Oneidas' "ear" during delegations with American officials. Educated and literate in English, Otsiquette petitioned New York State in 1791 for his own personal land along the border of the Oneida's unceded land. The state granted him title to the land but aimed to remove Otsiquette's family in the long-term, since the agreement guaranteed the title only to Otsiquette and his immediate offspring. At Smith's Old Fort Schuyler store, Otsiquette purchased a variety of clothing, subsistence commodities, and sundries including linen, soap, chintz, leggings, rum and spirits, silverware, strouding, mittens, a firearm, and a hoe for farming.[51]

Smith had become increasingly involved in Oneida land affairs. Operating as a trusted merchant bordering Oneida lands and exchanging mutually sought-after necessities with his Native neighbors, Smith worked through Oneida intermediaries to expand his land speculation interests. In an October 20, 1792, letter to Smith, his English-speaking Oneida associate Jacob Reed mentioned his expectation that during Smith's trip to Kanonwalohale, he would "converse with the chiefs about lands," affirming that "most all of the chiefs are willing to let you have it."[52] That month, Smith secured a lease on a major tract of Oneida land, promising "credit and future payments" to the Oneida, as well as to speculators and cross-cultural power brokers including Reed, James Dean, Samuel Kirkland, and Ebenezer Caulkins. Despite a reaffirmation of Oneida sovereignty guaranteed by the 1788 Treaty of Fort Schuyler, state officials capitalized on opportunities to acquire swaths of Oneida land in Central New York that had been cleared and were ripe for American settlement and commercial expansion.[53]

Old Fort Schuyler grew exponentially more cosmopolitan as an expansion-minded and industrious commercial community. A 1792 visitor to the growing village described it as "an extensive well-built town, surrounded by highly cultivated fields."[54] Writing to Holland Land Company agent Adam Mappa from his Ulster County farm near Kingston on July 15, 1792, Dutch immigrant and agriculturalist Francis Adrian van der Kemp advocated for American expansion westward through Central and Western New York. He wrote that he wished to see "Old Fort Schuyler nearly the central part of intercourse between the North and West, transformed in[to] an opulent mercantile city, where future Lorenzos will foster and protect arts and sciences, where the tomahawk and scalping knife are replaced by the chisel and pencil, and the wigwam by marble palaces." Here, van der Kemp clearly borrowed from the persistent settler-colonial mythology that Indigenous peoples were "uncivilized" and culturally inferior to white people, requiring Euro-American lifeways and

---

51. Wonderley, "'Good Peter's Narrative of Several Transactions respecting Indian Land,'" 262–63; Smith, *Old Fort Schuyler Indian Blotter*, 1788–1802.
52. Jacob Reed to Peter Smith, October 20, 1792, Box 1, PSP-SUL.
53. Taylor, *The Divided Ground*, 172, 229–31; Tiro, *People of the Standing Stone*, 93.
54. Edward Countryman, "From Revolution to Statehood (1776–1825)," in *The Empire State: A History of New York*, ed. Milton M. Klein (Ithaca, NY: Cornell University Press, 2001), 258.

Christianity for "guidance."[55] He went on to call New York State "the most desirable, advantageous market" and labeled Old Fort Schuyler "nearly the central part of intercourse between the North and West," explaining that once Britain surrendered its Great Lakes posts, the "commerce of our State receive nourishment" leaving "the markets of New York, Albany and Schenectadi, glutted with the produce of the West." Ignoring the implications of his proposals on the welfare of Indigenous peoples, van der Kemp nationalistically defined the global implications of moving through and eventually beyond New York's borderlands , proclaiming that national and local "commerce is increasing daily; our merchantmen cross every sea our flag is treated with respect in the Indies, while those of the Pacific Ocean have become acquainted with its thirteen stripes."[56]

At Old Fort Schuyler, Peter Smith worked to fulfill van der Kemp's Panglossian view of extending state and national borders. While the shrewd merchant maneuvered to acquire western land, he simultaneously positioned himself as a major supplier to settler families moving west. Between January and February 1792, migrant Andrew Backus purchased linen, buttons, wine, shot, sugar, rice, spirits, and other sundries en route to Western New York. Additionally, Backus exchanged twelve days of his services to carry a "Load [of goods] to Canadasago [Geneva]," as well as his committing his services as a distant exchange agent and middleman between Smith and the Indian trade farther west.[57] Between 1791 and May 1794, Jacobus Mabee remained a frequent customer of Smith's during his migration to a new home near present-day Rochester. From this distant countryside, Mabee and his wife, Christina, bartered moderately sized stocks of muskrats, bear, mink, otter, fisher, deer, raccoon, and bobcat skins to Smith in exchange for teacups, saucers, plates, bowls and other dishware, pork, linen, silk, tea, buttons, and knives, some of which they purchased. These were items essential to building the Mabee's homestead in Western New York.[58]

As New York's private interests pushed farther west of Old Fort Schuyler and Whitestown, Peter Smith stood at the forefront of pressuring the Oneida to cede remaining lands. In a February 1793 letter, Oneida interpreter Jacob Reed explained that "if the Assembly should confirm your Lease, then you would reward me for what I have done in aiding you to obtain the Lease of our nation." Reed continues, "don't mention it to no Living soul . . . keep

55. John F. Seymour, Centennial Address Delivered at Trenton, N.Y., July 4, 1876, by John F. Seymour, with Letters from Francis Adrian Van der Kemp, written in 1792, and Other Documents Relating to the First Settlement of Trenton and Central New York (Utica, NY: White & Floyd, 1877), 51; Preston, Texture of Contact, 160. See also Anton Treuer, Everything You Wanted to Know about Indians but Were Afraid to Ask (St. Paul, MN: Borealis Books, 2012).

56. Seymour, Centennial Address Delivered at Trenton, N.Y., 51, 53, 55.

57. Smith, Old Fort Schuyler Blotter C, 1792–1793, pp. 33, 135, Box 7, PSP-SUL.

58. Peter Smith, Old Fort Schuyler Blotter B, 1791, p. 143, Box 6, Oversize 2, PSP-SUL; Smith, Old Fort Schuyler Blotter C, 1792–1793, pp. 153, 374, Box 6 ; Peter Smith, Old Fort Schuyler Ledger B, 1791–1798, p. 87, Box 8, PSP-SUL; William Farley Peck, History of Rochester and Monroe County New York From the Earliest Historic Times to the Beginning of 1907, 2 vols. (New York: Pioneering Publishing, 1908), 1:503.

it all in Secrecy."[59] For a personal stake in Smith's assertive acquisition of Oneida lands, Reed secretly bartered his help as an insider. Later that spring, Reed relayed to Smith that "the three sober men will go with the surveyors or you," as some Oneida sought rum and alcohol from Smith's stock at his Old Fort Schuyler store in exchange for help mapping out land cessions.[60] In an April 29 letter to Oneida confidant and former missionary Samuel Kirkland, Smith explains, "I should wish the Indians all to be Satisfied" regarding payment for his newly acquired lands. Smith further states his hope for the Oneida to "collect together & appoint a Committee of Six of the principal Chiefs to Receive their Rent of 400 Dollars."[61] The following month, agent Ebenezer Caulking wrote to Smith from Kanonwalohale that "half the Castle" aimed to meet Smith regarding land deals, while Caulking relayed to the Oneida Smith's request "only for one of from each tribe—but the matter is agreed upon and they must Go to Smith's 'Treaty'—Rum I Suppose is their object."[62] Not only did Caulking echo stereotypes of Oneida drunkenness, he reinforced the pressure that Smith placed on the nation to cede land.

Trekking across New York's drastically changing landscape, increasingly home to new saw and grist mills, ash factories, and increasing numbers of brick and limestone mansions, surveyor Joseph Annin mapped the remaining Oneida lands as their autonomy gradually gave way to the pressures of American expansion. Annin surveyed allotments along Peter Smith's New Petersburgh tract, a swath of territory consisting of former Oneida lands bordering roughly twenty townships farther west of Whitestown.[63] Smith's New York City business associate John Jacob Astor explained that the State Assembly "was very Glad to heare" about Smith's nearly wholesale acquisition of Oneida lands.[64] Astor himself entered Smith's scheme alongside New York City businessman William Laight. This triumvirate believed that land value in New York's gradually developing borderlands would double with increased investment. Together, Astor and Laight partnered and backed Smith's acquisition of roughly fifty thousand acres of former Oneida lands in the present-day Oneida and Madison County townships of Augusta, Stockbridge, Smithfield, Fenner, and northern

---

59. Jacob Reed to Peter Smith, February 3, 1793, Box 1, PSP-SUL.
60. Jacob Reed to Peter Smith, April 7, and May 9, 1793, Box 1, PSP-SUL; Tiro, *People of the Standing Stone*, 78.
61. Hauptman, *Conspiracy of Interests*, 71; Peter Smith to Samuel Kirkland, April 29, 1793, Samuel Kirkland Collection, Burke Library, Hamilton College, Clinton, NY, available through Hamilton College Library Digital Collections at http://contentdm6.hamilton.edu/cdm/compoundobject /collection/arc-kir/id/1846/rec/1. In an October 1801 letter to Smith, Kirkland grudgingly reflected on his collaboration with Smith to obtain Oneida land. He explains Smith's actions in "soliciting my influence with the Oneidas on behalf of your purchase, or Lease of Land. Were Jacob Reed & Capt John living (& were it proper to make public) they could witness to my friendly aid & repeated exerting in your favor, even to the riske of my comfort, if not character." See Samuel Kirkland to Peter Smith, October 17, 1801, Box 1, PSP-SUL.
62. Ebenezer Caulking to Peter Smith, May 10, 1793, Box 1, PSP-SUL.
63. Joseph Annin to Peter Smith, May 28, 1793, Box 1, PSP-SUL; Peter Smith, New Petersburgh Land Field Book, 1793, Box 20, PSP-SUL.
64. John Jacob Astor to Peter Smith, March 10, 1793, Box 1, PSP-SUL.

Cazenovia, as well as along the Byrne and Charlotte Rivers in New York's Schoharie Valley. The team aimed to sell and lease land to settlers, even offering the first three years rent free.[65]

During the mid-1790s, the acquisition of Haudenosaunee lands paved the way for state and private interests to absorb Western New York into its developing political economy. In March 1794, the New York State legislature passed a law "laying out and improving a public road or highway to begin at Old Fort Schuyler on the Mohawk river" and end at Canandaigua. Aiming to connect the developing Central New York countryside with the expanding western reaches of the state, New York officials practiced a form of eminent domain, compensating private landowners for properties and designating Western New York's "unappropriated lands" as a "western district" of the state, thus ignoring Oneida pleas like those of Good Peter and his allies.[66] In April 1794, Holland Land Company agent and Cazenovia settler John Lincklaen requested a small parcel of Peter Smith's "Lease Lands" along the developing western roads "in some agreement that would secure these lands to me whenever they will be sold by the Indians."[67] Lincklaen's bid for Smith's lands demonstrates the Old Fort Schuyler merchant's alignment with statewide goals shared by New York's settlers and state officials, all but declaring the acquisition of Haudenosaunee land as inevitable. The combined efforts of these forces cemented Old Fort Schuyler's centrality in generating new opportunities for targeting Oneida lands, continuing the countryside's demographic boom, and steering demand for settler-colonial prosperity in an expanding backcountry exchange economy.

In Fall 1794, the Oneida and their former Haudenosaunee partners met with federal commissioner Timothy Pickering and others to sign the vitally important Treaty of Canandaigua. In August that year, after several prior military losses, American forces won decisively at the Battle of Fallen Timbers, somewhat soothing fears of a British and Indian attack in the vulnerable borderlands. Representing the federal government, Pickering believed achieving peace, balance, and reciprocity in New York's borderlands was possible through this treaty. Land cessions and speculative pressures were front and center, but federal goals of maintaining diplomacy with the Six Nations played into the affair as well. Over 1,600 Haudenosaunee representatives met, 150 of them Oneida, Tuscarora, and a few Onondaga refugees living on their reservation, many of whom likely shopped at Smith's Old Fort Schuyler store. Collectively, the Haudenosaunee representatives aimed to renegotiate the limiting geographical boundaries imposed a decade earlier at Fort Stanwix and to restore the Covenant Chain with the United States. Peter Smith's acquisition of over

---

65. John Jacob Astor to Peter Smith, March 2, 1794, Box 1 PSP-SUL; Hauptman, *Conspiracy of Interests*, 45; Ellis, *Landlords and Farmers*, 58. Ellis explains that Smith paid off Astor's and Laight's interest on the land for full ownership in 1829.

66. New York State and Hough, *Laws of the State of New York*, 3:504, 527; Higgins, *Expansion in New York*, 125-26.

67. John Lincklaen to Peter Smith, April 28, 1794, Box 1, PSP-SUL.

61,000 acres of Oneida land highlighted tense discussions between the Haudenosaunee and federal officials about easing land pressures. Pickering asserted that Smith's paltry annual rent of $200 to the Oneida was inadequate since the speculator profited from a tenancy of nearly 300 families on that same land. Ultimately, negotiations landed Pickering and Haudenosaunee representatives with an affirmation of territorial and cultural autonomy. Yet Pickering himself would not reverse land cessions of previous years; he offered them instead $5,000 in post treaty restitution for their losses. Furthermore, the federal government increased its annual annuity to the Six Nations from $1500 to $4500 for purchasing subsistence equipment and American supplies in a veiled attempt to acculturate the Oneida and their Indigenous neighbors to settler-colonial lifeways. Ironically, places like Smith's store were likely the destination for those seeking American goods.[68] Soon after, New York State and ravenous private land speculators aimed to put these federal promises to the test.

In the aftermath of the Treaty of Canandaigua, the convergence between state and private interests involving Smith, Old Fort Schuyler, and expansion to western lands peaked. In 1795, New York officials signed a treaty with the Oneida imbuing the state with the power to purchase much of Smith's leased Oneida lands. Soon after, Smith paid the state for title to 22,300 acres of land in Central New York, while the state government compensated him for the remaining territory. He took advantage of religious and socioeconomic fractures among the Oneida and found aid in the likes of colluders such as Jacob Reed and even respected Oneida elder Skenandoa.[69] From New York City's bustling courts, John Livingston wrote to Smith that New York Legislators issued a bill giving Smith the "right to purchase of the state the Lands you have ceased from the Oneide."[70] Via private acquisition from Old Fort Schuyler, Smith worked through intermediaries, agents, and speculators, positioning himself as a major land dealer among white settlers. In a September 1795 letter to Smith, Astor wrote, "I am told your making a grate fourtione & very fast."[71] Smith's position at the crossroads of Central and Western New York and his relationship with other powerful land speculators earned him wealth, power, and swathes of leasable land. While Smith paved the way at the frontline of Oneida dispossession and New York's steady settler-colonial expansion, American officials formally applied similar tactics on the Midwest's Native American communities. The aftermath of the 1795 Treaty of Greenville, for example, opened the door for settler-colonial actors to push past agreed upon boundaries in the Ohio River valley, a

68. Oberg, *Peacemakers*, 98–104, 108–11, 113–15, 131–34, 191. Oberg's detailed study provides granular accounts of the council's proceedings and expert analysis of Treaty itself; Taylor, "The Divided Ground," 61–65. See Smith, *Old Fort Schuyler Indian Blotter*, 1788–1802, for more on Smith's Haudenosaunee customers.

69. Hauptman, *Conspiracy of Interests*, 45. Smith obtained these lands at $3.53 per acre, and he continued to lease them at a markup to settlers. See Taylor, *The Divided Ground*, 306–7 and Tiro, *People of the Standing Stone*, 92–93.

70. John Livingston to Peter Smith, July 20, 1795, Box 1, PSP-SUL. Additionally, Smith established Peterboro in 1795, a settlement on a portion of his land in Madison County. See Dann, *Practical Dreamer*, 95.

71. John Jacob Astor to Peter Smith, September 10, 1795, Box 1, PSP-SUL.

formerly contested borderland that came to represent prosperity for the United States and "human misery" for dispossessed Indian nations. Closer to home for the Oneida, federal agents on the borderlands had few resources with which to check New York's attempts to obtain Haudenosaunee lands from the United States' former wartime allies.[72]

Utica, Upstate Commerce, and Fading Reciprocity

Settlers arrived to its grided streets, growing stores and warehouses, and more elaborate buildings, and Old Fort Schuyler grew exponentially during late 1790s. Residents, many recently arrived from eastern New York and New England, as well as some Haudenosaunee and Oneida, contributed to a growing local market economy, paying in cash and land for goods and services. The largely white landed migrants and local businesspeople mutually benefited from economic and territorial expansion, as farmers, settlers, and laborers purchased, or bought on credit, pork, rum, brandy, wine, cloth, linen, silk, and other fabrics, farming equipment, tea, needles, knives, while furs, lumber, and grains that filtered through Old Fort Schuyler to Albany's and New York City's export markets.[73] In 1797, Albany became New York State's capital city. Turnpikes and roadway improvements connected the new capital to the burgeoning commercial expansion extending from Central New York westward.[74] As residents improved local infrastructure, constructed bridges across the Mohawk River, and sustained a local economy, Old Fort Schuyler remained for a hub, ensuring that state boundaries continued their extension westward.[75] On April 3, 1798, New York State formally recognized community leaders' incorporation of the former colonial post into the village of Utica and created Oneida County in Central New York.[76]

---

72. Andrew R. L. Clayton, "'Noble Actors' upon 'the Theatre of Honour': Power and Civility in the Treaty of Greenville," in *Contact Points: American Frontiers from the Mohawk Valley to the Mississippi*, 1750–1830, ed. Andrew R. L. Clayton and Fredrika J. Teute (Chapel Hill: University of North Carolina Press, 1998), 268–69; Oberg, *Peacemakers*, 139–41.

73. John Post to Charles C. Brodhead, August 29, 1795, Broadhead Family Papers, 1795-1848, Oneida County History Center, Utica, NY. A former Schenectady trader, Post sent pork, rum, and brandy to Old Fort Schuyler surveyor Brodhead, explaining, "Your men appeared to be much in want." Additionally, Post sold goods from his successful store in the village. Old Fort Schuyler customers included Watts Sherman, John Budlong, Jedediah Kingsley, Moses Bagg, James S. Kip, and Rhode Island migrants Benjamin Ballou and Uriah Alverson. See John Post Ledger, 1791–1800, pp. 3, 8–9, 23-24, 28, 61, 66, 81, 84, Oneida County History Center, Utica, NY (the ledger's contents date from 1795 to 1800).

74. Brooks, *Frontier Settlement and Market Revolution*, 10–12; Wyckoff, *Developer's Frontier*, 2–4, 104; William Chazanof, *Joseph Ellicott and the Holland Land Company: The Opening of Western New York* (Syracuse, NY: Syracuse University Press, 1970), 34; Ellis, *Landlords and Farmers*, 85–86.

75. John Post Ledger, 1791–1800, pp. 65-80; New York State and Hough, *Laws of the State of New York*, 4:82. On March 28, 1797, state officials reimbursed Old Fort Schuyler villagers John Post, Nathan Smith, and Isaac Brayton for a bridge construction payment.

76. New York State and Hough, *Laws of the State of New York*, 4:253-54; Ellis, *Landlords and Farmers*, 37.

By 1798, Haudenosaunee rights to their ancestral lands were severely limited.[77] While Central New York's Six Nations populations were forced to cope and struggle with dispossession, the newly named village of Utica adopted a more cosmopolitan image. Meanwhile, Peter Smith continued building his fortune through rent collection and from state compensation for 22,299½ acres of his New Petersburgh lands in Whitestown.[78] Remaining Oneida settled on their small parcels of unceded land, like Chief Skenendoah, for example, who continued visiting Smith's store for food and supplies.[79] However, as with interactions between the British and Six Nations in the first three-quarters of the eighteenth century, the Oneida and elements of the Haudenosaunee were never fully dispossessed. In some cases, the Oneida adopted their own autonomous commercial ventures in the form of small-scale agriculture and performative and salable handicrafts, even as Euro-American pressures circumvented long-held covenants of reciprocity regarding land. Despite high levels of dispossession and numerous families' relocation to land in Wisconsin, the Oneida maintained an attachment to what remained of their ancestral home in Central New York.[80]

By the close of the eighteenth century, Old Fort Schuyler's incorporation into the village of Utica and the formation of Oneida County illustrated Central New York's quickening commercial industrial development, as it outpaced its culturally entangled origins. By then, New York State's population had ballooned, increasing from 340,120 in 1790 to over 589,000 in 1800, while the Oneida population hovered at just under 690 people.[81] Despite decades of cultural coexistence and occasional periods of diplomacy and violence, the economic growth that New York State and private actors like Smith found in dispossession proved too tempting. Economic and demographic growth fueled by burgeoning territorial expansion had, in many ways, eclipsed some of the guarantees that the United States promised to the Haudenosaunee earlier in the decade at Canandaigua. Less geographically centered settlements sprang up throughout the state's growing western borderlands, as the settler-colonists continued building communities along developing turnpikes extending from the Mohawk Valley to Genesee Country.[82]

As the eighteenth century ended, New York's borderlands gradually gave way to commercial industrial development and to both state and private agendas toward extending its borders. By April 1806, Smith carried his fortune off to Peterboro and established a new

77. Kline, "The 'New' New York," 16.
78. Peter Smith, New Petersburgh Land Sales Book A, 1797–1831, pp. 154–59, Box 12, PSP-SUL (Box 12); New York State and Hough, Laws of the State of New York, 4:104-5.
79. Smith, Old Fort Schuyler Indian Blotter, 1788–1802. See especially the 1797–1799 portions of the ledger.
80. Gail D. MacLeitch, Imperial Entanglements: Iroquois Change and Persistence on the Frontiers of Empire (Philadelphia: University of Pennsylvania Press, 2011), 5, 245–47; Oberg, Peacemakers, 144–45; Tiro, People of the Standing Stone, xv, 154.
81. Ellis, "Rise of the Empire State," 6; Tiro, People of the Standing Stone, 193.
82. Mary P. Ryan, Cradle of the Middle Class: The Family in Oneida County, New York, 1790–1865 (Cambridge, UK: Cambridge University Press, 1981), 20–21; Taylor, The Divided Ground, 385; New York State and Hough, Laws of the State of New York, 4:559, 563.

Figure 2. *View of Utica from the Hotel, September 1807.* This sketch shows a quickly developing commercial center at Utica. COURTESY OF THE MIRIAM AND IRA D. WALLACH DIVISION OF ART, PRINTS AND PHOTOGRAPHS, NEW YORK PUBLIC LIBRARY, HTTPS:// DIGITALCOLLECTIONS.NYPL.ORG/ITEMS/510D47D9-7B49-A3D9-E040-E00A18064A99.

estate from which to manage his landed empire in Central New York.[83] Scouting the Mohawk Valley and Western corridor for a potential canal path in 1810, future New York Governor DeWitt Clinton observed that Smith acquired "an immense body of excellent land at a low price, and is now very opulent."[84] On August 27, 1818, cholera claimed the life of Smith's wife, Elizabeth Livingston, dealing a clear blow to the wealthy businessman. Her death led Smith to step back from handling his major business interests. In November 1819, Smith's business passed to his son, Gerrit, and his Johnstown nephew, Daniel Cady.[85] After carving an empire out of New York's evolving countryside in the 1790s, capitalizing on Oneida dispossession and partnering with migrant intermediaries and commercially connected metropolitan merchants, Smith remained in Peterboro until 1815, when he relocated to Schenectady, where he later died in 1837.

The threshold of New York State's expansion extended westward from Utica in the

---

83. Peter Smith, Old Fort Schuyler Blotter F, 1803–, p. 65, Box 6, PSP-SUL.
84. DeWitt Clinton, "Private Canal Journal, 1810," in *The Life and Writings of De Witt Clinton*, ed. William W. Campbell (New York: Baker and Scribner, 1849), 190. Additionally, Dr. Alexander Coventry observed the same year that "Mr. Smith is the richest man in this Western country: has a fine (large) house, completely finished and furnished." See Coventry, *Memoirs of an Emigrant*, 1109–10.
85. Robert E. Powers, "The Letters of John Jacob Astor and William B. Astor to Peter and Gerrit Smith" (PhD diss., Syracuse University, 1949), 14.; Milton C. Sernett, *North Star Country: Upstate New York and the Crusade for African American Freedom* (Syracuse, NY: Syracuse University Press, 2002), 198, 293n62; Dann, *Practical Dreamer*, 22.

early nineteenth century. By 1811, the continuously growing, centrally located village retained four hundred houses, six taverns, fifteen stores, two breweries, and three printing
offices.[86] After Robert Fulton unveiled his steamboat in 1807 and when other industrial
commerce and transportation technology ushered in a new industrial age for the Hudson
Valley, Utica and Oneida Counties experienced a wave of industrialization and cosmopolitan development. Cotton mills, glass factories, and mechanized looms and textile works
grew exponentially.[87] A January 1817 Utica *Patrol* issue referenced the "growing wealth of
the village and its vicinity," as the considerable industrialization of Central New York shat-
tered its agrarian underpinnings.[88] The Embargo Act, War of 1812, and the depression of
1819 resulted in statewide economic turmoil, but the start of the Erie Canal in 1817 and its
completion across ancestral Haudenosaunee lands in 1825 cemented the connection between the transatlantic world, New York City, and the Great Lakes. By the 1840s, grains,
flour, salt, and the bounty of the Midwest passed through Buffalo as New York's new "gateway to the west."[89]

By the start of the nineteenth century, Old Fort Schuyler had grown from a small
backwater post to a burgeoning commercial thoroughfare. Its story constitutes a microcosm of the foundational ideas that precipitated the erosion of diplomacy, reciprocity, and
coexistence with Indigenous peoples in favor of a commercialized agrarian-industrial economy in the borderlands of the early Republic. Geographically, commercially, and ideolog-
ically, the village and its economy promoted migration and settler colonialism. It became
an early "gateway to the west," a moniker bestowed on Utica by regional nineteenth century
writers. While agrarian-based subsistence culture and capital-focused market ambassadors
diverged at times, both retained the mutual goal of expanding American economic hegemony through the control of land via the erosion of the sovereignty of its Indigenous neighbors.[90] As Utica functioned as a major import-export site after the Erie Canal's completion
in 1825, other Upstate New York cities exploded commercially and even more rapidly than
the once-small upper Mohawk Valley settlement. Peter Smith's role in capitalizing on the
removal of his Indian neighbors, as well as the ways he interfaced with key players in New
York's borderlands, puts him on par with major commercial figures like William Cooper,
Philip Schuyler, and the Holland Land Company. Furthermore, his presence at Utica, the

86. Chazanof, *Joseph Ellicott and the Holland Land Company*, 96.
87. Cynthia Owen Philip, "The Triumph of 'Fulton's Folly,'" *Hudson River Valley Review* 25, no. 9
(Spring 2009): 21; Robert Frederick Berkhofer, "Industrial History of Oneida County, New York, to
1850" (PhD diss., Cornell University, 1955), 12, 16–17, 42, 49.
88. Madeline B. Sterns, *William Williams: Pioneer Printer of Utica, New York, 1787–1850* (Charlottesville, VA: Bibliographical Society of the University of Virginia, 1951), 9–10; Countryman, "From
Revolution to Statehood (1776–1825)," 291.
89. Brooks, *Frontier Development and Market Revolution*, 37, 65; Marvin A. Rapp, "New York's
Trace on the Great Lakes, 1800–1840," *New York History* 39, no. 1 (January 1958): 22–23, 27, 32;
Sernett, *North Star Country*, 12.
90. Sellers, *Market Revolution*, 4–5, 20; Brooks, *Frontier Settlement and Market Revolution*, 2–4, 9.

terminus of arguably the most important economic byway for the Dutch, English, and later, the United States in the Mohawk Valley, secured crucial victories for the American settler-colonial project. Simultaneously, New York's efforts to extend its territorial and economic reach through public-private enterprise constituted the foundations of a developing ideology of American continental domination through political economy that was tested in the borderlands of the early Republic.

Roebling's Niagara Railway Suspension Bridge

Paul C. King

The nineteenth century witnessed a gradual succession from horses and carriages on un-improved roads, to canals, to steamboats, and then to railroads. As modes of transportation evolved, bridges needed to adapt. Once a primary form of transportation, rivers that had been a source of liberation to a growing America were now obstacles to overcome. As the century began, spanning rivers meant the construction of falsework, a wooden structure that sat on the riverbed as temporary support, while a permanent wood or stone bridge was built above. Only when the bridge was self-supporting could falsework be removed.

Wood and stone bridges rely primarily on compression, with the weight of the bridge itself contributing to their stability. Suspension bridges, by contrast, rely on tension, and it would take the development of wrought-iron chains and wire cables at the start of the nineteenth century to modernize its implementation (figure 1).

In places like Niagara, below the great falls, where the gorge was wide and the waters deep and turbulent, the river stood as an impassable barrier. Filled with ice in winter, it possessed the power to destroy the piers of a river span—if one could even be built. With the construction of falsework impracticable, it would take the "suspension method" to overcome these obstacles. So long as the first rope could be put across, a railway could now extend 245 feet above the river.

Suspension bridges were not introduced to America and Europe without great difficulty. As their engineering was not well understood, they often fell down as quickly as they were put up, from rhythmic motion caused by storms, from the weight of winter ice and snow, or from the crossing of cattle, or troops who had yet to understand the importance of breaking step.

Figure 1. Bird's-eye view of the Niagara Suspension Bridge, 1859. PHOTOGRAPH BY
WILLIAM ENGLAND. COURTESY OF GETTY IMAGES.

Early Iron Suspension Bridges

The introduction of cast and wrought iron, which lent themselves to different roles in the
construction of bridges, spurred the development of modern suspension bridges. Cast iron,
when melted, poured into a mold, and allowed to cool, is hard like stone. It works well
in compression and is easily cast into components like anchor plates, saddles, and rollers. Wrought or "worked iron" by comparison, is relatively soft, has greater malleability
and strength in tension, making it invaluable for suspension cables or chains, for rod and
wire suspenders and stays, and for anchor chains. Drawn into wires it increases in tensile strength, and when used for the cables of suspension bridges, it can be stressed and
stretched, but returns to its original length when the cause of the stress, like a passing train,
is removed.

In 1801, using large wrought-iron links, Judge James Finley built America's first chain
suspension bridge across Jacob's Creek in Pennsylvania. Finley's innovation was the introduction of vertical suspenders of varying length to allow for a level deck suitable for
carriages. His ideas traveled to Great Britain and then to France, where the concept continued to evolve.[1] While British engineers were deferential to iron chains, French engineers

1. J. Finley, "Finley's Chain Bridge," *The Port Folio 3*, no. 6 (June 1810): 441–53.

embraced iron wires for their suspension bridges before the concept returned to America with the work of Charles Ellet Jr. and John A. Roebling.

In Britain, Capt. Samuel Brown and Thomas Telford embraced Finley's ingenuity. Brown's 1820 Union Bridge modified Finley's simple large iron links to introduce pairs of long round-section bars with short coupling shackles. A 437-foot span, Brown's Union chain bridge was the longest in the world until 1826, when Telford completed his more ambitious 579-foot span across the Menai Straights.[2] Telford flattened Brown's long round bars and introduced multiple flat, parallel chain links to suspend his bridges, making this method standard for British suspension bridges.

While Brown's bridge separating England from Scotland sat a moderate 27 feet above the River Tweed, Telford's bridge spanned an active channel connecting Wales to the Isle of Anglesea. Allowing the passage of tall ships required a deck height close to 100 feet, making it the world's first true long span suspension bridge, built at a site that made it the target of fierce winds.

In France, Claude-Louis Navier, Marc Seguin, Henri Guillaume Dufour, and Joseph Chaley continued the development of suspension bridges. Navier, a member of the French École des Ponts et Chaussees (School of Bridges and Roads) traveled to Britain in 1821 and 1823 to learn their methods, and in 1823 he published *Rapport et memoire sur les ponts suspendus* (Report and Memoir on Suspension Bridges), introducing suspension bridges to French engineers. A mathematician, Navier is credited with developing the first detailed structural analysis of suspension bridges.

Navier's one attempt to build, was a 557′-long chain suspension bridge, just 22 feet shy of Telford's Menai Bridge, and 120′ longer than Brown's Union Bridge. In July 1826, soon after the chains were hung, the foundations failed—in part due to a water-main break. The bridge was dismantled, minimizing Navier's influence to promote British-style chain bridges in France. While the bridge could be repaired, his Egyptian towers and eighteen heavy iron chains were viewed as a visual affront to the historic Les Invalides in Paris, where it was sited.

In 1822, Marc Seguin and his brothers replaced British chains with iron-wire cables, building a 59-foot experimental footbridge on their father's property, across the Rhone at Annonay. As private citizens, the Seguin brothers sought authorization to build a bridge at Tournon at their own cost in exchange for a ninety-nine-year concession to collect tolls. With no precedent for such an arrangement, it would take until August of 1825 for the bridge to be complete. It marked the construction of the first permanent, wire-supported roadway bridge in the world.[3] In response to inquiries, Seguin wrote of his new bridge and

2. S. Smiles, *The Life of Thomas Telford, Civil Engineer: With an Introductory History of Roads and Travelling in Great Britain* (London: J. Murray, 1867), 262–79.
3. M. Seguin, *Des ponts en fil de fer* (Paris: Bachelier, 1824), viii.

methods in his 1826 treatise *Des ponts en fil de fer* (Bridges of iron wire). Distributed to French engineers by the École des Ponts et Chaussees, wire suspension bridges became the predominant form in France and the rest of Europe. Seguin and his brothers would go on to establish a bridge-building company and erect hundreds of wire suspension bridges.

In August 1823, while Seguin waited for approval, Henri Guillaume Dufour was to build the first permanent, wire-supported footbridge in Europe. Working from designs developed by Seguin, Dufour completed the two-span St. Antoine footbridge at the fortifications in Geneva, predating Seguin's Tain-Tournon by almost two years.

In 1834, Joseph Chaley surpassed Telford's Menai Bridge and completed an 895-foot iron-wire span across the Sarine River in Fribourg, Switzerland. At 167 feet above the river, Chaley's Fribourg Bridge became the new model for long-span suspension bridges and remained the world's longest until 1849, when American Charles Ellet Jr. completed a 1,010-foot span across the Ohio River, in Wheeling, West Virginia.

To the French, iron-wire suspension cables had advantages over the solid iron chains of British bridges. Testing proved that an equal cross section of wires, when compared to bars, had far superior tensile strength, and where a bar might have an unseen defect that could cause failure, the many parallel wires in a cable provided redundancy. This meant a wire bridge of greater strength required less material and was more economical to build than a chain bridge.

While exact techniques among French engineers varied, they were consistent in their use of multiple smaller, prefabricated wire cables tied together periodically along their length, to support their suspension bridges. As these cables needed to be transported and then lifted in place using block and tackle, they were limited in both length and weight. This meant longer spans required shorter cables spliced together to make longer lengths; the splicing creating an inherent weakness in the cables. While Dufour pioneered a technique of pre-tensioning his wires as he made his cables, and the Seguin brothers were careful constructors, an 1831 report on suspension bridges in the Rhone Valley by Louis Vicat pointed to deficiencies. Most notably, uneven tension in the individual wires caused some to be slack and others to be overstressed, and the greater surface area of the many smaller cables increased the risk of oxidation.[4]

The French had yet to conceive of making and anchoring a single large and continuously wrapped suspension cable. Common to today's suspension bridges and first perfected by Roebling, his method of aerial spinning solved the unequal tension of individual wires and his continuous wrapping provided superior protection from oxidation.

The 1820s in Great Britain and France; was a time of experimentation and discovery as engineers tested new ideas and built their first suspension bridges. Still young men, Johann August Roebling and Charles Ellet Jr. were exposed to this creative thinking, with

---

4. Louis Vicat, "Rapport sur les ponts en fil de fer sur le Rhône, " *Annales des Pont et Chaussees*, pt. 1 (1831): 93–145.

Roebling attending the Berlin Bauakademie in 1824, and Ellet in Paris at the École des Ponts et Chausses in 1830, where he observed the construction of French wire suspension bridges.

The story of Roebling and Ellet is the story of three bridges, the Fairmont in Philadelphia, America's first permanent wire rope suspension bridge; the Niagara, first to connect the United States to Canada; and the Wheeling in West Virginia, the longest span in the world at the time of its completion. Their construction would contrast different schools of thought, Ellet using the methods of French engineers and Roebling innovating to develop his own. When it came time to consider a suspension railway bridge across the Niagara Gorge, the two men were quick to propose solutions, and only time would tell whose methods would be proven best.

Selecting an Engineer

The spanning of Niagara would be championed by Canadian William H. Merritt who was inspired by Chaley's span at Fribourg and American Charles B. Stuart, who was working to locate a route to connect the Great Western Railway of Canada and the New York Central Railroad.[5] Although they possessed little knowledge of suspension bridges, the two men led the effort to see one built, and they helped to set the location of the bridge—between the "falls" and the "whirlpool."

Suspension bridges were uncommon in America, and rarer still was a railway suspension bridge; there had been only one previous attempt made—in 1830 by Captain Brown across the River Tees. Brown's iron chain bridge failed on its first test, with its deck deforming in an s-curve in front of the locomotive, requiring the bridge be propped up midspan by a trestle. Afterwards, British engineers led by Robert Stephenson considered suspension bridges unsuitable for railways and instead built wrought-iron tubular box girders with multiple short spans and mid-river piers, a solution not applicable to the deep and wide gorge at Niagara.[6]

Quick to see an opportunity, Ellet reached out to both Merritt and Stuart as early as 1845, obtaining a lead that Roebling would find difficult to overcome in a race that would last until November 1847. In November 1845, Ellet proposed a bridge above the falls near the whirlpool for railway purposes at a cost of $220,000. Following French methods using separate, small suspension cables, it included "a single railway track in the centre, and 2 lateral ways for common travel, and 2 foot ways . . . a single sweep of 750 feet . . . supported

---

5. William Hamilton Merritt. *Biography of the Hon. W. H. Merritt, M. P. of Lincoln, district of Niagara, including an account of the origin, progress and completion of some of the most important public works in Canada* (St. Catharines, Ont.: E. S. Leavenworth, 1875), 279 and C. B. Stuart, *Lives and Works of Civil and Military Engineers of America* (New York: D. Van Nostrand, 1871), 269–74.

6. Stuart, *Lives and Works of Civil and Military Engineers*, 306–9; Roebling to Stuart, January 7, 1847. Available at Archive.org.

by twenty cables of iron wire—10 on each side—each of which will be nearly 5 inches in diameter, 1000 feet long."[7]

In January 1846, D. K. Minor, editor of the *American Railroad Journal*, published Ellet's proposal and, in an editorial, suggested a "spirited" competition between Ellet and Roebling. While in public he appeared neutral; in private he wrote to Roebling, "Mr. E—is indefatigable in whatever he undertakes...you must move in this matter, promptly vigorously and judiciously if you would inscribe your name on the rocks of Niagara Falls for all time to come."[8]

At the start of 1846, Stuart was certain the contract would soon be awarded to Ellet, but his expectations were premature. It would take until the end of the year for Canada to form the Niagara Falls Suspension Bridge Company and for New York State to incorporate the Niagara Falls International Bridge Company.[9] As D. K. Minor encouraged a healthy competition, the two engineers returned to their respective canal projects, with Ellet serving as president of the Schuylkill Navigation Company and Roebling starting his suspension aqueducts for the Delaware & Hudson (D&H) Canal.

As 1847 began, an open call went out for proposals.[10] Most historical narratives based on Stuart's account, identifies four engineers who answered the call. In addition to Roebling, this short list included fellow Americans Ellet and Edward Serrell along with Canadian Samuel Keefer, all of whom followed French methods. By 1869, each of these men would complete a suspension bridge across the Niagara River between the falls and Lake Ontario. There was, in fact, a fifth proposal, from Canadian Architect William Thomas, that had been sent to William Hamilton Merritt.

By 1847, Keefer had completed a single suspension bridge, the Union Bridge (1844) across the Ottawa and Chaudière Falls, a 234' 6" span, designed in the French style with four small-wire suspension cables on each side of the deck.[11] To Ellet's credit, he had completed the Fairmont Bridge in Philadelphia (1842), and in July 1847, six months before the Niagara contract was awarded, he had bested Roebling in competition for the Wheeling Suspension Bridge. Roebling was actively involved in the construction of four suspension aqueducts for the D&H Canal and had completed two suspension bridges in Pittsburgh, the Allegheny Aqueduct (1845) at the terminus of the Pennsylvania Main Line Canal, and the Monongahela Roadway Bridge (1846). Like Ellet, Roebling was a popular contributor

---

7. "Niagara Suspension Bridge," *American Railroad Journal* 19 (January 17, 1846): 35–37.

8. D. K. Minor to Johann August Roebling (JAR), January 2, 1846, MC.654, Reel 1: 1839–46 Correspondence, Roebling Family Papers, Rutgers University Library.

9. Charter acts and amendments of the Niagara Falls International Bridge Co., and Niagara Falls Suspension Bridge Co. See also Articles of Association by State of New York (1856).

10. C. B. Stuart, *Lives and Works of Civil and Military Engineers*, 270.

11. Plan of the Union Suspension Bridge, between Bytown and Hull,... Office of the Board of Works, 1842, Government of Canada, Library and Archives, accessed September 15, 2022, https://www.bac-lac.gc.ca/eng/CollectionSearch/Pages/record.aspx?app=fonandcol&IdNumber=4149828&new=-8585697207453882902.

to the *American Railroad Journal* on topics including suspension bridges, and with the success of his wire rope business, his expertise was never in question. Ironically, Serrell, who had yet to build a suspension bridge at all, would be first to span the gorge with a world-record 1040-foot span in 1851.

Interestingly, Thomas's proposal for a chain bridge in the style of Telford provides a point of contrast between the work of Serrell, Keefer, and Ellet, who followed French methods. Thomas restates the arguments of British engineers in their preference for "iron chains," noting two primary deficiencies of the French method (1) that wires in the suspension cables cannot be made to have equal tension, and (2) that when comparing an equal cross section of iron bar to wires, the greater surface area of the wires are more susceptible to oxidation. Three days after his proposal is rejected by the board (who will only consider a wire suspension bridge due to its economy), Thomas abandons his arguments and submits a proposal for a wire bridge—at a considerable reduction in cost.[12]

In May, as Roebling presents his proposal, Ellet shifts $30,000 of his fee to capital stock, effectively lowering his price to $190,000, a strategy he often employed to win competitive bids.[13] Unlike Ellet's single deck, Roebling proposed a double-deck span segregating railway traffic from the carriageway forming a wooden lattice box truss, supported by four large suspension cables. Roebling underbid Ellet, offering to complete his bridge for $180,000 plus $20,000 in bridge stock.[14] The long double-deck lattice truss, Roebling argued, separated horses from "railroad trains with their puffing and panting locomotives" and a "great depth of framing will be formed in the direction of the bridge, which will greatly add to the stiffness of the structure"[15]

In June, Roebling was convinced he would soon undertake several "large works" including "the Niagara Br [Bridge], the Wheeling," and "Cincinnati"; but by November, as he agreed to a final interview with the bridge directors, he knew he could not overcome "Ellet's Influence."[16]

On November 9, 1847, after an "act of union" the Niagara Falls Suspension Bridge Company of Canada and the Niagara Falls International Bridge Company of New York, the contract was awarded to Ellet.[17] At $190,000, Ellet's railway suspension bridge to be

12. William Thomas to Board, November 8, 1847, Box 2_1, Thomas Fisher Rare Book Library, University of Toronto.

13. Ellet to Washington Hunt, May 14, 1847, in G. D. Lewis, Charles Ellet, Jr. (Urbana: University of Illinois Press, 1968), 109–10.

14. Stuart, *Lives and Works of Civil and Military Engineers*, 309.

15. Specification of the Niagara Bridge by John A. Roebling Civil Engineer, Pittsburgh, May 1847, MC.04 Box 37F9, Roebling Collection, Rensselaer Polytechnic Institute, Troy, NY (hereafter RPI).

16. Roebling to Archbald, June 5, 1847, Archbald Papers, Lackawanna Valley Historical Society, Scranton, PA; Roebling to R. F. Lord, D & H Canal, October 20, 1847, R. F. Lord Papers, Minisink Valley Historical Society, Port Jervis, NY.

17. Charter acts and amendments of the Niagara Falls International Bridge Co., and Niagara Falls Suspension Bridge Co. See also Articles of Association by State of New York (1856).

complete by May 1, 1849.[18] called for a span of 800 feet supported by sixteen wire cables, with a deck 28 feet wide divided into two 7½ foot carriageways, two 4 foot walkways, and a central railway designed for maximum train weight of 24 tons pulled by a six-ton locomotive.[19] Despite his lower bid and the efforts of D. K. Minor, Ellet's award of the Wheeling commission and his early negotiations with Merritt and Stuart, proved too much for Roebling to overcome.

Ellet's Niagara

Ellet's short but eventful time at Niagara would do much to demonstrate the character of the man, his flair for the theatrical, and his willingness to litigate.

As 1848 began, he tackled a practical problem: How to get the first rope across the gorge with the whirlpool rapids below? One evening at dinner, a solution was proposed: hold a kite-flying contest, challenging competitors to get the first string across the gorge (see figure 2). Local youth came and after three days, on January 30, 1848, Homan Walsh succeeded in getting his kite across to secure the $5 prize.[20]

Using this first string to pull successively thicker ropes across, Ellet secured a 36-strand cable of No. 10 wires. On Monday March 13, 1848, with his cable secured, Ellet stepped into a small iron basket designed to ferry materials and rode suspended high above the river—the first person ever to cross from the American to the Canadian side above the Niagara Gorge. (see figure 3).[21] Word of the spectacle spread, with accounts reprinted in newspapers, enhancing Ellet's reputation on both sides of the gorge.

Next, eight prefabricated suspension cables of 72 strands each, were drawn across, and the first of two temporary footbridges, each 3 feet wide, began to extend from both sides. During construction of the second footbridge, the hazards of the site became apparent when a tornado caused severe damage, stranding several men precariously above the gorge. As fierce rains continued, the ferry basket was let out to the middle of the gorge, and a ladder was extended to the men, who made their way to safety one at a time. After repairs were made, the two smaller footbridges were drawn together to construct a more substantial 7½-foot wide footbridge below (figure 4).[22]

18. Stuart, *Lives and Works of Civil and Military Engineers*, 273.

19. Niagara Falls Suspension Bridge Difficulties, October 17, 1847, Box 26, Ellet Papers, University of Michigan, Special Collections Research Center (hereafter UM-SCRC); and Ellet to Merritt comparing the construction of his bridge to Keefer's proposal, February 28, 1848, Box 1_1, Thomas Fisher Rare Book Library, University of Toronto.

20. Lewis, *Charles Ellet, Jr.*, 111. Homan Walsh was the first to fly a kite across the gorge. Different accounts describe a $5 or $10 prize. See also M. Robinson, "The Kite That Bridged a River," Kite History, accessed September 15, 2022, http://www.kitehistory.com/Miscellaneous/Homan_Walsh.htm.

21. Stuart, *Lives and Works of Civil and Military Engineers*, 274–75. In a letter to Charles Stuart Ellet describes the details of his first trip across the gorge in a basket hung from a wire rope.

22. Niagara Falls Suspension Bridge Difficulties – Theodore G. Hulett & Jonathan Baldwin, October 17, 1847, Box 9-5, Ellet Papers, UM-SCRC.

Figure 2. Kite-flying contest at Niagara, January 1848. COURTESY OF WIKIMEDIA COMMONS.

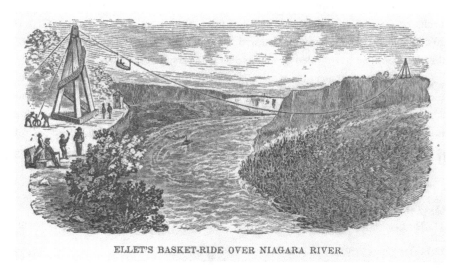

ELLET'S BASKET-RIDE OVER NIAGARA RIVER.

Figure 3. "Ellet's first basket ride across the Niagara Gorge in March 1848." FROM C. B. STUART, *LIVES AND WORKS OF CIVIL AND MILITARY ENGINEERS OF AMERICA* (NEW YORK: D. VAN NOSTRAND, 1871), 274.

At the end of July, with the larger footbridge complete but for guardrails,[23] Ellet again took to the stage to perform a feat of daring, first riding a "high-spirited" horse and buggy across the narrow span, and then pulling a fully loaded test carriage weighing 3,000 pounds.[24]

Behind the scenes, Ellet was challenged by directors from separate countries, who lacked organization and provided inadequate financial support. While stock was fully subscribed, the directors were slow to collect funds and often short of cash, forcing Ellet to extend credit to pay his workers. By February, a month after the kite contest, there were already indications that a lack of funds would impact the progress of the work. By March, as Ellet rode triumphant in his basket across the gorge, the directors considered a reduction of scope and a delay of the railway, an idea to which Ellet strenuously objected.[25] Despite his best efforts, at the start of April, Ellet accepted a modified contract for $145,000 for a bridge without a central railroad track.[26]

The relationship between Ellet and the directors became additionally strained when Ellet's began collecting tolls, first for those brave enough to ride across in his basket and later 25 cents for each person who crossed the footbridge. As the directors were not providing sufficient funds for the construction of the bridge, Ellet as the contractor in charge, chose to keep these fees for himself.

In mid-July, Ellet wrote the board stating his intention to stop work and secure his tools until funds were made available, an action the board perceived as a threat.[27] Working simultaneously on two large commissions, the railway bridge at Niagara and the Wheeling Bridge across the Ohio, Ellet divided his time traveling back and forth to Virginia. On August 1, taking advantage of his absence and just days after his heroic "spirited ride" across the gorge, the joint board voted to remove Ellet as the engineer in charge.[28]

A protracted battle ensued at the bridge and in the courts, as groups of men from each side fought for control.[29] On August 14, 1848, the directors took to the offensive and attempted to seize the bridge, storming the gates on the Canadian side and imprisoning two of Ellet's men, including his brother Alfred.[30] Within days, the directors gained control of the bridge by order of the New York Supreme Court. At the end of September, after the

---

23. Niagara Falls Suspension Bridge Difficulties – Theodore G. Hulett & Jonathan Baldwin, October 17, 1847.
24. "The Suspension Bridge at the Falls of Niagara," *Mechanics Magazine* 49 (September 30, 1848): 332.
25. Ellet to Stuart, February 27, 1848, Box 9-5, Ellet Papers, UM-SCRC.
26. Handwritten Updated Contract, April 1, 1848, Box 1_1, Thomas Fisher Rare Book Library, University of Toronto.
27. July 10, 1848, Box 1_2, Thomas Fisher Rare Book Library, University of Toronto.
28. Board Secy Colton to Ellet, August 5, 1848, Box 10-2, Ellet Papers, UM-SCRC.
29. Niagara Falls Suspension Bridge Difficulties—Theodore G. Hulett & Jonathan Baldwin, October 17, 1847, Box 9-5, Ellet Papers, UM-SCRC.
30. Ellie to Ellet, August 16, 1848, Box 10-2, Ellet Papers, UM-SCRC. Ellet's wife refers to his brother Alfred being at Niagara.

Figure 4. William Endicott lithograph of Ellet's Niagara Suspension Bridge, 1849.
COURTESY OF THE LIBRARY OF CONGRESS, PRINTS AND PHOTOGRAPHS DIVISION,
LC-DIG-PGA-06293.

court order was vacated, Ellet's men regained partial control, removed some of the wooden planks at the center of the bridge, and rendered the span impassable at the international border.[31] To protect their interests, Ellet's men placed a "3 pound canon" at the center and set an axe at the ready near the gate, to cut the cables, should all be lost.[32]

Lawsuits were filed on both sides, and with each in possession of half a bridge, the stalemate forced negotiations. By December 1848, all cases were dismissed as the two sides settled. Ellet gave up control, was compensated for his costs, and was given an additional $12,000.[33] Leaving for Wheeling to complete his world-record span, Ellet knew he would always be first to have crossed the gorge hundreds of feet above the river.

Roebling's Niagara

After events of 1848 between Ellet and the joint board, Roebling was likely glad to have been passed over by the directors in favor of Ellet. While he left Niagara angered by the

---

31. Various correspondence to Ellet, August 7–August 18, 1848, Box 10, Ellet Papers, UM-SCRC; and September 23, 1848, Supreme Court Decision.
32. R. Haw, *Engineering America: The Life and Times of John A. Roebling* (New York: Oxford University Press, 2020), 334.
33. Lewis, Charles Ellet, Jr., 115–16. Lewis gives the amount as $10,000. Haw, *Engineering America*, 334, uses the amount of $12,000.

selection process, Roebling continued to correspond with Merritt, president of the Canadian board, as Ellet progressed with his work. In December 1847, just as Roebling lost the Niagara contract, Merritt asked him to develop a proposal for a pedestrian bridge across the gorge, closer to the falls. Keeping their communications secret, Roebling proposed a two-span footbridge just below the falls, with a center pier on goat island. Unable to refrain from expressing his displeasure over recent events, he describes his bridge as "far more attractive than Ellet's structure ever will be" and pressed to move the project forward to prove "those men at Lockport, that they are mistaken"[34]

In May, there was a second inquiry by Merritt regarding the footbridge across the Niagara near Clifton House, but nothing came from the discussion. Writing as he completed the first of his four aqueducts for the D&H Canal, Roebling again criticized Ellet. Boasting of his well wrapped cables, "two solid and smooth iron cylinders of eight and 1/4 inch diameter, perfectly smooth and round," he declared that Ellet, "has no idea yet of the manner, in which I construct my cables." [35]

The Niagara Railway Bridge represents a crossroads in Roebling's career. A comparison of Ellet's and Roebling's different approaches to the same problem highlights the differences not so much between the two men as it does the difference in methodology of French engineers as represented by Ellet and the innovative work of John Roebling. At a span of 821' 4" from tower to tower, and with the railway deck 245 feet above the whirlpool rapids, Roebling's Niagara railway bridge represents his first true long-span suspension bridge and marks his transition from the use of solid iron bars to wire ropes for his suspenders and stays. While he had already completed six bridges by the time construction began in 1852, five aqueducts (one in Pittsburgh and four for the D&H), and the Monongahela Roadway Bridge in Pittsburgh, these were all relatively short spans with decks at modest heights above the water.

Ellet's proposed railway bridge at Niagara was to follow French methods, with sixteen small-diameter suspension cables (eight on each side), tied together periodically along their length. Described as a "garland" by Seguin, who developed the technique, many parallel strands of wire were laid out and then their ends were lifted into place.[36] This "lifting" created a critical deficiency as the wires near the bottom were stretched (over-tensioned) while those at the top were more lax, resulting in unequal tension in the wires across the cable. When supporting a load, wires at the bottom took on greater stress, while those near the top did little to provide support. The greater the diameter of the cable and the greater the number of wires—the greater this imbalance.

---

34. Roebling to Merritt, November 22, 1847, Box 1_1, Thomas Fisher Rare Book Library, University of Toronto.
35. Roebling to Merritt, May 22, 1848, Box 2_1, Thomas Fisher Rare Book Library, University of Toronto.
36. Seguin, *Des ponts en fil de fer*.

In the defense of their iron chains, British engineers were quick to cite the deficiencies of French wire suspension bridges. Both Samuel Brown and Thomas Telford tested the strength of iron bars and iron wires, and while they observed that the process of drawing iron wire added to its strength, they continued to prefer iron chains for their bridges.

While Ellet replicated French methods, Roebling chose to innovate surpassing the methods of both British and French engineers. Taking full advantage of the greater tensile strength of iron wires, Roebling developed a means of "aerial spinning" large suspension cables in place creating wires of equal tension across their section, and then "wrapping" the wires to create a protective layer eliminating oxidation.

Nowhere was this more important than at the Niagara Gorge, in sight of the great cataract and high above the whirlpool rapids. Ellet's methods were inefficient. He had spent six months and $30,000 building footbridges that hung from temporary towers, none of which was capable of supporting a railway (see figure 4).[37] He then planned on starting his permanent towers and pulling his smaller cables across one at a time to support his railway deck. While Roebling would make use of Ellet's bridge to ferry men and materials, his typical sequence of construction did not require these preliminary steps. Roebling instead began construction with permanent anchorages and towers; then extending wire ropes across, hung a work bridge from his towers, following a curve similar in deflection to his final suspension cables—all in preparation for spinning his cables in place, one wire at a time. Using his work bridge, Roebling then erected a lateral work platform from which workmen could "regulate the tension of the wires" as they were spun across the gorge.

In 1847, in contemplation of a bridge across the Niagara Gorge, Roebling patented an "Improvements in apparatus for passing suspension wires for bridges across rivers" (see figure 5). To spin wires in place, an endless rope is strung across from anchorage to anchorage. Similar to the manner in which a clothesline operates, this rope is secured on either end with rotating wheels positioned horizontally. From this rope hang two "traveling wheels" one at each side of the gorge; pulled across using "horse-power."

On one end of the span, a wire shed is positioned, as shown in the patent drawing symbolically on the left (see figure 5) as a spool of cable. A single wire is taken from the spool and secured at the anchorage, then looped around the "traveling wheel," and pulled across the span. Since the main spool of wire is stationary, two wires are pulled across with each pass. Once on the other side, the wire is looped around a cast-iron "shoe" designed to attach to the anchor chains; and then the "traveling wheel" returns. As there are two reciprocating wheels on opposite sides of the endless rope, two cables are spun at once; and with each pass, a wire is always pulled across.

Aligned with a guide rope, cables were spun to one-third of their final deflection, allowing the wires to stretch under load, to their designed alignment. By repeating this many

37. Haw, *Engineering America*, 353.

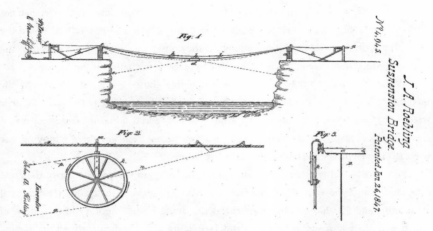

Figure 5. Apparatus for passing suspension wires for bridges across rivers, 1847. COURTESY U.S. PATENT OFFICE, PATENT US4945 1847.

times, wires were run until each "strand" was complete. Using this method, the wires all had equal tension and could equally share the load of a passing train.

To make handling hundreds of wires manageable, Roebling grouped his wires into smaller bundles called "strands." Knowing that seven circles of equal size create a round form, Roebling used 7 strands to form his suspension cables, until the Brooklyn Bridge, which uses cables of 19 strands each, adding 12 more strands around an inner core of 7 (see figure 6). Each strand was tied together with "temporary bands" at intervals of 9", and when 7 strands were complete and pinned to the anchor chains, the cables were ready for wrapping (see figure 7).

At Niagara, each of the four suspension cables had averaged 3,640 No. 9–gauge wires (0.14" in diameter). Together, the 7 strands of 520-wires each were 10" in diameter, the largest cable Roebling had yet made. As was his practice, all the wire was tested to sustain minimal tensile strength when "suspended between two posts, 400 feet apart" and to withstand bending by "pair of pliars [sic], and, rebending, without rupture"[38]

The wire shed located on the Canadian side behind the anchorages housed fourteen reels of wire. It was there the wires were prepared for spinning, straightened, coated in oil, and spliced to create a single continuous length. "The mode of splicing consists in overlapping the ends of the two wires, after having been filed tapering, and wrapping them with fine wire."[39] Roebling's splice proved stronger than the wire on either side.

In 1842, when Roebling patented his "Method of and machine for manufacturing wire

---

38. J. A. Roebling, Final Report on the Niagara Railway Suspension Bridge (1855), 24–26.
39. Niagara Suspension Bridge Handwritten History, MC.04.S2 Box 14.F39, Roebling Collection, RPI.

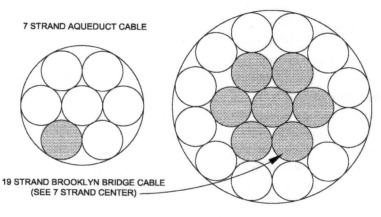

Figure 6. Typical 7-strand cable and 19-strand cable used for the Brooklyn Bridge. IMAGE BY THE AUTHOR.

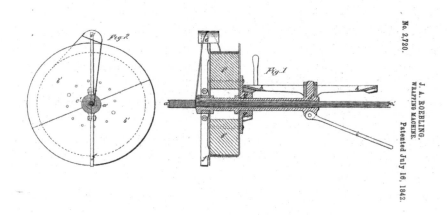

Figure 7. Patent 4945 for wire-wrapping machine to manufacture wire ropes, 1842. COURTESY U.S. PATENT OFFICE, PATENT US2720 1842.

ropes," he included a machine to add an outer wrapping. At the time, Roebling was developing his first wire ropes for the inclined planes of the Allegheny Portage Railroad. Located where the Pennsylvania Main Line Canal crossed the Allegheny Mountains, the portage loaded canal boats onto large railway cars on inclined planes and pulled them up and over the mountains, powered by endless hemp ropes connected to stationary steam engines. Roebling believed an outer wrapping would help his wire ropes hold to the sheaves, making it easier to attach the rail cars, and creating a durable wire rope as a replacement for the larger hemp ropes. Interestingly, before they became competitors, Ellet corresponded with Roebling about his ropes. Ellet discouraged wrapping of the wires, predicting the failure of the ropes as they went around the sheaves.[40] After testing, Roebling abandoned the wrapping of wire ropes used for haulage and developed instead a rope with 7 strands, similar to his suspension cables.[41] While it had not been his primary intention, Roebling recognized "the same machine might with equal advantage be applicable to the wrapping of cables for suspension bridges."[42] While the wrapping failed for his wire ropes, it proved a great success on his suspension cables.

As the wrapping machine moved along the cable, it compressed the 7 strands into a round form. The individual wires, coated in linseed oil during the spinning process, were again coated with oil and painted, then tightly wrapped with an outer annealed wire, and again coated with a protective layer of paint. This method of wrapping, oiling, and painting successfully protected the inner wires from oxidation.[43]

The Anchorages

Before spinning and wrapping the cables, Roebling first built his anchorages and towers with cast-iron saddles. At Niagara, he modified his 1846 patent method of "Anchoring suspension chains for bridges," another innovation from the approach of British and French engineers, who constructed open accessible chambers. While open chambers allowed for easy inspection, the anchor chains were exposed to moisture and susceptible to corrosion, so protecting them required regular maintenance.

Developed as he completed the Monongahela Bridge in Pittsburgh, this patent was intended for conditions where bedrock was not readily available. The anchor chains are sets of parallel bars, similar to the suspension chains of Telford bridges. Roebling's application of the system at Niagara is a hybrid, as the first four vertical bars sit in a 3 × 7 foot shaft in the bedrock that is enlarged at the bottom to a prism shaped chamber of 8 × 8 feet to hold a 6½ × 6½ cast-iron anchor plate (see figure 8). The remaining anchor chain bars extend above the natural grade and curve to align with the suspension cables. Following the system of the original patent, their joints are pinned and rest on small cast-iron plates and large stone blocks to maintain their position.[44] Using four suspension cables for the first time, the Niagara anchorage is doubled, with eight shafts 25 feet deep into the limestone, four on each side of the river.

---

40. Ellet to Roebling, December 12, 1840, RG17.470, Box 8: 1829–43, Pennsylvania State Archives, Harrisburg, PA.

41. D. Sayenga, ed., "Washington Roebling's Father: A Memoir of John A. Roebling," *American Society of Civil Engineers* (October 2008): 69.

42. Roebling to Ellet, December 16, 1840, Box 5-16, Ellet Papers, UM-SCRC.

43. Roebling, Final Report on the Niagara Railway Suspension Bridge (1855), 26.

44. Niagara Suspension Bridge Handwritten History, MC.04.S2 Box 14.F39, Roebling Collection, RPI.

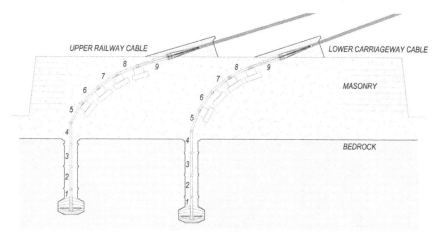

Figure 8. Double anchorage for upper and lower cables showing shafts, anchor plates, and bars. IMAGE BY THE AUTHOR.

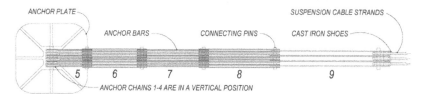

Figure 9. Plan view of anchor-plate pinned to anchor-chains pinned to shoes holding cable strands. IMAGE BY THE AUTHOR.

Each anchor plate had seven slotted holes to accept the first set of parallel wrought-iron anchor bars (see figure 9). Next a set of eight bars (six full-thickness bars with two thinner outer bars), and then alternating from nine to eight until the last set, which are pinned to "cast-iron shoes" designed to hold the 7 strands of the suspension cables. Each set of bars is 7 feet long until the last set, which are 10 feet and split into two groups (see figure 10). Of this last set, the top four bars are pinned to shoes holding three strands, and the bottom five bars are pinned to hold the four remaining strands.[45]

As each strand passes around a cast-iron shoe, it divides into 2 smaller strands, so a view of the anchorage would show 14 smaller strands extending from the wrapped suspension cable to the anchor chains. To exclude moisture and make the anchorage maintenance free, the iron bars were coated in linseed oil, "painted twice with zinc paint and Spanish

45. Roebling, Final Report on the Niagara Railway Suspension Bridge (1855),17.

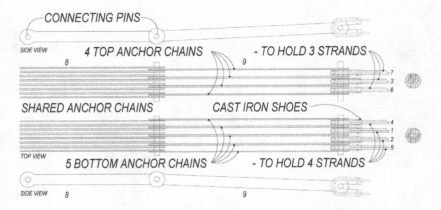

Figure 10.: Anchor-chain to shoe to 7-strand suspension cable transition. IMAGE BY THE AUTHOR.

Figure 11. Full span showing upper and lower suspension cables and double anchorages. IMAGE BY THE AUTHOR.

Brown," surrounded by a layer of hydraulic cement, with the shafts then filled with masonry and cement mortar.[46]

The Suspension Cables

Roebling's tall, slender masonry towers at Niagara were designed in an Egyptian style, similar to Navier's Pont des Invalides and Ellet's towers for the Fairmont Bridge. Like the bridges of Telford in Britain, the cables sat on saddles with cast-iron rollers to minimize the transfer of movement from the suspension cables of the primary span to the land cables, which extended back from the towers to the anchorages (see figure 11).

Roebling made two critical adjustments to assure the upper and lower suspension cables stayed in equilibrium during expansion and contraction from changes in temperature or the passing of trains. The deflection of the cables differed by 10 feet with the upper cables

46. J. A. Roebling, "Anchoring Suspension-Chains for Bridges" (jno a. roebling, of pittsburgh, pennsylvania), U.S. Patent No. US4710 (Washington, DC: U.S. Patent and Trademark Office, 1846).

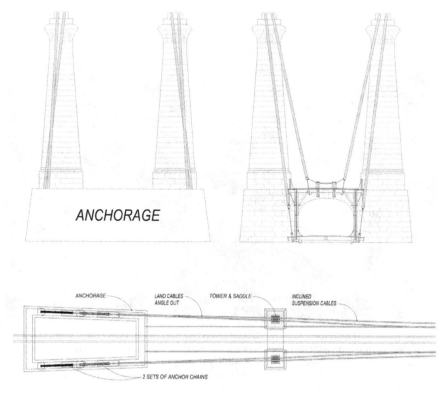

Figure 12. (Top) Elevations at anchorage showing outward land cables, and view from bridge center showing inclined suspension cables. IMAGE BY THE AUTHOR. (Bottom) Plan at anchorage showing line of land and suspension cables. IMAGE BY THE AUTHOR.

supporting the railway deck 54 feet below the saddles on the towers, and the lower cables supporting the carriageway at 64 feet, making for different lengths of cable across the span. To equalize this difference, the upper cable extended farther back at the rear anchorage, so the total length of the two cables matched.[47]

Some of Roebling's engineering is subtle, and the principles he employed are difficult to visualize without drawings. To provide additional lateral stability to his bridge, Roebling inclined his suspension cables (so they were closer together at the midspan of the bridge than at the towers), a technique he employed on all his bridges (see figure 12, top). This cradle form stabilized the bridge from side to side but also created an inward pull on the

---

47. Roebling, Final Report on the Niagara Railway Suspension Bridge (1855), 46; J. A. Roebling, Report to the Directors of the Niagara Falls International and Suspension Bridge Companies (1852), 9–10.

Figure 13. This 1868 photograph by Charles Bierstadt shows the suspenders and stays for main suspension span. COURTESY OF WIKIMEDIA COMMONS. To make his Niagara Bridge safe for railway traffic, Roebling gave it stability through a combination of "Weight, Girders, Trusses_and Stays" to ensure stiffness "and to resist either the action of trains, or the violence of storms."

separate towers that needed to be balanced. At Niagara, Roebling's tall, independent "obelisk" towers needed to account for these forces. He carefully aligned each of the cables so the inward vector of the "suspension cables" across the span was balanced by the outward direction of the "land cables" extending back to the anchorage. Visible in plan or when looking directly in line with the towers, these subtle adjustments are visible (see figure 12, bottom). Roebling describes this "lateral stability" in his 1855 final report. "The inclination of the tangents of the suspension cables very nearly coincide with the angles of the land cables, consequently their united tensions will produce a vertical pressure through the axis of each tower."[48]

To stabilize his bridge at Niagra, "weight" is employed by a combination of the cable superstructure and masonry towers which exert downward forces, deep wooden "Girders" run the length of the upper deck directly below the track rails, "Trusses" are formed by a wood lattice with diagonal iron tension bars, and wire rope "Stays" run from the towers to

---

48. Roebling, Final Report on the Niagara Railway Suspension Bridge (1855), 21.

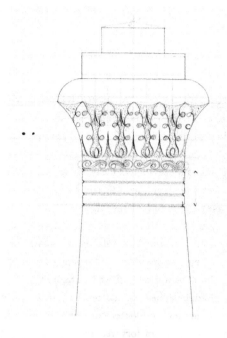

Figures 14a. Niagara masonry carving details at the top of the towers. Courtesy of the Roebling Collection, Box 37.F8, Rensselaer Polytechnic Institute, Troy, NY.

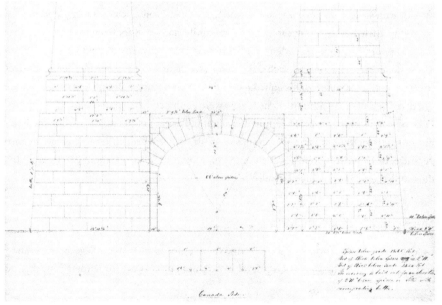

Figures 14b. Niagara stonework at base of towers showing connecting arch. COURTESY OF THE ROEBLING COLLECTION, BOX 37.F8, RENSSELAER POLYTECHNIC INSTITUTE, TROY, NY.

the decks, crossing the vertical suspenders to form rigid triangles (see figure 13). Roebling cautions, "no suspension bridge is safe without some of these appliances" to protect against the "violence of storms."[49]

Masonry Towers and Cast-Iron Saddles

Roebling's Egyptian towers sat on top of a 20 × 60 foot base with a center arch 19 feet wide. The railway ran across the top of the arch, and common traffic entered the lower deck through the archway. The towers continued up an additional 60 feet and were 15 feet square at the base and 8 feet square at the top.

To accommodate a height difference between the two sides of the gorge, the base on the American side was taller, at 28 feet high, 10 feet more than the 18-foot-high Canadian side. Drawings from 1853 show the first three courses of each tower 6 feet high with a 16-inch top molding, followed by twenty-one courses almost 2 feet thick and six upper courses, also close to 2 feet thick (see figure 14b). The specification required careful attention to the stonework, with alternating courses offset and the upper courses doweled together for greater stability. The ornamental detail was cut after the stone was set in place (see figure 14a).

Made of limestone, the specification required the stone to be quarried from their respective countries, and none could be taken "within a distance of 200 feet above or below the sight of the bridge on the banks of the river." The masonry contractors were responsible to "hoist the cast-iron saddles on top of the towers and to set them . . . on a bed of cement mortar." [50]

Atop each tower, a moveable cast-iron saddle had an 8-foot-square baseplate 2½″ thick, supporting two independent saddles, one for each suspension cable, resting on ten 5″-diameter cast-iron rollers, each 25½″ long (see figure 15). For all Roebling's bridges (other than the river piers of his aqueducts and the Monongahela Bridge that used a unique system of bell-crank pendulums), the towers were equipped with similar moveable saddles. "The object of these rollers is to admit of a slight movement of the saddles, when the equilibrium between the land and the suspension cables is disturbed, either by changes of temperature, or by passing trains." When tested on March 18, 1855, a train of 326 tons shifted the saddles less than a ½ inch laterally.[51]

The Hybrid Suspension Bridge

By definition "suspension bridges" like those of Telford's in Britain, Seguin's in France, and Ellet's in America supported a level deck hung by "vertical suspenders" attached to

49. Roebling, Final Report on the Niagara Railway Suspension Bridge (1855), 7.
50. Niagara Railway Suspension Bridge Specification for the Erection of Masonry, MC.04 Box 5.F31, Roebling Collection, RPI.
51. Roebling, Final Report on the Niagara Railway Suspension Bridge (1855), 22. 5

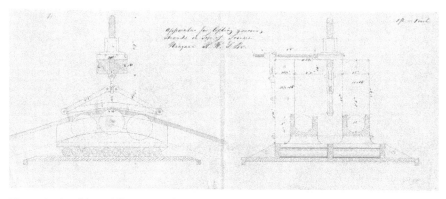

Figure 15. Double Saddle on top of tower at Niagara Suspension Bridge. COURTESY OF THE ROEBLING COLLECTION, BOX 37.F6, RENSSELAER POLYTECHNIC INSTITUTE, TROY, NY.

suspension cables or chains spanning from tower to tower. A second means of securing the deck is the use of "diagonal stays," which connect from the towers direct to the deck but do not run from tower to tower. Roebling promoted many unique ideas including the concept of a "hybrid suspension bridge," which integrated the use of "vertical suspenders" with "diagonal stays," the intersection of which gives the Brooklyn Bridge its iconic look.

At Niagara, sixty-four above-deck diagonal stays stiffened the span and assisted the main suspension cables. Made of 1 3/8″ wire ropes, there were sixteen stays for each of the four suspension cables, with eight stays connected to the moveable saddles at each end (see figure 16). As the stays crossed the vertical suspenders, they were lashed together with "small wrappings," forming triangles to lend rigidity to the bridge. Roebling understood that the "the triangle is the only geometrical figure whose corners cannot be shifted, consequently by keeping those stays under a good tension, we formed so many stationary points in the flooring, as we have stays."[52]

Up to this point in his career, Roebling's suspenders and diagonal stays were made using solid iron bars and not the more flexible wire ropes employed here and on his later bridges. Often misstated by historians, Roebling's first use of wire rope suspenders was not for the Delaware Aqueduct but was in fact at Niagara.[53] This represents a shift in thinking, as his 1847 proposal showed a preference for solid suspenders, "made of charcoal bar iron to wire suspender, the latter adding too much to the limberness of the structure giving it a trifling appearance and increasing unnecessarily the surface of iron to be kept in paint."[54]

52. Roebling, Final Report on the Niagara Railway Suspension Bridge (1855), 15.
53. D. B. Steinman, *The Builders of the Bridge: the Story of John Roebling and His Son* (New York: Harcourt, Brace, 1950), 103–104. Steinman incorrectly states that the Delaware Aqueduct was Roebling's first use of wire rope suspenders. This mistake has been carried forward by many authors.
54. Niagara Railway Suspension Bridge Superstructure Specification, May 1847, MC.04 Box 37.F9, Roebling Collection, RPI.

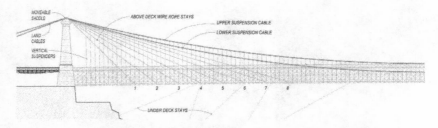

Figure 16. Half-span showing vertical suspenders with above and under the deck stays.
IMAGE BY THE AUTHOR.

By 1852, drawings show his intention to use wire rope suspenders, a change likely due to the great length required to reach from the tall towers to the upper and lower decks. He did, however, continue to rely on solid iron bars for shorter suspenders closer to the center of the span, a choice he also made for the Cincinnati-Covington and Brooklyn Bridges to follow.

Another fifty-six "under deck stays" were secured to the cliffs of the gorge to prevent uplift and to "insure against horizontal as well as vertical motions. Their principle duty is to guard against the force of winds, but at the same time they contribute materially to preserve the equilibrium of the structure during the passage of trains."[55]

Unlike his unique use of above-deck stays, the under-deck stays were a common strategy employed by the engineers who built suspension bridges across the windy Niagara Gorge. In fact, the 1864 destruction of Edward Serrell's Lewiston-Queenston Bridge in a windstorm, the first permanent suspension bridge to cross the gorge, occurred after the under-deck stays had been temporarily detached from the cliffs to protect them from the encroaching ice of the river.[56]

Roebling's vertical suspenders were attached to the suspension cables by a friction strap that was similar in design to those later used on the Brooklyn Bridge (see figure 17). For the lower suspension cables, suspenders extended to the outer edge of the lower deck, where they transitioned to U-shaped solid iron stirrups that passed between a lower pair of crossbeams and around a wood-block and cast-iron collar, with a groove to accept the iron bar. The wire suspenders ran from the collar of the friction strap down to a small cast-iron "transition block" with three holes—one in the center for the wire rope and two on the outside, to connect the U-shaped stirrup that was secured at its threaded ends like a bolt. To hold the wire cable ends, each was splayed to form a cone shape by bending the individual wires back on themselves.

For the upper cables, the wire rope suspenders transitioned to solid iron bars or short

55. Roebling, Final Report on the Niagara Railway Suspension Bridge (1855), 16.
56. F. Griggs and A. Griggs, "General Edward W. Serrell," *Structure Magazine*, February 2012.

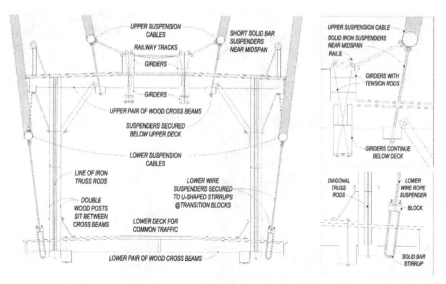

Figure 17. Cross-section of the wooden box truss showing the suspension cable and suspender connections. IMAGE BY THE AUTHOR.

solid iron bars (near the center of the span), which passed through the upper deck and were secured to a wooden block and cast-iron plate that sat below the upper pair of wood cross beams.

The Double-Deck Lattice Box Truss

While cast-iron and wrought-iron components were used for the wire cable superstructure, saddles, and anchorages, Roebling's span across the Niagara was still primarily a wooden bridge. Roebling did not begin to integrate iron beams to support his decks and railings until after he returned to Pittsburgh in 1859 to build the St. Clair Street Bridge across the Allegheny. It was the Cincinnati-Covington Bridge where Roebling first implemented a full iron truss.

At the time of the Niagara Railway Bridge, the development of rolled iron beams in America was in its infancy, and the Bessemer process, which removed impurities from molten iron and reduced carbon to create steel, would not be patented until 1856, a year after the bridge was complete. Steel wire would not be used until the Brooklyn Bridge, marking an end of the era of "iron wire" suspension bridges.

Early designs for the box truss show the sides inclined to match the line of the lower suspension cables; but, as built, the box was square: 18 feet from deck to deck, 24 feet across at the bottom, and 25 feet across at the top (see figure 18). At 821' 4" and his longest span to date, Roebling added camber, curving the box truss along its length, so it rose in the center

Figure 18. Interior of Niagara Suspension Bridge, 1859. PHOTOGRAPH BY WILLIAM
ENGLAND. COURTESY OF WIKIMEDIA COMMONS.

to resist the flattening that would occur when a heavy train passed over the span. Spaced
every five feet to match the suspenders, wooden cross-frames made of pairs of Canadian
pine beams 16 × 4 inches, supported the upper and lower decks and straddled pairs of
vertical wooden posts on each side, spaced to allow for wrought-iron tension rods, 1″ thick
with 1 1/8″ screw ends. Viewed from the side, these iron truss rods ran at 45 degrees to the
decks, crossing to form a "diamond work," providing a second opportunity for Roebling to
apply the stability of the triangle for stiffness and further reduce "undulations, caused by
wind."[57]

Sequence of Construction

Just as the details of Roebling's bridges reveal his ingenuity, so too does the sequence of
construction he followed. The bridge was built in two phases, with the carriageway deck
and lower cables completed by June 1854 and the railway deck and upper cables ready in
March 1855.

---

57. Roebling, Final Report on the Niagara Railway Suspension Bridge (1855), 8, 12–13.

Having received his contract in June 1852, Roebling submitted his preliminary report to the directors in July, and by September began work on the anchorages, first with shafts for the anchors and chains, followed by the construction of the masonry towers, both of which took more than a year to complete. In December 1853, the spinning of the lower cables began, and despite delays due to strong winds, by January 1854, Roebling's aerial spinning was running as many as sixty wires a day, powered by two horses taking turns.[58]

On May 17, 1854, as the suspension cables neared completion and the rope suspenders were hung and the wood frames of the lower carriageway began to extend from the sides of the gorge to meet in the middle, Charles Ellet Jr. would unintentionally disrupt Roebling's plans at Niagara when his Wheeling Bridge was destroyed in a windstorm. Just four days later on May 21, 1854, Roebling wrote urgently to Charles Swan, who ran his wire rope business in Trenton, requesting he quickly ship more wire rope to Niagara, to add additional under-deck stays and assure the bridge's safety, "The destruction of the Wheeling bridge is a fact. I wrote to you to send me 2000 foot more of rope 7 × 7 No 9 3 lbs. per ft. for stays. Do not neglect this. I must have this rope very soon to render our new floor safe. If possible send more as fast as you can make it."[59]

Roebling knew that his bridge was at its most vulnerable in the months it would take to complete the railway deck. In its unfinished state, the carriageway was a single deck, not yet stiffened by the full construction of the wooden box truss and iron truss rods, supported only by the strength of the lower suspension cables. The collapse at Wheeling could not be ignored, and Roebling addressed it directly in his final report, to assure the bridge directors and the public that his bridge was safe. "The destruction of the Wheeling Bridge by a high wind on the 17th of May last year, the greatest disaster of the kind on record, has naturally given rise to doubts as to the safety of suspension bridges generally. ... That bridge was destroyed by the momentum acquired by its own dead weight, when swayed up and down by the force of the wind." Referring to the four primary means employed to stabilize the bridge he adds, "The destruction of that bridge was clearly owing to a want of *stability*, and not to a want of *strength*. This want of *stiffness* could have been supplied by *over floor stays*, *truss railings*, *under floor stays*, or cable stays."[60]

In June, 1854 Roebling's carriageway opened to public use with little fanfare, a contrast to Ellet's spectacle on horseback, showing the difference in the character of the men. For Roebling, it was about the work. It would take almost a year for the upper suspension cables and railway deck to be ready for the first locomotive. Roebling again looked to test the deck with little notice, attempting to keep the timing secret by misleading the newspapers, but with too many locals involved in the work, word quickly spread. On March 8, 1855, the

---

58. Technological. Journal Entry Niagara January 2, 1854, Reel 8: Writings, ca. 1837–1869, Roebling Family Papers, Rutgers University Library.
59. JAR to Swan, May 21, 1854, Reel 1: 1839–46 Correspondence.
60. J. A. Roebling, Final Report to the Presidents and Directors of the Niagara Falls Suspension and Niagara Falls International Bridge Companies (Rochester, NY: Lee and Mann, 1855), 37, 39.

twenty-three-ton *London* made its way out onto the span above the gorge with Roebling on board and covered by men like bees on a hive.[61] As he had predicted, there was little movement of the bridge and the increased deflection of the cables as they stretched from the added weight, measured no more than three inches. On March 20, 1855, Roebling officially opened the bridge to railway traffic, with twenty trains crossing in the first twenty-four hours; by March 25, thirty trains a day were making their way across (see figure 19).[62]

If anyone was qualified to judge John Roebling's engineering skill, it was his son Washington, who took over as chief engineer of the East River Bridge in 1869, after his father's untimely death. Washington had a unique window into his father's life as an engineer, having witnessed his first attempts to make wire rope at their Saxonburg farm, and having accompanied his father to Pittsburgh at age of eight to attend school while the Allegheny Aqueduct and the Monongahela Bridges were built. In February 1850, after his father injured his hand in a new wire rope machine at the Trenton ropeworks, Washington, age twelve, accompanied his father as "assistant" and "scribe" to the D&H Canal, as the Neversink and High Falls Aqueducts were finished.[63] In 1852, as his father began work at Niagara, Washington was two years from enrolling at Rensselaer Institute in Troy, New York, to study engineering.

At Niagara, Washington reflected on the finer points of his fathers' methods, "not generally recognized by the engineers of the time," describing with admiration the manner in which he balanced the loads of his suspension cables, adjusting their deflection by careful placement of the anchorages. While the phased construction allowed the lower carriageway to begin to collect tolls in advance of the railway, the independent construction of the upper cable and deck presented a unique challenge: How to join the two decks? Having been in service for almost a year, the cables of the lower deck were fully tensioned, while those of the railway level had yet to support a true load. It would be critical that the two be joined in such a manner that the upper and lower cables act in unison as a train crossed. Only after the two decks were joined could the installation of the iron tension rods be completed, thus tying the decks together to act in unison as a lattice box truss. Washington describes the joining: "Then came the *experimentum crucis*, to unite the two floors, to make due allowance for the lower cables which had already stretched and forced the upper cable down to their ultimate place—This could only be achieved by loading the upper floors with 400 tons of stone, thus stretching the upper cables artificially—this plan succeeded admirably—both cables carrying their equal share when a train passed over."[64]

Completion of the bridge gained great notice of the general public and also the reluctant admiration of British engineer Robert Stephenson, who earlier had dismissed the

---

61. Haw, *Engineering America*, 375.
62. *Niagara Falls Gazette*, March 14, 1855, p. 2, fig. 2.
63. Sayenga, "Washington Roebling's Father," 126–27, 129.
64. Sayenga, 150.

Figure 19. Upper Railway Deck with locomotive, 1859. PHOTOGRAPH BY WILLIAM ENGLAND. COURTESY OF GETTY IMAGES.

application of the "suspension method" for railway bridges. After visiting Niagara and reviewing Roebling's final report he wrote, "no other system of bridge-building yet devised could cope with the large span of 800 feet which was there absolutely called for . . . no one appreciates more than I do, the skill and science displayed by Mr. Roebling in overcoming the striking engineering difficulties by which he was surrounded."[65]

Roebling's 1860 Report

While five years of successful operation had made Roebling famous worldwide, other engineers and the public, out of ignorance, criticized the Niagara Suspension Bridge with newspapers warning, "the bridge is giving way rapidly" as the cables expanded in the summer heat. Roebling had calculated this movement and knew that with cables of such a great length, the height at the center of the bridge in summer would vary as much at two feet, from the cold of the winter.[66]

During the five years since the bridge opened, people became accustomed to faster rail travel and questioned the speed limit of trains crossing the span. Roebling had been explicit in his instructions for the use of the bridge based on design loads. With safety in mind, trains were to pass no faster than five miles per hour, and on the lower carriageway, "public processions, marching to the sound of music, or bodies of soldiers" needed to break step and "droves of cattle are . . . to be divided off in troops of 20" with no more than "60 to be allowed on the bridge at one time."[67]

In July 1860, Roebling returned to Niagara at the behest of the bridge company and spent three days examining his bridge. After making assurances of safety, Roebling with poetic license, notes the unique beauty of the falls at Niagara when addressing the speed of trains: "What would be gained by a higher speed? Nothing whatever. The bridge forms a link between two termini, and there is always time to make connections. Passengers will prefer to cross at a slow rate in order to enjoy the splendid scenery during the passage."[68]

Not the only one to see the uniqueness of the site and his bridge, both Harriet Tubman and Mark Twain reflected upon crossing. Serving as the last link on the underground railroad, Tubman's biographer describes an 1856 trip across, leading a group of escaped slaves to freedom in Canada: "The cars began to cross the bridge. Harriet was very anxious to have her companions see the falls. . . . At length Harriet knew by the rise in the center of the bridge, and the descent on the other side, that they had crossed the line."[69]

65. J. Hodges, Construction of the great Victoria Bridge in Canada by James Hodges, engineer, to Messrs. Peto, Brassey, and Betts, contractors (London: J. Weale, 1860), 85–99. See, esp. the letter to the chairman and directors of the Grand Chunk Railway of Canada Company (98).

66. Niagara JAR Letter to Commercial Journal regarding Expansion and Contraction of Cables, August 6, 1859, MC.04 Box 5.F30, Roebling Collection, RPI.

67. J. A. Roebling (1855), Final Report to the Presidents and Directors.

68. J. A. Roebling, Report on the Condition of the Niagara Railway Suspension Bridge (1860), 5.

69. S. H. Bradford, The Scenes in the life of Harriet Tubman (Auburn: J. Moses Printer, 1869), 33.

And Twain perhaps reflects a more honest sense of crossing, "Then you drive over to suspension bridge, and divide your misery between the chances of smashing down 200 feet into the river below, and the chances of having the railway train overhead smashing down onto you. Either possibility is discomforting taken by itself, but, mixed together, they amount in the aggregate to positive unhappiness."[70]

Niagara was a turning point for both John A. Roebling and Charles Ellet Jr. In 1847, as Ellet began work on his two large commissions at Niagara and Wheeling, he was the best known and most successful civil engineer and builder of suspension bridges in America. Despite Ellet's short tenure at Niagara and the success of Wheeling, he would see his reputation grow as his bridge become known in Great Britain, France, and the rest of Europe as the longest span in the world. For the two men, over the eight years from 1847 to 1855, from when they first competed for the Niagara and Wheeling commissions until Roebling's railway bridge was complete, there would be a reversal of fortunes, with Ellet as America's most famous engineer at the start and Roebling in that position at the end.

Roebling had built the world's first and only successful railway suspension bridge, earning the praise of British engineer Robert Stephenson, who had earlier dismissed suspension bridges for railways in favor of his own tubular system. Ellet's career as a builder of bridges ended with the collapse of the bridge at Wheeling a year before Roebling finished his Niagara. Roebling's ingenuity not only demonstrated the technical superiority of his methods over those of French and British engineers his work continues to influence how we build to the present day, with modern bridge cables spun in the air and wrapped much as Roebling did in the nineteenth century. After 1855, Roebling now held the title of America's greatest civil engineer and would go on to design his two most monumental works, the Cincinnati-Covington Bridge across the Ohio and his crowning achievement, the East River Bridge in New York.

70. M. Twain, "A Visit to Niagara," in *Sketches New and Old*, 70–80. (New York: Harper & Brothers, 1903), 71.

Goodbye Old 1910
Encounters with the Market in the 1910 Diary of a Rural New York Woman

Hamilton Craig

In 1910, Mary Brainard, a sixty-eight-year-old home producer and farmer's wife who lived in the rural Upstate New York community of Wilton, the town she grew up in, kept a diary in which she recorded the daily activities of her household.[1] Mundane on its surface, this diary reveals much about a traditional community in a process of transformation. In the year the diary was written, Mary Brainard and the members of her social network mounted a quiet resistance to industrial capitalism even as their community was dispersed by farm-to-factory migration. They resisted by maintaining bonds of community that stretched between the farm and the factory, the countryside and the town.

Country Values

Scholars have disagreed about the place of rural northeastern communities like Wilton in the transition to capitalism. Some scholars have portrayed northeastern farm neighborhoods as sites of resistance to the hegemony of the market, embracing instead values of self-sufficiency that were inherently opposed to capitalism. Against this interpretation, others have argued that the members of these communities participated in the market economy and therefore were agents of change rather than victims of or defenders against capitalism. Some scholars have critiqued the assumptions of such arguments, which accept a clear distinction between a precapitalist northeastern agriculture based on subsistence and a

---

1. Mary Brainard lived in Wilton from at most the age of twelve to at least the age of twenty-seven. She would return there from Saratoga Springs in 1888, when she was forty-five. For the earliest record showing Mary Brainard in Wilton, see *1855 New York State Census*, Saratoga County, population schedule, Wilton Township, dwelling 442, family 534; Ancestry.com, s.v. "Nancy Gailor." For the last record showing Mary Brainard in Wilton prior to her time in Saratoga Springs, see *1870 U.S. Census, New York State*, Saratoga County, population schedule, Wilton Township, dwelling 17, family 17; Ancestry.com, s.v. "Nancy Gailor."

capitalist agriculture based on participation in the market.[2] For instance, Richard Bushman posited the "composite farm," the farm that sent some produce to market but also provided for the needs of family members, as a "conciliatory concept" in "multiple economies" where "subsistence and market production co-existed." Bushman held that, while even the earliest northeastern farmers were willing to engage in the commodity markets of their time, the wellbeing of the family was their primary goal. According to Bushman, this goal was served both by trade and by the subsistence production that helped to insulate farmers and their families from the vagaries of the market into the nineteenth century and beyond.[3]

Hal Barron investigated the persistence of agrarian values after the market revolution. In his book *Mixed Harvest: The Second Great Transformation in American Agriculture*, he described the period from 1870 to 1930 as marked by the rise of consumer culture, corporate entities, and centralized government. Northern farmers, he held, met these changes in ways still informed by an attachment to family farms and local communities. Barron saw the story of farmers in this period as "a story of change and continuity and of accommodation as well as resistance," in that farmers successfully resisted some changes, like school consolidation, while embracing others, like the rise of mail-order houses catering to rural people, that could be married to an agrarian ethos.[4]

Other scholars took up the subject of how farmers negotiated social changes in this period. Ronald Kline, in *Consumers in the Country*, argued that while farmers adopted new consumer technologies in the early twentieth century, they did so selectively, always informed by their own identities and needs. While advertisers and extension agents sought to "urbanize" rural people by turning them into consumers, farmers created distinctly rural versions of technological modernity, such as party-line telephone systems modeled on rural visiting practices.[5] Mary Neth, in *Preserving the Family Farm: Women, Community, and the Foundations of Agribusiness in the Midwest: 1900–1940*, focused on how farm families in the Midwest contested the visions of extension agents who sought to impose commercial agriculture and middle-class family values on their communities. They adopted some new methods but employed them in the service of preserving small family farms rather than

2. For discussion of this debate, see Alan Kulikoff, "The Transition to Capitalism in Rural America," *William and Mary Quarterly* 46, no.1 (1989): 120–44; Naomi R. Lamoreaux, "Rethinking the Transition to Capitalism in the Early American Northeast," *Journal of American History* 90, no. 2 (2003): 472–61; Daniel Vickers, "Errors Expected: The Culture of Credit in Rural New England, 1750–1800," *Economic History Review*, 63, no. 4 (2010): 1032–57; and Christopher Clark, "The View from the Farmhouse: Rural Lives in the Early Republic," in *Whither the Republic: A Forum on the Future of the Field*, ed. John Lauritz Larson and Michael A. Morisson (Philadelphia: University of Philadelphia Press, 2005), 48–57.
3. Richard Lyman Bushman, "Markets and Composite Farms in Early America," *William and Mary Quarterly* 55, no. 3 (1998): 374.
4. Hal S. Barron, *Mixed Harvest: The Second Great Transformation in American Agriculture* (Chapel Hill: University of North Carolina Press, 1997), 8, 12, 76–77, 240–41.
5. Ronald R. Kline, *Consumers in the Country: Technology and Social Change in Rural America* (Baltimore, MD: Johns Hopkins University Press, 2000), 6–10, 18–19, 50–54.

Figure 1. An undated photo of two Wilton men, Albert and Will Pettis, driving a horse team and cart. John Brainard and John Winney may have looked much the same when they rode out together. *Albert and Will Pettis*, n.d., by unknown photographer. COURTESY OF THE WILTON HERITAGE SOCIETY AND KAREN JAMES, WILTON TOWN HISTORIAN.

attempting to found large operations.[6] Nancy Grey Osterud, in *Bonds of Community: The Lives of Farm Women in Nineteenth Century New York*, held that in the late nineteenth century farmers continued to rely on communal labor and home production to resist "both the capitalist market and capitalist notions of value" at the turn of the century.[7] Neth, Kline, Barron, and Osterud were all concerned with the ways rural people met the modernizing and commercializing influences of the late nineteenth and early twentieth centuries on their own terms, retaining an ethos grounded in community, family, and productive labor.

The Ties That Bound

The diary that Mary Brainard kept from December 1909 through December 1910 adds to this scholarship by presenting an intimate portrait of a farm community grappling with change in New York's capital district. It reveals the importance of communal work practices and home production methods, both of which served to maintain a degree of neighborhood and family independence from the marketplace. It shows Mary Brainard and her family

---

6. Mary Neth, *Preserving the Family Farm: Women, Community, and the Foundations of Agribusiness in the Midwest: 1900–1940* (Baltimore, MD: Johns Hopkins University Press, 1995), 143–46, 212–13, 237–40.
7. Nancy Grey Osterud, *Bonds of Community: The Lives of Farm Women in Nineteenth-Century New York* (Ithaca, NY: Cornell University Press, 1991), 207.

engaging with the commercial world on their own terms, incorporating store-bought products into rural practices of home production and nonmonetary exchange. The diary also
offers a view of the rural response to demographic contraction, as farm-to-factory migrants
retained important connections to the Wilton community. Mary Brainard's diary affords
a microhistorical study of the rural effort to meet the "Great Transformation" of the late
nineteenth and early twentieth century in a manner that accorded with agrarian values.

When Mary Brainard wrote her diary, Wilton, which is now a developed suburb of
over 16,000 people, was a small, rural community of about 900 people.[8] Situated just north
of Saratoga Springs, the area was first occupied by settlers in the eighteenth century and
was incorporated in 1818.[9] By 1910, Wilton was a long-settled place with extensive social and
familial connections between its residents. Contrary to some stereotypes of rural people,
Mary Brainard was not isolated, but deeply enmeshed in the traditions and social networks
that defined her village.

At the time the diary was written, Mary Brainard was living in a farmhouse in Wilton
with her husband, John, and the family of her younger nephew John Winney, including his
wife, Jennie, and their daughters, Ada, Gladys, and Ethel (until Ethel married Vincent Varney in February 1910).[10] Mary had moved to Wilton with her husband from the village of
Saratoga Springs twenty-two years earlier, and John Brainard still owned his former home
there.[11] Mary also co-owned another house in Saratoga Springs with her nephew. Typically

---

8. The current population count is available via the U.S Census bureau website. See "Quick facts,
Wilton Town, Saratoga County, New York," U.S. Census Bureau, accessed January 22, 2022,
https://www.census.gov/quickfacts/wiltontownsaratogacountynewyork. The population count for
1910 was garnered from the U.S. census of that year; at Ancestry.com.
9. For an overview of Wilton's early history, see Nathaniel Bartlett Sylvester, *History of Saratoga
County, New York, with Illustrations and Biographical Sketches of Some of Its Prominent Men and
Pioneers* (Philadelphia: Everts and Ensign, 1877), 462–71.
10. 1910 U.S. Census, Saratoga County, New York, population schedule, Wilton Township, dwelling 18, family 21; Ancestry.com, s.v. "Mary A. Brainard." For the marriage, see Brainard, Diary
(typescript), February 10, 1910.
11. The 1880 Federal Census shows John Brainard and Mary Brainard living in a farmhouse on
Catherine Street in Saratoga Springs. 1880 Federal Census, Saratoga County, population schedule,
Saratoga Springs, dwelling 304, family 336; Ancestry.com, s.v. "John Brainard." In her diary, Mary
Brainard wrote on March 29, 1910: "22 years ago to day we moved from the villag [sic] out here," in-
dicating that they left the house in 1888; see Brainard, Diary (typescript). A deed from 1904 records
the transfer of this house from John Winney to John Brainard. See "John Winney to John Brainard,
June 1, 1904," in Saratoga County Deeds, bk. 248, p. 428. This deed also gives the earlier history of the
property, which indicates that at the time that John Brainard and Mary Brainard lived there, it was
owned by Chauncey Gailor, a relative of Mary Brainard née Gailor. A deed from 1926 indicates that
John Brainard eventually returned the property to John Winney. See "John Brainard to John Winney,
September 9, 1925," in Saratoga County Deeds, bk. 336, p. 231. The trading back and forth of this
property between kin members and its use as a resource by kin members reflects Osterud's assertion
that "local farmers were not speculative in their attitude toward land . . . they did not regard land as
a short-term investment made for the sake of individual profit. Rather, they engaged in a myriad of
market transactions for familial ends." See Osterud, *Bonds of Community*, 63. For the house on Maple
Avenue that Mary Brainard and John Winney co-owned, see "Mary A. Brainard and John Winney,"
Saratoga Town Tax Rolls, 1910, Vault at the Saratoga Springs Visitors Center, Saratoga Springs, NY.

for a northern rural family, kin relationships were central to their lives. As Nancy Grey Osterud writes, in northern rural communities "kinship was a lifelong bond of mutual aid."[12]
This bond was expressed by the cohabitation of Mary Brainard and her nephew, as well as
by the fact that he rented the land he farmed from her and would be granted ownership of
it in 1911. Kin relationships were foremost among the connections that enabled farmers to
maintain some independence, granting them access to property and labor apart from the
mainstream marketplace.

In addition to cohabiting with his aunt's family, John Winney farmed land he rented
from her. This rented land was a ninety-one-acre property that Mary had inherited from
her father, James M. Gailor, who had died intestate.[13] She finally transferred the land by
deed to John Winney in 1911, the year after her surviving diary ended.[14] Both cohabitation
and rental indicate the utility of kin relationships, which provided valuable support and
conferred attachments and obligations outside of the demands of the market.

The Winneys and Brainards depended upon one another for many kinds of help
within the home. Jennie Winney and Mary Brainard exchanged work on both a paid and
an informal basis.[15] Ada Winney assisted Mary with clothing production and gardening.[16]
John Winney cleaned and fixed Mary's stove.[17] He also helped till her and John's vegetable garden.[18] John Winney and John Brainard worked together to shovel paths and "break
roads."[19] The women of both households worked together to gather berries.[20] The Winneys and Brainards exchanged gifts, and when Ethel Winney was married, Mary Brainard

---

12. Osterud, *Bonds of Community*, 61.
13. For James M. Gailor's probate record, see Surrogates Court (Saratoga County), Probate Records, 1815–1923, Index, 1878–1904, Saratoga, New York, 1896; Ancestry.com, s.v. "James Gailor."
14. For evidence of the rental, see "Mary Brainard," in Saratoga County Tax Rolls, Wilton, 1905,
1906, 1907, 1910, Saratoga County Historians Office, Ballston Spa, NY. For the 1911 transfer,
see "Mary Brainard to John Winney, April 4, 1911," in Saratoga County Deeds, bk. 276, p. 167. It
should be noted that in the Nanticoke Valley it would have been highly unusual for a woman to
receive farmland at all. Writes Osterud, "one pattern stands out: sons were given land, but daughters received household furnishings when they married.... This gender difference... was as deeply
rooted in the kinship system as the most fundamental conceptions of the mutual obligations of
parents and children." Osterud, *Bonds of Community*, 64. Mary Brainard's possession of the land
may have stemmed from her father dying without making a will. See Osterud's discussion of estate
division (66).
15. For descriptions of work-sharing between these women, see Brainard, Diary (typescript), December 27, 1909; and January 27, 1910; February 7, 22, 28, 1910; April 4, 5, 18, 22, 25, 1910; May
2, 9, 10, 16, 17, 23, 27, 1910; June 6, 13, 20, 27, 1910; July 5, 11, 18, 25, 1910; August 1, 8, 15, 22, 29,
1910; September 5, 12, 19, 26, 1910; October 3, 10, 17, 24, 31, 1910; November 14, 15, 21, 28, 1910.
16. Brainard, Diary (typescript), April 6 and 8, 1910.
17. Brainard, Diary (typescript), April 25, September 29, and November 30, 1910.
18. Brainard, Diary (typescript), June 10, 1910.
19. Brainard, Diary (typescript), December 27, 1909; January 7, 1910; February 4, 5, 18, 1910.
Nancy Grey Osterud has observed that this activity may have constituted a formal labor duty the
men owed to the village as property owners.
20. Brainard, Diary (typescript), June 17, 21, 24, 1910; July 22 and August 9, 1910.

hosted her wedding party in her parlor.[21] The closeness of the cohabiting families found material expression in a variety of ways, and reciprocity between kin helped meet needs for resources and work outside of the market economy.

Reciprocity extended beyond the household as well. As Mary Neth writes of midwestern farm communities, "Neighboring extended the patterns of mutuality formed in families to create a system of reciprocity that went beyond the ties of kinship to larger community groups."[22] An example of reciprocity is given by the relationship between John Winney and Seymour Linendoll. Seymour Linendoll, an independent Wilton farmer, was one of the most consistent and significant sources of outside help to John Winney's farming operation.[23] He threshed wheat for John Winney in the spring on an apparently informal schedule, and John repaid Seymour for his labor in a variety of ways, such as by mowing hay and butchering pigs.[24] The reciprocity that operated between the two men illustrates a system of labor distinct from the wage labor associated with capitalism.

An anecdote from the diary gives a poignant illustration of the extent to which the principle of community reciprocity defined the world Mary Brainard inhabited. It is worth quoting in its entirety. On June 27, 1910, Mary Brainard wrote,

> A swarm of bees came and lit on a limb of the little tree by the doghouse about ten o'clock, Johnnie came in from the corn field and went over to Irelands for a hive and got a lot of them in, then they all came out and started to go in the tree again and he went down to Dave Easterbrooks for another hive and got one with some comb in it and they did not think they would stay then but started to go away and John and Johnnie drove them back with water and sand then they lit on a post in the hen yard and then they smoked them in.[25]

In mounting an effort to harness the resource of the bee swarm, members of four families (the Irelands, the Easterbrooks, the Winneys, and the Brainards) cooperated. This entry presents today's reader with a succinct word picture of a world in which mutuality was an unquestioned part of daily life.

Modes of life associated with insulation *from* the market could be extended to shape interactions *with* the market. An example of this can be found in the ways that home production of clothing was blended with commercial consumption. Women in the Winney and Brainard households produced clothing using store-bought cloth and patterns rather

21. Brainard, Diary (typescript), January 4, July 3, September 8, September 20, and December 7, 1910; and March 6, April 6, July 24, and September 17, 1910.
22. Neth, Preserving the Family Farm, 41.
23. <18XX> U.S. Census, Saratoga County, New York, population schedule, Wilton Township, dwelling 30, family 34; Ancestry.com, s.v. "Seymour Linendoll."
24. Brainard, Diary (typescript), March 7, 8, 10, 11, 17, 1910. See also December 10, 1909; January 11, January 26, March 30, July 11, July 20, September 6, December 7, and February 20, 1910.
25. Brainard, Diary (typescript), June 27, 1910.

than buying ready-made clothing from stores. In this way they combined purchasing with traditional home production. This evidences the way that farm women interacted with the market on their own terms, in a manner shaped by traditional practices of "making do."[26] Nancy Grey Osterud and Mary Neth both write about how women's home production was valued as a part of the farm family enterprise that enabled independence from the market.[27] The growing availability of ready-made goods in the twentieth century presented many attractions but also threatened the status farm women held as producers.[28] While economics may have been their foremost concern, the practices of Mary Brainard and her housemates also reflect attachments to their productive roles and a rural policy of making do that shaped their behavior as consumers.

Mary Brainard and her husband similarly blended commercial consumption with traditional practices in the way they obtained and paid for butter. The Brainards did not produce their own butter, nor did they buy it through the market. Rather than purchasing butter from a store, they obtained it through the Winneys, who typically gave them butter on credit.[29] Sometimes the Brainards paid their debt to the Winneys in cash, but often they used store-bought goods to make up the balance as when, on June 25, Mary Brainard wrote, "John got 20 pounds of sugar for Johnnie when he went to town after supper. That would merely pay for the jar of butter."[30] This suggests a complex relationship between the Brainards and the marketplace. They preferred acquiring butter, which could be produced locally, through their kin rather than through the intermediary of merchants. When they did buy goods through a store, these goods could be integrated into their own kin and community-based economy to settle debts via barter. Thus, traditional practices that supported independence shaped the ways that the people of Wilton engaged with the market economy.

On the Move

People from Wilton did not lose their connections to networks of reciprocity even when they entered the world of industrial work. An example of this can be found in the relationship the Brainards maintained with Nancy Gailor, a woman from Wilton who was likely Mary Brainard's first cousin.[31] Nancy Gailor was one of seven children; she moved

26. For references to sewing with store-bought materials, see Brainard, Diary (typescript), August 8, October 8, October 20, and December 27, 1910.
27. Neth, *Preserving the Family Farm*, 30; Osterud, *Bonds of Community*, 212–15
28. Neth, *Preserving the Family Farm*, 242–43.
29. For example, see Brainard, Diary (typescript), April 8, June 5, June 13, June 26, and July 6, 1910.
30. Brainard, Diary (typescript), July 25, 1910.
31. It is difficult to prove that Mary Brainard and Nancy Gailor were cousins because of the lack of records proving that their fathers were brothers. However, there is evidence that suggests this was the case. A census record from 1855 shows Nancy Gailor living with her father, Jacob Gailor, in a

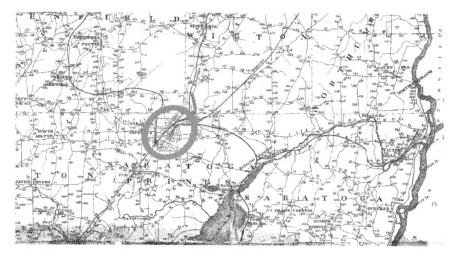

Figure 2. This map shows the location of the James M. Gailor farm, where Mary Brainard grew up, and the Brainard farm in 1890. The Brainard household is indicated by the X to the south. The Gailor farm is indicated by the X to the north. Saratoga Springs is circled. *Farmer's Pocket Directory and Map of Saratoga County, N.Y.* (Valatie: Lant and Silvernail, 1890). COURTESY OF THE SARATOGA COUNTY HISTORICAL SOCIETY ARCHIVES AT BROOKSIDE MUSEUM AND FIELD HORNE.

to Saratoga Springs to work in a cotton mill by the time she was nineteen.[32] The Brainards' properties in Saratoga Springs were a source of support to Nancy's household. Most of the work on these properties was done by John Winney and John Brainard, but Nancy Gailor's husband, Eph Butler, a "metal warper," was given the work of fixing the sewers on both

---

household that also included Jacob's father, John Gailor. See 1855 U.S. Census, Saratoga County, New York, population schedule, Wilton Township, dwelling 442, family 534; Ancestry.com, s.v. "Nancy Gailor." In 1850, John Gailor lived with one Daniel Gailor and, although the 1850 census did not state that John was Daniel's father, it seems probable that Daniel and Jacob were brothers who took turns housing their aged father. See 1850 U.S. Census, Saratoga County, New York, population schedule, Wilton Township, dwelling 222, family 236; Ancestry.com, s.v. "John Gailor." This interpretation is supported by a member-created family tree on Ancestry.com, entitled "H. Jewell Family Tree," which holds Jacob, Daniel, and James M. Gailor to be the sons of John Gailor. See markgwen1, "H Jewell Family Tree," profile for John Gailor (1783–1870), unsourced "Public Member Tree" entry, Ancestry.com, accessed June 15, 2021. Given that the records this author has located support the view that Daniel and Jacob were brothers, and given that Mary and Nancy retained close ties, it seems likely that the H Jewell tree is correct, and Mary and Nancy were first cousins.
32. 1855 New York State Census, Saratoga County, population schedule, Wilton Township, dwelling 442, family 534; Ancestry.com, s.v. "Nancy Gailor." 1870 U.S. Census, Saratoga County, New York, population schedule, City of Saratoga Springs, dwelling 479, family 501; Ancestry.com, s.v. "Nancy Gailor." It has not, thus far, been possible for this author, who is not a trained genealogist, to establish the precise kin relationship between Nancy Gailor and Mary Brainard née Gailor. It is nigh indisputable that they were related by blood, given their shared name, proximity, and documented relationship.

properties.[33] Thereby, the Brainards and Winneys involved the husband of their relation in the shared labors of the clan. Even as a worker in the nonagricultural labor market, Butler's relationship with the Brainards and Winneys was tinged with an intimacy and informality that reflected the tradition of mutual aid. John Brainard borrowed his tools for the purpose of putting a roof on the Wilton farmhouse after the sewers were fixed.[34] Also, Mary Brainard often paid visits to Nancy Gailor when she was in Saratoga.[35] Thus, not only did Nancy Gailor not leave the farm society of Wilton by taking up urban wage labor, her husband was also incorporated into it.

Nancy Gailor's farm-to-factory journey was part of a pattern. Between 1880 and 1910, the population of the town of Wilton declined from 1,118 to 908.[36] Outmigration from rural communities in the late nineteenth century initially served to increase homogeneity in the communities, and it ensured an adequate supply of farmland for those who remained.[37] But as outmigration increased during the twentieth century, it threatened to erode farm communities from within.[38] As Osterud explains this phenomenon in south-central New York: "The high wages offered by factory jobs, coupled with the rapid inflation of prices for consumer goods, drew unprecedented numbers of young men and women into the cities."[39] The *Report of the Country Life Commission*, a federal government study, released in 1909, argued that the superior amenities and opportunities of cities drove a growing level of outmigration.[40] The census suggests that the economic changes that impinged on

---

33. For John Winney and John Brainard's work, see Brainard, Diary (typescript), February 14 and 16, 1910; April 23, 1910. For Eph Butler, see 1910 U.S. Census, Saratoga County, New York, population schedule, City of Saratoga Springs, dwelling 1, family 4; Ancestry.com, s.v. "Ephraim Butler." For Eph's work on the Saratoga properties, see Brainard, Diary (typescript), April 23 and August 1, 1910.

34. Brainard, Diary (typescript), September 12, 1910.

35. Brainard, Diary (typescript), February 11, September 6, and December 9, 1910.

36. 1880 U.S. Census, Saratoga County, New York, population schedule, Wilton Township; Ancestry.com. 1910 U.S. Census, Saratoga County, New York, population schedule, Wilton Township; Ancestry.com. These numbers were obtained using keyword searches within both censuses on the genealogy website Ancestry.com. This search engine appears to be highly accurate, but some allowance must be made for possible misinterpretations of handwritten words.

37. Nancy Grey Osterud, "Farm Crisis and Rural Revitalization in South-Central New York during the Early Twentieth Century," *Agricultural History* 80, no. 2 (Spring 2010): 145l; Osterud, *Bonds of Community*, 43–46; Neth, *Preserving the Family Farm*, 10. See also Hal S. Barron, *Those Who Stayed Behind: Rural Society in Nineteenth-Century New England* (New York: Cambridge University Press, 1984).

38. Osterud, "Farm Crisis": 145–48; Neth, *Preserving the Family Farm*, 11.

39. Osterud, "Farm Crisis": 145.

40. Country Life Commission, *Report of the Country Life Commission: Special Message From the President of the United States Transmitting the Report of the Country Life Commission* (Washington, DC: Government Printing Office, 1909), 35, 42, 43, 44, 49. The report identifies the problems of American farmers as rooted in the antagonism between their traditional agrarian culture and the increasingly centralized economy: "There has been a complete and fundamental change in our whole economic system within the past century. This has resulted in profound social changes and the redirection of our point of view on life. In all the great series of farm occupations the readjustment has been the most tardy, because the whole structure of a traditional and fundamental

small farms were partly to blame for Wilton's decline. At the same time as Wilton's population declined, those listed on the census as "farmers" (not including farm laborers) went from constituting 65 percent of heads of household to only 49 percent.[41] Mary Brainard's community was experiencing a decline arguably driven by the great social and economic transformations of the late nineteenth and early twentieth centuries.

The story of the Thorn family of Wilton tells of the changes Wilton was undergoing in 1910. Jesse B. Thorn, who was a widower by 1910, was the patriarch of a large Wilton family and owned 82.5 acres of farmland valued in the 1910 tax assessment records at $700.[42] His two sons, Jesse S. Thorn and Fred Thorn, moved to Reading, Massachusetts, to work for wages at a rubber mill rather than take over their shares of the family farm.[43] In 1911, Jesse B. Thorn sold his farm property to Eugene Wiswall of Saratoga Springs.[44] By 1910, Jesse B. Thorn was already living in Reading, Massachusetts.[45] The initial catalyst for the migration of the Thorns may have been Jesse S. Thorn's marriage to Nellie Parker, a woman from Reading, in 1890.[46] However, the outmigration of the Thorn family clearly reflected the social transformations of an era when farming was becoming less viable, and urban labor more attractive, for the heirs of farm families. But, if the migration of the Thorns was representative of the contraction affecting farm communities in this period, their relationship with the Brainards, which was expressed in both social and material support, represented the strength of community ties that were leveraged in response to this dissolution.

The Brainards maintained strong relationships with the Reading Thorns and others in their kin network during the period covered by the diary. This may be partly because

---

system has been involved. It is not strange, therefore, that development is still arrested in certain respects; that marked inequalities have arisen; or that positive injustices may prevail even to a very marked and widespread extent" (21). For more on the Country Life Commission and its arguably chauvinistic way of relating to rural communities, see Osterud, "Farm Crisis," 147–48; Neth, *Preserving the Family Farm*, 102.

41. See note 36.

42. "Jesse B. Thorn," in Saratoga County Tax Rolls, Wilton, 1910, Saratoga County Historians Office, Ballston Spa, NY. For Jesse B. Thorn's complete family, see 1880 New York Census, Saratoga County, population schedule, Wilton Township, dwelling 15, family 16; Ancestry.com, s.v. "Jesse B. Thorn."

43. 1910 U.S. Census, Middlesex County, Massachusetts, population schedule, City of Reading, dwelling 51, family 61; Ancestry.com, s.v. "Jesse S. Thomas [sic]"; 1910 U.S. Census, Middlesex County, Massachusetts, population schedule, City of Reading, dwelling 29, family 31; Ancestry .com, s.v. "Fred Thorn."

44. "Jesse B. Thorn to Eugene Wiswall, October 30, 1911," in Saratoga County Deeds, bk. 278, p. 166.

45. In the diary, Mary Brainard describes John Brainard writing to a Jesse Thorn in Reading. It can be assumed that this was Jesse B. Thorn because he was the only Jesse Thorn who owned property in Wilton in 1910, and Mary Brainard writes that John Brainard paid the property tax of the Jess Thorn with whom he corresponded; see notes 46 and 47 below. For 1920, see 1920 U.S. Census, Middlesex County, Massachusetts, population schedule, City of Reading, dwelling 79, family 107; Ancestry.com, s.v. "Jesse B. Thorn."

46. "Massachusetts, U.S., Marriage Records, 1840–1915"; Ancestry.com, s.v. "Jesse S. Thorn" (married December 26, 1891).

the Thorns were tangentially connected to the Brainards' kin network, as Jesse B. Thorn's daughter, Gertrude Thorn, had married William Gailor Jr., the grandson of Jacob Gailor, who was likely Mary Brainard's uncle.[47] Thus, Gertrude Thorn was, by marriage, Mary Brainard's first cousin once removed. Such a remote family connection would carry little weight with many Americans today, but as Osterud has asserted, even distant kin ties furnished the basis for the networks of mutual aid that farmers depended on. While John Brainard corresponded with Jesse B. Thorn, Mary Brainard corresponded with Lizzie Thorn, his daughter-in-law who also lived in Reading.[48] The Brainards tried to stay abreast of events in the lives of the Reading Thorns, such as when Mary Brainard wrote, on February 11, 1909, "We heard the Thorns were all quarantined for small-pox at Reading Mass" (they recovered). Mary Brainard also periodically visited Jesse B. Thorn's daughter Emma, who lived with her husband, Owen Shaver, a wage-earning railcar repairer, in Saratoga Springs.[49] Thus, both the Brainards made efforts to maintain relationships with the dispersed members of the Thorn family. Clearly, they felt these relationships, which derived from the fabric of the Wilton community, continued to be important even across physical distances.

The Brainards also offered important material support to Jesse B. Thorn during the time he resided in Reading. Prior to Thorn selling his land in Wilton in 1911, John Brainard had paid Thorn's taxes to the town. The evidence for this consists of three entries in Mary Brainard's diary. The first, dated January 11, 1910, reads: "John Winney went to Wilton and paid all the taxes Jess Thorns and ours."[50] It seems John Winney was merely conveying funds provided by the Brainards, because subsequent entries suggest that paying Jess Thorn's taxes fell under John Brainard's purview. On February 1, Mary Brainard wrote, "John [Brainard] sent a letter to Jess Thorn with his tax receipt," and on December 30, 1910, she wrote, John "paid Jess Thorn's school tax to Smith the collector of that district."[51] Another entry suggests that there was an element of reciprocity involved in John Brainard's payment of Jess's taxes, in that the Brainards derived a material benefit from the relationship. On January 10, they collected payment of $25 from Will Perry in exchange for the

---

47. "New York State, Marriage Index, 1861-1967"; Ancestry.com s.v. "William Gailor Jr." (married December 31, 1907).
48. 1910 U.S. Census, Middlesex County, Massachusetts, population schedule, City of Reading, dwelling 51, family 61; Ancestry.com, s.v. "Jesse S. Thomas [sic]." For references to correspondence, see Brainard, Diary (typescript) December 29, 1909; February 8 and 14, 1910; March 10 and 26, 1910; October 22 and December 21, 1910.
49. For visits, see Brainard, Diary (typescript), February 15, May 10 and 31, August 28, and September 14, 1910. For residence see 1910 U.S. Census, Saratoga County, New York, population schedule, City of Saratoga Springs, dwelling 137, family 103; Ancestry.com, s.v. "Emma B. Shaver. For Emma Shaver, nee Thorn's marriage to Owen Shaver, see "New York State Marriage Index 1881–1967," Ancestry.com, s.v. "Emma B. Thorn." For Emma as Jesse Thorn's daughter, see 1892 New York State Census, Saratoga County, population schedule, Wilton Township, dwelling n.a., family n.a.; Ancestry.com, s.v. "Emma B Thorn.
50. Brainard, Diary (typescript), January 10, 1910.
51. Brainard, Diary (typescript), February 1, and December 30, 1910.

Figure 3.: An undated photo of the farmhouse owned by Dallas Varney, cousin of Vincent Varney. This image gives a sense of what a homestead in early-twentieth-century Wilton looked like. *Dallas Varney House*, n.d., by unknown photographer. COURTESY OF THE WILTON HERITAGE SOCIETY AND KAREN JAMES, WILTON TOWN HISTORIAN.

right to mow the hay on Jess Thorn's land.[52] This could mean that John Brainard had obtained haying rights to the Thorn land in exchange for paying Jess's taxes. Jess's continued payment of taxes through the Brainards indicates his desire to maintain a foothold in his home community before he sold the land. To assist him, Jess solicited the aid of a fellow community member, John Brainard, engaging the traditional reciprocity at the heart of Wilton farm society from a distance.

One more entry gives moving and symbolically charged testament to Jess's deep attachment to Wilton. On October 26, 1910, Mary Brainard wrote, "John ordered 8 cases of Spring water to Jess Thorn this morning."[53] The water of the Wilton mineral Springs was highly praised, advertised as "The King of Table Waters."[54] It is likely that Jess Thorn, living out his old age in a strange factory town, wished for a taste of home and sought to draw strength and renewal from a familiar source.

---

52. Brainard, Diary (typescript), July 2, 1910.
53. Brainard, Diary (typescript), October 26, 1910.
54. For a vintage photograph of the springs in 1914, see Jeannine Woutersz, *Wilton* (Mount Pleasant, SC: Arcadia, 2003), 68. For more on the Springs, see Claudia Shrock, "Town of Wilton," in *Saratoga County Heritage*, ed. Violet B. Dunn (Saratoga County, NY: n.p., 1974), 522. It is common folk knowledge that the springs of Saratoga are supposed to have healing properties. It may be that the same view was taken of the Wilton springs.

Conclusions

Approaching the end of the extant diary, on New Year's Eve, Mary Brainard wrote the eerie, poetic phrase, "Good by old 1910 tomorrow…you will have gone never to return to us again in this world."[55] Looking back on this document today, the line reads as elegiac, an evocation of a past world in decline and change. While its contents are mundane, Mary Brainard's diary, considered in combination with tax rolls and deed and census records, presents a powerful story of people who sought to encounter this changing world on their own terms. While they engaged with the market by making purchases and producing commodities, they used methods such as home production, reliance on kin, and work-sharing to maintain their independence. Farm-to-factory migration certainly would have challenged this way of life, but migration did not altogether sever the bonds of community. As much as migration took individuals away from the community, it also extended the community outward, as migrants maintained connections back home and continued to engage in reciprocal relationships with former neighbors. Such practices constituted a subtle resistance to the industrial/commercial order, a resistance that deserves to be examined further by historians of capitalism and anticapitalism.

55. Brainard, Diary (typescript), January 31, 1910.

War Comes to Westchester
The Killing of William Lounsbury

Dillon Streifeneder

On the morning of August 29, 1776, Pvt. Samuel Miller awoke to marching orders. An informant had come in during the night, and Miller learned that a group of Tories were enlisting men for the "royal cause" near the village of Mamaroneck. By the summer of 1776, Miller was used to such reports, but this one had added gravity. Eight days prior, nearly twenty-thousand soldiers of William Howe's invasion force had come ashore in neighboring King's County. While Miller might not have known it when he awoke on that morning, Howe's army had defeated George Washington's forces on Long Island, and the American Army was in retreat. The war had come to New York.[1]

After having volunteered in the winter of 1775 in Capt. Micah Townsend's company of "rangers," Miller had, since the end of June 1776, been working closely with the Westchester County Committee of Safety at White Plains, "taking up and disbanding the Tories and disaffected who were Engaged in collecting together and concerting measures to destroy the said Committee and opposing the cause of Revolution."[2] While similar to previous intelligence gained from informants, the Committee responded to this report with particular urgency. With the British advancing on Long Island and having already called out the militia in response to British warships menacing the shoreline, the possibility of internal enemies acting in concert with an external invasion force threatened the entire revolutionary movement.[3] The Committee was determined to suppress the threat immediately and called on its quick reaction force—Townsend's company of rangers—to apprehend the Loyalists. Before daylight, Townsend, together with Miller and about twenty others, headed southeast from

---

1. Samuel Miller, pension, June 8, 1832, "Revolutionary War Pension and Bounty–Land Warrant Application Files," microfilm publication M804 (Washington, DC: National Archives and Records Service, 1980), Roll 2450. Hereafter RWP M804.
2. Samuel Miller, pension, June 8, 1832, RWP M804, Roll 2450.
3. *Calendar of Historical Manuscripts, relating to the War of the Revolution, in the Office of the Secretary of State, Albany, N.Y.*, 2 vols. (Albany: Weed, Parsons, 1868), 1:464.

White Plains, following the informant toward an area of dense woods and rocks known as the Great Lots, just north of Mamaroneck.[4]

Finding the Loyalist hiding place, Capt. Townsend's men encircled the encampment. Aroused, Loyalist leader William Lounsbury fired his musket at the approaching militia.[5] In the smoke and confusion that ensued, Lounsbury escaped and fled to a nearby cave; he then collapsed, wounded. Refusing to surrender to the pursuing militia, he tried to fend them off, wielding his musket as a club. In this turmoil, a handful of Patriots closed in and finished him off with a bayonet.[6]

As a local resident recalled nearly seventy years later, "Lounsberry was the first person killed in Westchester county" during the American Revolution.[7] He was also, in a sense, the last casualty of the battle of Long Island. His death marked the coming of war to Westchester; it also marked a key moment of transition for the engine of the Revolution, the local committee system.[8]

While scholars have noted the importance of the Revolutionary committees, there are few studies that closely examine the evolution of committee activity at the local level outside of New England.[9] This is problematic for two reasons. First, it has led to two starkly

---

4. Samuel Miller, pension, June 8, 1832, RWP M804, Roll 2450.

5. Caleb Tompkins, October 11, 1851, MacDonald Papers, 1083-84, Westchester County Historical Society, Elmsford, NY. The MacDonald Papers are a collection of 407 oral interviews with 241 different persons from Westchester County conducted between 1844 and 1851 by John M. Mac-Donald, a local antiquarian. The interviews consist of recollections of Westchester County during the American Revolution and late colonial period, totaling 1,100 pages of hand-written notes. This collection does have its limitations and they should be used with caution. Those interviewed were between seventy and ninety-six years old. More than sixty years elapsed since the end of the Revolution before MacDonald began his interviews. Those interviewed were quite old and most experienced the American Revolution as children or adolescents, or were recounting stories passed down by relatives and neighbors. Additionally, MacDonald had no formal training for conducting oral interviews. Moreover, he left behind no indication of the types of questions he asked. Regardless of these limitations, a critical approach to these documents provides an invaluable source to better understand the everyday experience of the Revolution for common New Yorkers.

6. Stephen Hall, November 5, 1846, 396-97; Nelson Schofield, November 11, 1846, 388-89; Caleb Tompkins, October 11, 1851, 1083-84, MacDonald Papers; Journal of the Provincial Congress of the State of New York, 1775-1777, 2 vols. (Albany, 1842), 1:599-600; Calendar of Historical Manuscripts, 1:465.

7. Caleb Tompkins, October 11, 1851, 1084, MacDonald Papers.

8. For a general overview of the Revolution in Westchester County see Jacob Judd's chapter "Westchester County," in The Other New York: The American Revolution Beyond New York City, 1763–1787, ed. Joseph S. Tiedemann and Eugene R. Finger (Albany, NY: State University of New York Press, 2005), 107–26.

9. Bernard Mason, The Road to Independence: The Revolutionary Movement in New York, 1773-1777 (Lexington: University Press of Kentucky, 1966); Richard Ketchum, Divided Loyalties: How the American Revolution Came to New York (New York: Macmillan, 2002); Michael Kammen, "The American Revolution as a Crise de Conscience: The Case of New York," in Society, Freedom, and Conscience: The American Revolution in Virginia, Massachusetts, and New York, ed. Richard M. Jellison (New York: Norton, 1976); Howard Pashman, Building a Revolutionary State: The Legal Transformation of New York, 1776-1783 (Chicago: University of Chicago Press, 2018); Philip Ranlet, The New York Loyalists (Knoxville: University of Tennessee Press, 1986).The newest study

different portrayals of the committees. One group of historians views the committees primarily as "schools of revolution," that "seldom allowed the policing of popular ideology to get out of hand."[10] A second group of historians has asserted that committees were at their core "an apparatus of oppression and terror."[11]

The second concern is one of time and change. While not exclusively tied to the peaceable portrayal of the committees, most of these works examining the role of committees conclude their studies prior to 1776. The committees that have been studied acted as a political network, playing their role from the Stamp Act crisis until 1775, after which they lost their relevance as American Revolution transitioned into Revolutionary War. Another

---

on New York's committee system similarly focuses on the state-level Committee that emerged in mid-1776: Joshua Canale, "'When a State Abounds in Rascals': New York's Revolutionary Era Committees for Public Safety, 1775–1783," *Journal of the Early Republic* 39, no. 2 (Summer 2019): 203–38; Edward Countryman's *A People in Revolution: The American Revolution and Political Society in New York, 1760–1790* (Baltimore, MD: Johns Hopkins University Press, 1981) provides a clear overview of committee development, but is primarily focused on initial political mobilization. See also Christopher F. Minty, "'Of One Hart and One Mind': Local Institutions and Allegiance during the American Revolution," *Early American Studies* 15, no. 1 (Winter 2017): 99–132.

10. T. H. Breen, *American Insurgents, American Patriots: The Revolution of the People* (New York: Hill and Wang, 2010), 162–64, 185–86, 208, 212–15; David Ammerman, *In the Common Cause: American Response to the Coercive Acts of 1774* (Charlottesville: University Press of Virginia, 1974), 103–24; Richard D. Brown, *Revolutionary Politics in Massachusetts: The Boston Committee of Correspondence and the Towns, 1772–1774* (Cambridge, MA: Harvard University Press, 1970); Larry R. Gerlach, *Prologue to Independence: New Jersey in the Coming of the American Revolution* (New Brunswick, NJ: Rutgers University Press, 1976); Jonathan Clark, "The Problem of Allegiance in Revolutionary Poughkeepsie," in *Saints and Revolutionaries: Essays on Early American History*, ed. David D. Hall, John M. Murrin, and Thad W. Tate (New York: Norton, 1982), 285–317; Judith L. Van Buskirk, *Generous Enemies: Patriots and Loyalists in Revolutionary New York* (Philadelphia: University of Pennsylvania Press, 2002). See also Bernard Bailyn, *The Ideological Origins of the American Revolution* (Cambridge, MA: Belknap Press, 1967); Pauline Maier, *From Resistance to Revolution: Colonial Radicals and the Development of American Opposition to Britain, 1765–1776* (New York: A. A. Knopf, 1972); Gordon S. Wood, *The Radicalism of the American Revolution* (New York: Vintage Books, 1991).

11. Holger Hoock, *Scars of Independence: America's Violent Birth* (New York: Crown, 2017), 19–20, 29–31, 50–51; Harry Ward, *Between the Lines: Banditti of the American Revolution* (Santa Barbara: Praeger Books, 2002), 17–32; Mike Rapport, *The Unruly City: Paris, London and New York in the Age of Revolution* (New York: Basic Books, 2017), 73–97; Jeffery H. Richards, "Revolution, Domestic Life, and the End of 'Common Mercy' in Crévecoeur's 'Landscapes,'" *William and Mary Quarterly* 55, no. 2 (April 1998), 281–96; T. Cole Jones, *Captives of Liberty: Prisoners of War and the Politics of Vengeance in the American Revolution* (Philadelphia: University of Pennsylvania Press, 2019); Sharon Block, "Rape in the American Revolution: Process, Reaction, and Public Re-Creation," in *Sexual Violence in Conflict Zones: From the Ancient World to the Era of Human Rights*, ed. Elizabeth Heineman (Philadelphia: University of Pennsylvania Press, 2011), 25–38; Richard Maxwell Brown, "Violence and the American Revolution," in *Essays on the American Revolution*, ed. Stephen G. Kurtz and James H. Huston (Chapel Hill: University of North Carolina Press, 1973), 81–120; For a more nuanced interpretation of revolutionary violence, see Glenn A. Moots and Phillip Hamilton, *Justifying Revolution: Law, Virtue, and Violence in the American War of Independence* (Norman: University of Oklahoma Press, 2018). On violence in Westchester County, see Sung Bok Kim, "The Limits of Politicization in the American Revolution: The Experience of Westchester County, New York," *Journal of American History* 80, no. 3 (December 1993): 868–89.

body of work on committees has a similar problem. This second group of studies either begins their look at committees amid full-scale war after the British military invasion in 1776
or does not acknowledge that any change occurred in how people and institutions acted
when war came to the neighborhood. Both interpretations are tied to a larger problem of
historians not engaging with the social history of war-making.[12]

In New York, the committees neither disappeared by 1776 nor were they stagnant.
War directly impacted the committees and forced them to change and adapt, most notably in their tactics for dealing with Loyalists. First emerging as political networks in 1774
and 1775, by 1776 the committees in New York transformed into imperfect agencies for
war-making and acted as the precursor for the nascent revolutionary state. Lost in national narratives and origin stories, this change occurred in different localities at various
times and was intimately tied to the larger context of the evolving revolutionary movement
and war.

This article examines that evolution of the role committees fulfilled by presenting a
story about a particular place: Westchester County, New York. As with other histories of a
place and its particularities, this study uses local stories to help illuminate the texture and
complexities that form the fabric of the larger narrative of the American Revolution.[13] The
contrast with neighboring New England and other localities is strong. Yet Westchester's case
is not one of absolute differences; instead, it demonstrates the diversity of experience across
the whole of the American colonies that, together, formed a common process of revolution.

In this article I provide a narrative of committee action that moves between three
interconnected stories centered on local committees, Britain's military and ministers, and
the Loyalist William Lounsbury. In doing so, I trace how Westchester's committees moved
day to day—often too slowly according to radical New England Whigs—not knowing what
lay ahead. As the threat of war approached, Westchester's committees adopted coercive
tactics in direct response to military action in and around New York Harbor. I also focus
on William Lounsbury's actions, most notably his sabotage of hundreds of Patriot cannon,
to show how Westchester's committees responded to Loyalist threats. Culminating with
Lounsbury's death, I argue that the Westchester committees completed their transition
from political networking to the use of coercion and violence but that they did so only after
the war arrived. They grew into imperfect war-making organizations waging a war against
Great Britain's military and their Loyalist neighbors.

---

12. John Shy, "The American Revolution: The Military Conflict Considered as a Revolutionary
War," in Kurtz and Huston, *Essays on the American Revolution*, 121–56; Don Higginbotham, *War
and Society in Revolutionary America: The Wider Dimensions of Conflict* (Columbia: University of
South Carolina Press, 1988).
13. For two recent discussions on the connection between local places and larger questions, see
John-Paul A. Ghobrial, "Seeing the World like a Microhistorian," *Past and Present* 242 (November
2019): 1–22; Nicole Etcheson, "Local History, National Contexts: Exploring Microhistory in Hen-
derson Kentucky," *Register of the Kentucky Historical Society* 113, no. 4 (Autumn 2015): 591–600.

Lounsbury was killed at the direction of the Westchester Committee, but two years earlier no such institution had existed. Cautious to act, one observer described Westchester's inhabitants' response to the revolutionary movement as "very indolent."[14] By mid-summer in 1774, however, a handful of Whig-minded local officials began to organize and convince their neighbors to join the nascent movement. Responding to the New York City Committee's second circular letter urging the counties to elect delegates to send to Philadelphia, at least three of Westchester's towns held meetings that August.[15] On August 22, 1774, officials organized a countywide meeting. While the local meetings proposed more radical resolves, including calls to establish committees in each town and to collect donations "for the poor and distressed people of Boston," the county meeting took a decidedly conservative approach.[16] Chaired by Frederick Philipse—a conservative Assemblyman, wealthy manor lord, and future Loyalist—the county meeting at White Plains issued the following resolves: first, they reasserted their allegiance to the King of Great Britain; second, they resolved that Parliament's imposition of taxes without their consent did require redress; and third, to obtain redress, they tentatively supported a meeting of "a general Congress" but refrained from appointing their own delegates, deferring to those already elected from New York City.[17]

By the time the Continental Congress met in early September 1774, however, a vocal opposition had emerged to the town and county resolves, led by Philipse, fellow Assemblyman Isaac Wilkins, and Anglican minister Samuel Seabury. This opposition focused on the Continental Congress's actions, most notably rebuked in Seabury's pamphlets under the pseudonym "a Farmer." Similar pamphlets and newspaper articles appeared throughout the fall and winter of 1774 and into 1775, all aimed at rejecting local attempts to organize committees and congresses while enforcing the General Association adopted by the Continental Congress.[18] In Cortlandt's Manor, a group of inhabitants went as far as signing a counterassociation, resolving to "pay no regard to any resolves, or restrictions, but such are enjoined us by our CONSTITUTIONAL DELEGATES."[19]

14. *New-York Gazette and Weekly Mercury*, June 19, 1775.

15. Peter Force, ed., *American Archives: Consisting of Authentic Records, State Papers, Debates, and Letters and other Notices of Public Affairs*, 4th ser., 6 vols.; 5th ser., 3 vols (Washington, DC, 1837–1853), 4th ser., 1:325.

16. *New-York Gazette and Weekly Mercury*, August 15, 1774; August 29, 1774.

17. Force, *American Archives*, 4th ser., 1:325, 1188–89; Worthington C. Ford et al., eds., *Journals of the Continental Congress, 1774–1789* (Washington, DC, 1904–37), 1:19. While not directly represented by a delegate, the New York City delegates included John Jay who was from Westchester but by 1774 lived in New York City.

18. Isaac Wilkins, *Short Advice to the Counties of New-York* (New York: Rivington, 1774); *New-York Gazette and Weekly Mercury*, October 13, 1774; Rivington's *New York Gazetteer; or, the Connecticut, New-Jersey, Hudson's-River, and Quebec Weekly Advertiser*, January 12, 1775.

19. Rivington's *New York Gazetteer*, February 16, 1775.

Throughout 1774 and into 1775, pro-Crown advocates rallied around the argument that the dispute between the colonies and Britain required "a speedy reconciliation," but that reconciliation was to be pursued exclusively by the General Assembly.[20] As the Cortlandt Manor counterassociation asserted, "Everything to the contrary, we deem ILLEGAL."[21] This position found strong support across the county, including from some of its leading officeholders. Isaac Wilkins made similar statements in a pamphlet distributed in 1774, and on the Assembly floor in 1775, he forcefully called on fellow members "to put a stop to the illegal and disorderly proceedings and resolutions of Committees, Associations, and Congresses."[22]

Despite their strong words, however, the county's "friends of Government" failed to form a coherent countermovement. With Governor William Tryon away in England from April 1774 until late June 1775, pro-Crown advocates lacked clear leadership and coordination. Loyalist control in Westchester was at its height in January and February of 1775, but by early May, it had dissolved. Shutting down discourse at legal government functions, such as at the sitting of the county supervisors and at town meetings worked initially, but such tactics became ineffective when Whig leaders shifted the discourse on Britain's actions into private homes, taverns, and places of worship. By refusing to organize similar "illegal" associations, the Loyalists in Westchester, therefore, allowed Whig-minded ideology to dominate mobilization efforts and local responses to Parliament.

When the Assembly failed to appoint delegates to attend the Second Continental Congress in May, for instance, pro-Crown supporters believed the matter settled. As the New York City Committee proceeded to elect deputies anyway and encouraged the other counties to do the same, the Loyalists failed to respond. Conversely, Whig leaders in Westchester responded by calling for "a general meeting of the Freeholders" on April 11, 1775, at White Plains to vote on whether the county should follow the City's lead.[23]

Aware of the meeting, the county's leading Loyalists rallied supporters to attend and vote "to oppose a measure so replete with ruin and misery."[24] Led by Philipse, Wilkins, and Seabury, nearly three hundred "friends of Government" gathered at White Plains, including William Lounsbury.[25] But when it came time to vote, the Loyalist leadership "declared that they would not join in the business of the Day." Proclaiming the proceedings "illegal and unconstitutional," they refused to vote and marched to a nearby tavern instead. Without any opposition, the remaining crowd "unanimously" passed the motion to elect

---

20. *New-York Gazette and Weekly Mercury*, April 10, 1775.

21. *Rivington's New York Gazetteer*, February 16, 1775.

22. Wilkins, *Short Advice to the Counties of New-York*; Force, *American Archives*, 4th ser., 1:1293–97.

23. *New-York Gazette and Weekly Mercury*, April 17, 1775.

24. *Rivington's New York Gazetteer*, April 6, 1775.

25. *Rivington's New York Gazetteer*, April 20, 1775.

delegates.[26] By refusing to participate, the Loyalists abdicated all influence and ability to stop or alter the direction of the revolutionary movement. Furthermore, their decision to act only in "legal" organizations stymied the creation of a coherent countermovement and left mobilization efforts in the hands of the pro-Whig committees.[27]

This process accelerated following the fighting at Lexington and Concord, as any remaining Patriot hesitancy and foot-dragging disappeared.[28] From April 20 to 23, 1775, eight deputies from Westchester met in New York City with their counterparts from the other counties and resolved to encourage every county to elect representatives to form a "Provincial Congress" to convene in the City on May 22.[29] Responding to this call, Westchester's Patriot leadership held a meeting on May 8 and appointed a "Committee of 90 persons," along with eleven delegates "to represent the said county in Provincial Convention."[30] Delegates were chosen, and the Committee proceeded with a public signing of the General Association "and appointed Sub-Committees to superintend the signing of the same throughout the county."[31]

When their elected representatives met in New York City for the first time on May 22, 1775, the Westchester committees focused on gaining popular support and organizing a coherent platform of resistance toward British imperial policies. Having engaged in a series of newspaper and pamphlet wars with Loyalists throughout 1774 and early 1775, by June, the Westchester committees expanded their efforts beyond print. Organizing public meetings and going door-to-door, the committee members worked to convince their neighbors to sign the General Association, denounce the actions of Parliament, and demand reconciliation based on American terms.[32]

---

26. *New-York Gazette and Weekly Mercury*, April 17, 1775.

27. Leopold Launitz-Schurer Jr., *Loyal Whigs and Revolutionaries: The Making of the Revolution in New York, 1765–1776* (New York: New York University Press, 1980), 141-44.

28. For the immediate reaction to the arrival of news of the fighting at Concord, see entries of April 29 and May 1, 1775, in William Smith, *Historical Memoirs of William Smith from 16 March 1763 to 9 July 1776*, ed. William Sabine (New York: New York Public Library, 1956), 222-23;, Cadwallader Colden, "Colden to Governor Carleton, May 3, 1775," in *The Colden Letter Books*, vol. 2: 1765–1775 (New York: New-York Historical Society, 1876–-1877), 2: 403–4. Launitz-Schurer Jr., *Loyal Whigs and Revolutionaries*, 154–58.

29. *New-York Gazette and Weekly Mercury*, April 17, 1775; *New-York Journal, or General Advertiser*, April 27, 1775; *Calendar of Historical Manuscripts*, 1:4.

30. *Rivington's New York Gazetteer*, May 11, 1775. The only known surviving minute books of committee activity in New York are for Albany and Tryon County, with town or precinct committee minutes for King's District in Albany County, and the Northeast Precinct in Dutchess County. While no similar minutes for the Westchester Committee have been found, it is possible to examine Westchester's committee activity by consolidating disparate accounts from contemporary newspapers, the Journals of the Provincial Congress, the American Archives collections compiled by Peter Force, and the revolutionary manuscript transcriptions published by New York State known as the *Calendar of Historical Manuscripts*.

31. *Rivington's New York Gazetteer*, May 11, 1775; *Calendar of Historical Manuscripts*, 1:20.

32. *Journal of the Provincial Congress*, 1:145. For an examination of the effectiveness of the committee-led canvassing effort for signatures to the General Association, see Clark, "The Problem of Allegiance in Revolutionary Poughkeepsie," 290–92.

In an effort to bolster their legitimacy, the committees consciously courted colonial magistrates, bringing a considerable number of them into their ranks.[33] With many New Yorkers hesitant to completely reject the authority of the King, colonial magistrates formed an important bridge between royal authority and committee governance. In some cases, the justices simply adopted the mantle of "committeeman" while continuing to perform duties under commissions granted by the King, without any apparent contradiction.

Others took more convincing. Such was the case with Gilbert Merrit, a justice of the peace from Rye who had signed a resolution in 1774 reaffirming his loyalty to the King.[34] Merrit was an influential member in a neighborhood with many staunch Loyalists (including William Lounsbury), so gaining the support of someone like him was an important part of how the committees added adherents to the revolutionary cause. Over time, Merrit proved amenable to the steady flow of revolutionary rhetoric provided by the committees. By 1775, Merrit sided with the Patriot movement, continuing in his role as "one of his Majestys Justices of the peace," yet acting on behalf of the committees.[35]

Not all the colonial magistrates, however, were redeemable in the eyes of the committee, as was the case with William Sutton of Mamaroneck. In 1775, Sutton converted his residence on Budd's Neck from a place for holding proceedings as a justice of the peace to a node for organizing Loyalist support.[36] Sutton's obnoxious commentary and conspicuous support of the Crown—like that of numerous other justices of the peace—rendered him incapable of making the transition from King's magistrate to people's justice. Initially ostracized and excluded, the committees eventually used force to remove such incorrigible holdovers of the Crown's authority.[37]

---

33. Of the colonial Justices of the Peace, 48 percent became Patriots while 42 percent remained loyal. For more on the fluidity of opinion and its coalescence into Patriot and Loyalist poles across the colonies, see Mary Beth Norton, *1774: The Long Year of Revolution* (New York: Vintage Books, 2020), 219–36, 268–69, 322–25. In Westchester, that fluidity and coalescence of opinion Norton ties to 1774 persisted into 1776.

34. *Rivington's New York Gazetteer*, October 13, 1774.

35. "Gilbert Merrit Proceedings," 1773–1779, Slater Family Papers Collection, Rye Historical Society, The Knapp House Archives, Rye, NY.

36. *Journal of the Provincial Congress*, 1:192-93, 221; 2:302-03.

37. Much of the process of revolution involved the inclusion and exclusion of particular groups in an effort to create a cohesive movement. The Revolution caught up with everyone in its social disruption, and these processes were evident in Westchester, just as other works have demonstrated on a larger level. See Robert G. Parkinson, *The Common Cause: Creating Race and Nation in the American Revolution* (Chapel Hill: University of North Carolina Press, 2016); Woody Holton, *Forced Founders: Indians, Debtors, Slaves & the Making of the American Revolution in Virginia* (Chapel Hill: University of North Carolina Press, 1999); Gregory T. Knouff, *The Soldiers' Revolution: Pennsylvanians in Arms and the Forging of Early American Identity* (University Park: Pennsylvania State University Press, 2004). As for William Sutton, the Westchester Committee arrested him and eventually removed him from his community by sending him to Philadelphia to be imprisoned in July of 1776. Upon reaching Philadelphia, Sutton was paroled instead of imprisoned. He broke his parole when he returned to New York City in 1777 and joined the Loyalist forces waging war in Westchester. *Calendar of Historical Manuscripts*, 1:427-28, 433; *Journal of the Provincial Congress*, 1:547.

Yet forcible removal still lay in the future. Closely following the guidance of the Provincial Congress, the Westchester Committee refrained from the use of coercion throughout the spring. As per the resolves of the Provincial Congress outlined on May 29, 1775, "no Coercive steps ought to be used to induce any person to sign the Association."[38] The Westchester Committee would have been hard pressed to try coercing Loyalist behavior anyway, as they lacked the means of coercion.[39] This changed, however, following the fighting at Bunker Hill. In response, the Provincial Congress moved swiftly to gain control of the militia. By June 29, the Provincial Congress provided the Westchester Committee with the first of its new warrants for officers.[40] Significant reorganization followed, and during July and August of 1775, the Westchester committeemen oversaw the election of new militia officers, removed officers who were not "sincere friends of the Country," established new geographic jurisdictions, and conducted inspections of martial proficiency, all of which helped transform the militia into the "strong right arm of the local committee."[41]

The Westchester Committee, though, was slow to use its new police power. It was not until mid-August that the Committee took its first step in exercising its regulatory authority. Holding a meeting at White Plains, the Committee divided the county into "Districts or Beats, agreeable to the directions of the Provincial Congress." Next, they adopted two resolutions enforcing several aspects of the Articles of Association. The first outlawed the county's inhabitants from purchasing tea. The second ordered them "immediately to desist from Horse-racing and all kinds of gaming" to ensure "morality and good order."[42] The Committee warned that persons failing to adhere to these resolves would "be dealt with accordingly"; but, by early September they had yet to use coercive measures to enforce their resolves.

This changed, however, following military action in New York Harbor. Prior to the summer of 1775, British military presence in New York consisted of approximately one-hundred soldiers of the 18th Regiment of Foot, supported by a small frigate in the Harbor.[43]

---

38. *Journal of the Provincial Congress*, 1:18.
39. It is unlikely the committees could have coerced behavior prior to late summer or early autumn 1775. Clark, "The Problem of Allegiance in Revolutionary Poughkeepsie," 288–291.
40. *Calendar of Historical Manuscripts*, 1:105.
41. *Calendar of Historical Manuscripts*, , 1:105, 113, 121–23, 132–37, 140–41, 157, 160; *Journal of the Provincial Congress*, 1:104; 2:62; Force, *American Archives*, 4th ser., 2:1604–5; John Shy, *A People Numerous and Armed: Reflections on the Military Struggle for American Independence* (Ann Arbor: The University of Michigan Press, 1990), 175–76.
42. Force, *American Archives*, 4th ser., 3:150; These actions are from Article 3 and Article 8 of the Articles of Association adopted by the Continental Congress in October of 1774. *Journals of the Continental Congress*, 1774–1789 (Washington: Government Printing Office, 1904), 1:75–80.
43. While the British maintained a notable garrison in New York following the Seven Years' War, between 1774 and 1775, the garrison was drained of manpower. Following Thomas Gage's appointment as Governor of Massachusetts in 1774, he pulled all available soldiers to Boston, leaving around 100 infirm and disabled soldiers split between Fort George and the Upper Barracks in New York City. On movement and strength of troops in America, see appendices 3, 4, and 5 in Derek Beck, *Igniting the American Revolution* (Naperville, IL: Sourcebooks, 2015), 278–312. On Gage's

On May 26, 1775, though, the warship *Asia* arrived from Boston.[44] With a robust battery and detachment of Royal Marines aboard, the *Asia* stood as a formidable power to "awe the licentious & encourage the friends of Government."[45]

While it failed to awe the Patriots, the *Asia*, following the return of Governor William Tryon, acted as a beacon for Loyalists. Having uncontested control of the waters around New York, Tryon turned the *Asia* into a mobile printing press from which to disseminate pro-Crown pamphlets and a base from which to coordinate and support Loyalist resistance.[46] By late summer, the Provincial Congress had yet to counter or restrict access to the *Asia*, its landing parties, or Governor Tryon. That changed, however, in late August.

When the 18th Regiment of Foot evacuated New York City on June 6, they left the cannon in the battery below Fort George behind.[47] By August 1775, the Provincial Congress was determined to "procure" the cannon for fortifications being erected in the Highlands.[48] While the execution of this mission is not entirely clear, shortly after midnight on August 24, a detachment of militia accompanied by a young Alexander Hamilton and some of his classmates from Kings College seized the guns.[49] Apprised of this move by Loyalist informants, Capt. George Vandeput responded with force. After a landing boat came under fire from the battery, Vandeput drew up the *Asia* and "began a heavy and smart Fire" until the Patriots dispersed.[50]

The repercussions of this event are often overlooked, as both sides acted with extreme calm in the immediate aftermath. Vandeput apologized for firing on the city, citing his responsibility to protect all "Stores belonging to the King."[51] The Provincial Congress accepted his apology and responded with two resolutions agreeing to continue supplying the warship with provisions and "that no more cannon ... be removed."[52] The event proved

appointment and actions, see John Shy, "Thomas Gage: Weak Link of Empire," in *George Washington's Opponents: British Generals and Admirals in the American Revolution*, ed. George Athan Billias (New York: William Morrow and Company, 1969), 21–23.

44. "Letter from George Vandeput," in *The Letters and Papers of Cadwallader Colden, 1711–1775*, 9 vols. (New York: The New-York Historical Society, 1918–37), 7:298.

45. "Lieutenant-Governor Colden to Early of Dartmouth," in Edmund B. O'Callaghan and Fernold Berthold, eds., *Documents Relative to the Colonial History of the State of New York*, 15 vols. (Albany: Weed and Parsons, 1853–1887), 8:544.

46. *Calendar of Historical Manuscripts*, 1:200, 328–29, 340, 354, 358, 366; Governor Tryon To Lord George Germain," Documents Relative to the Colonial History of the State of New York, 8: 673; Records of the British Colonial Office, Class 5, 1,450 vols., The National Archives, United Kingdom. (Note that this work is often cited as "CO class/volume" followed by page number, which is how I will cite it hereafter.) CO 5/1107, 117–19; Force, American Archives, 4th ser., 4:590–91. Journal of the Provincial Congress, 1:105.

47. "Letter from Isaac Hamilton," Letters and Papers of Cadwallader Colden, 7:300.

48. *Journal of the Provincial Congress*, 1:113-114.

49. Ron Chernow, *Alexander Hamilton* (New York: Penguin, 2005), 67; Alan C. Aimone and Eric I. Manders, "A Note on New York City's Independent Companies, 1775–1776," *New York History* 63, no. 1 (January 1982), 64–65.

50. *New-York Gazette and Weekly Mercury*, August 28, 1775.

51. *New-York Gazette and Weekly Mercury*, August 28, 1775.

52. *Journal of the Provincial Congress*, 1:122, 129; 2:28.

incredibly significant, though, for local committee activity. The *Asia's* attack sparked a wave of Loyalist action that had been absent since the previous winter. In the ensuing days and weeks, hundreds of Loyalists mobilized support, making their way to the warship for weapons and to find leadership to counter the committees.

In response, on September 1, 1775, the Provincial Congress passed a series of sweeping resolves that led to the first significant efforts to coerce and suppress the Loyalists. Citing attempts "to promote discord," and "aid the ministerial army and navy," the Provincial Congress authorized the committees to imprison for up to three months any persons found "furnishing the ministerial army or navy...with provisions," or "holding a correspondence...for the purpose of giving information to the said army or navy." They also empowered the committees to "apprehend every inhabitant or resident of the colony, who now is or shall hereafter be discovered to be enlisted in arms against the liberties of America." Lastly, they authorized committee members to seize "all arms fit for use by troops found in the hands or custody of any person who has not signed the general association."[53]

By late September, as the reverberations of the *Asia's* action in the Harbor made their way to Westchester, the Westchester Committee took its first coercive action against the county's Loyalists. On September 28, 1775, Eunice Purdy, a spinster from Rye searched out Gilbert Drake, a committee member and lieutenant colonel in the militia. She told him that she had overheard a conversation in which Godfrey Hains bemoaned the recent committee resolutions requiring all military-aged men to perform militia duty. Additionally, she claimed that Hains "damned the Congresses and Committees frequently," and threatened the committee would be "cut down in a fortnight" with help from "the men of war."[54] After hearing this deposition, Drake took a detachment of militia to Rye, arrested Hains, searched his house, seized his weapons, and sent him to jail in New York City.[55]

As the first Loyalist arrest in Westchester, this episode demonstrates two things. First, just as the committees cultivated and developed a political movement opposing British imperial policies in their first phase of activity, they now cultivated and developed a network of informants to report on the actions and statements of persons who expressed real or purported sentiment inimical to the revolutionary movement. Second, the Westchester Committee prosecuted this case with caution and restraint. After arresting Hains and not knowing what to do with him, they sent him to the Provincial Congress for punishment. The following day though, the Provincial Congress returned him, informing the Westchester Committee that "the County Committees are altogether competent for punishing and confining persons guilty of a breach of the said resolutions."[56]

---

53. *Journal of the Provincial Congress*, 1:131–32, 149–50.
54. *Journal of the Provincial Congress*, 2:84.
55. *Journal of the Provincial Congress*, 2:84–85; *Calendar of Historical Manuscripts*, 1:162. A few days after his imprisonment, Haines broke out of jail and made his way to the British warship Asia. He eventually returned to Rye, where the committee arrested him again in the winter of 1776.
56. Force, *American Archives*, 4th ser., 3:916-17.

Reprimand aside, between October and December 1775, the Westchester Committee grew into its role of revolutionary enforcer, slowly ramping up efforts to suppress Loyalist actions by seizing the weapons of "any person who has not signed the general association" and restricting the movement of persons without a certificate from the Committee.[57] The committees and their network of informants proved porous though, and in the minds of militant radicals in Connecticut, the Whigs in Westchester moved too slowly and were too lenient. After an unsuccessful foray into Westchester to seize Isaac Wilkins in April 1775, another group of Connecticut Whigs led by Isaac Sears proved more successful that November. Riding into New York City, this group destroyed James Rivington's printing press and took him captive, returned through Westchester, where they seized Samuel Seabury and two other outspoken Loyalists and then made off with them into Connecticut.[58]

Writing to John Jay in the immediate aftermath, Alexander Hamilton condemned the intrusion of New Englanders into New York, but hoped that it might stir New York's "cautious and prudent" Whigs into action. Hamilton, like other leaders in New York City worried that it might make outsiders "imagine that the New Yorkers are totally, or a majority of them, disaffected to the American cause." In response, Hamilton concluded that it was "necessary to repress and overawe" the "insolent and clamorous" Tories.[59]

Repressing and overawing the Tories, though, was easier said than done, especially in an extensive county like Westchester, where Loyalists had access to British warships. In mid-December 1775, for instance, amid deep snow drifts and bitterly cold temperatures, two men near the borough of Westchester "put up about three or four hundred barrels [of beef], which they... conveyed on board the Asia man-of-war." Just up the coast at Mamaroneck, William Sutton stockpiled and barreled "twenty head of fat cattle" with similar plans. In both cases, the Westchester Committee arrived too late to seize the goods, already aboard the Asia. The delayed response drew the ire of their counterparts in New York City, who caustically remarked that "the proceedings of the Committee of that County appear rash, dilatory, weak, and inadequate to their unhappy circumstances."[60]

Taking such critique seriously, the Westchester Committee responded by expanding their jurisdictional reach from the roads to the water, passing a resolve on January 8, 1776, empowering the subcommittees "to examine into all cargoes of provisions that go out, and

---

57. *Journal of the Provincial Congress*, 1:146–50; Force, *American Archives*, 4th ser., 3:826.
58. *Journal of the Provincial Congress*, 1:213–14; "Alexander Hamilton to John Jay, November 26, 1775," in *The Papers of Alexander Hamilton Digital Edition*, ed. Harold C. Syrett (Charlottesville: University of Virginia Press, 2011); Mason, *The Road to Independence*, 54–60. See also the Connecticut militia incursion to Cortlandt Manor in November of 1775. Kim, "The Limits of Politicization in the American Revolution," 875.
59. "Alexander Hamilton to John Jay, November 26, 1775," in Syrett, *The Papers of Alexander Hamilton*, 176–178. Hamilton's concerns proved telling when ardent Whig soldiers from Connecticut burned houses at White Plains assuming the New Yorkers supported the Crown, see Benjamin L. Carp, "The Night the Yankees Burned Broadway: The New York City Fire of 1776," *Early American Studies* 4, no. 2 (Fall 2006), 503–4.
60. Force, *American Archives*, 4th ser., 4:590-91.

take, surely from those that carry it out."[61] Two days later, the committee at Poundridge took further steps, strictly forbidding any persons "to carry...by land or water, provisions of any kind" to the British.[62] Additionally, they directed "the Minute men, and all others that are friends to their county, to do their utmost to stop all drovers of fat cattle and sheep, hogs, poultry, or any other provision" from reaching the British warships.[63]

Other activities included disarming persons who had not signed the General Association or who had signed other documents in support of the Crown. On the morning of January 17, 1776, the combined committees of Bedford, Poundridge, and Salem summoned and examined three such men who had refused to sign the Association.[64] After the examination, the committee resolved to disarm one of the men, and labeled all three "enemies to their country."[65] The committee also published their names in the newspapers and "forbid any persons having any dealings with them."[66] Two weeks later, the committee did the same to Benjamin Close, citing an informant's accusation that Close cursed a "Presbyterian minister...doing the Devil's service."[67]

The committees also took an active role in suppressing the distribution of Loyalist pamphlets and other printed material. On the afternoon of January 17, 1776, the same committee "brought two men before them, on suspicion of their being enemies to their country."[68] Both men had come from New York City after meeting with Governor Tryon, who had fled aboard the *Duchess of Gordon* in October. Upon searching their persons, the committee discovered they had in their possession three copies of "The Address of the people of Great Britain to the inhabitants of America"—a pamphlet opposed to the revolutionary movement.[69] The committee ordered two of the pamphlets "burnt before their eyes, and kept one to shew the cause of their conduct with them."[70]

Proper self-confession and public humiliation, however, could prevent isolation and being labeled a "Tory." Two days after Benjamin Close's sentencing, Joseph Golding came forward to the same committee and confessed to speaking "against the Congress and the country, and in favour of the ministerial party."[71] Golding apologized and begged forgiveness, promising to "follow the rules of the committees." He also pledged that he would work for the committees, helping "discover any plots that come to my knowledge."[72] Golding's self-inflicted public humiliation before the committee, followed by the publication of his

---

61. *New-York Journal, or General Advertiser*, February 8, 1776.
62. *New-York Journal, or General Advertiser*, January 25, 1776.
63. *New-York Journal, or General Advertiser*.
64. *New-York Journal, or General Advertiser*, February 1, 1776.
65. *New-York Journal, or General Advertiser*.
66. *New-York Journal, or General Advertiser*, February 1, 1776.
67. *New-York Journal, or General Advertiser*, March 14, 1776.
68. *New-York Journal, or General Advertiser*, January 25, 1776.
69. *New-York Journal, or General Advertiser*.
70. *New-York Journal, or General Advertiser*.
71. *New-York Journal, or General Advertiser*, March 14, 1776.
72. *New-York Journal, or General Advertiser*.

confession in the newspaper, saved him from isolation and potential removal. For Golding, witnessing the social and economic isolation imposed on Close and other neighbors proved to be a powerful tool, making him turn from critic of the committee to one of its informants.

The window for redemption by joining the Patriot cause, however, was closing. As Governor Tryon shrewdly observed in early December of 1775, the coming winter stood as a "Critical Moment, to open our Commerce and restore our valuable Constitution." Privy to daily intelligence reports aboard the *Duchess of Gordon*, Tryon aptly understood that by early 1776, the established government had shifted to the Congress and committees. By labeling supporters of the Crown "enemies of their country," the Provincial Congress and local committees supplanted Provincial and British imperial institutions, asserting committee governance in their place. By forcing the Loyalists from all public positions and isolating and silencing vocal opposition, the revolutionary movement effectively seized the mantle of the establishment. Simultaneously, committee activity helped frame the understanding of the revolution that placed Loyalists outside of the emerging establishment and revolutionary society into that of an insurgency.

Recognizing this, Tryon responded as best he could. Throughout December 1775, he probed local informants to learn where the Patriots were weakest and where support for the Crown was strongest. In early January 1776, these efforts paid off when he learned of dedicated support in Mamaroneck and Budd's Neck in Westchester County—the same place from which William Sutton had provided British warships provisions earlier in December of the previous year.[73] Meeting with Sutton, a former justice of the peace, along with other Loyalists from Mamaroneck, Tryon realized he had supporters ready and willing to strike against the Patriots. Unable to provide them with direct military aid, however, such action required caution to succeed; it relied on insurgent tactics of espionage and sabotage by "concealed agents."

William Lounsbury was one of those "concealed agents." A prosperous weaver and small-scale farmer in his fifties, Lounsbury lived with his wife and son on a forty-acre parcel on Budd's Neck, a piece of land between Mamaroneck Harbor and the Long Island Sound.[74] From the 1750s onward, Lounsbury's neighbors had regularly elected him to lesser town offices ranging from fence viewer to constable, and he had briefly served as a lieutenant in the colonial militia.[75] Having expressed antirevolutionary sentiment early on, by October of 1775 he demonstrated his willingness to take physical action in a failed attempt

73. "Friends to Government on Budds Neck, Westchester County," and "Mamaroneck Friends to Government," December 15, 1775, in Governor Tryon's possession by January 5, 1775. CO 5/1107, 115.

74. Mary O'Connor English, ed., *Early Town Records of Mamaroneck, 1697–1881* (Mamaroneck, NY: Town of Mamaroneck, 1979), 10–11, 23–24.

75. O'Connor English, *Early Town Records of Mamaroneck*, 169–80; *Journal of the Provincial Congress*, 1:266–67.

to "cut down a Liberty Pole" in the town of North Castle.[76] In November 1775, statements he made deriding the Provincial Congress and the Westchester Committee brought him to the attention of the local committee, but when the informant declined to swear an oath to the accusations, the committee took no further action against him.[77]

Appearing on the list provided to Governor Tryon as a "Friend of Government," it is likely that William Sutton introduced Lounsbury to Tryon aboard his own sloop or aboard the *Duchess of Gordon* shortly after the New Year.[78] At one of these meetings, Lounsbury provided Tryon with information regarding fortifications and armaments near Kingsbridge, including the presence of a large collection of cannons in the vicinity of the bridge.[79] Already in Tryon's calculations, Lounsbury claimed the Governor had "advised disabling the cannon" if possible, in order to sever the communication between New York City and New England.[80] Upon his return to shore, Lounsbury passed along the information to a group of like-minded individuals who supported the Crown.

In uncovering the group who participated in the plot to sabotage the cannon at Kingsbridge, it is evident that there were nearly thirty different people involved. In recreating this network, William Lounsbury clearly stands out as the crucial node in planning, facilitating, and executing the sabotage, but he was not alone. There were two other key members—Joshua Gedney and Josiah Burrell, who played important secondary roles—as well as a handful of significant contributors.

Lounsbury, Gedney, and Burrell all lived on Budd's Neck within a mile of each other. Lounsbury had purchased his land from Joshua Gedney's cousin or uncle in 1760, and by 1775, Gedney lived on a plot of land bordering Lounsbury's, a mere two hundred meters from Lounsbury's house.[81] Gedney had signed a document opposed to the committees as early as 1774, and both men participated in the 1775 protest at White Plains. While Tryon's

76. Force, *American Archives*, 4th ser., 2:323–24; *The New-York Journal, or General Advertiser*, October 5, 1775; Prince Gedney, December 9, 1849, 899, MacDonald Papers.

77. *Journal of the Provincial Congress*, 1:192-93.

78. "Mamaroneck Friends to Government," CO 5/1107, 115; *Journal of the Provincial Congress*, 271–73.

79. Contemporary accounts place the number of cannon near 300. Returns for all cannon in or near New York City from March 10, 1776, showed 344 total. In April 1775, William Smith reported that some cannon were removed from New York City but did not specify which. On June 7, 1775, Cadwallader Colden stated that more than one hundred cannon "belonging to the Merchants" were removed to Kingsbridge, leaving behind "those belonging to the King." Benjamin Church informed his brother-in-law John Fleming, both Loyalists, that he counted "280 Pieces of Cannon from 24 to 3 Pounders at Kingsbridge," on July 23, 1775. William Smith, Historical Memoirs, 223; "Cadwallader Colden to Earl of Dartmouth," Documents Relative to the Colonial History of the State of New York, 8:580; "Benjamin Church to John Fleming, July 23, 1775," in *The Papers of George Washington Digital Edition* (Charlottesville: University of Virginia Press, 2008).

80. *Journal of the Provincial Congress*, 1:341-42.

81. O'Connor English, *Early Town Records of Mamaroneck*, 23–24; *Journal of the Provincial Congress*, 1:341-42; Charles W. Baird, *Chronicle of a Border Town: History of Rye, Westchester County, New York, 1660–1870* (New York: Anson D. F. Randolph, 1871), 469.

encouragement was crucial for making the sabotage happen, Gedney and Burrell had considered disabling the cannon at an earlier date but lacked the equipment to do so.[82] This played a major factor in the development of their plan, as they knew they needed to acquire tools to disable the cannon: the best method being to hammer steel files into the cannon touchholes (the hole through which the propellant is ignited to make the cannon fire). Acquiring such a large quantity of steel spikes, associated with hemp and flax farming, by men who farmed little of either, however, would surely have brought them to the attention of the local committee.

To ensure word did not get around about such a large acquisition, Lounsbury, Gedney, and Burrell approached two men whom they knew harbored pro-Crown sentiments to get the steel files. The first was Gedney's cousin, Isaac. He was a blacksmith, had served with Lounsbury in local government as a tax assessor, and was a vocal opponent of the committees and the revolutionary movement. The second was Joseph Purdy, another local blacksmith. Purdy harbored similar sentiments about the committees and was Lounsbury's neighbor. Both men agreed to help and spent the next few evenings forging somewhere between one and two hundred steel files.[83]

From Gedney and Burrell's previous reconnaissance, however, the conspirators knew they needed more files than the two blacksmiths could produce. With the help of William Sutton, Lounsbury arranged for a meeting with some of Sutton's connections in New York City, hiring local boatman John Flood, for transportation. These interactions proved fruitful, as Lounsbury found a willing seller "in the Broadway near St. Paul's church."[84] Rather than purchasing the files directly, however, Lounsbury returned to Westchester, stopping first at the town of Eastchester to meet John Fowler, another Loyalist previously accused of distributing pro-Crown pamphlets.[85] Fowler agreed to purchase thirty files for Lounsbury, who then arranged for his son James and the blacksmith Joseph Purdy to pick up and transport them using John Flood's boat—in order to avoid committee inspections of goods traveling along the roads.[86]

It took nearly two weeks to acquire the files, during which time Lounsbury, Gedney, and Burrell brought three other conspirators into their sabotage plan: William Hains, James Hains Jr., and Thomas Hains. This group personified the tight-knit world of colonial America, as all these men were neighbors on Budd's Neck, and four of them were related.[87] Between 1774 and 1775, these men most likely gathered at each other's homes over drink

---

82. *Journal of the Provincial Congress*, 1:341–42.
83. *Journal of the Provincial Congress*, 1:266–67.
84. *Journal of the Provincial Congress*, 1:262.
85. *Journal of the Provincial Congress*, 2:262, 270.
86. *Journal of the Provincial Congress*, 2:262-64, 266-67, 270.
87. James Hains Jr. and Thomas Hains of Rye were brothers and cousins of William Hains. All three were cousins with Joshua Gedney. Their uncle was Godfrey Hains, who helped educate and mobilize Loyalist sentiment among his nephews and neighbors. On the relationships and connections of these individuals, see O'Connor English, *Early Town Records of Mamaroneck*; Baird,

and food, engaged in political discourse, and encouraged like-minded political mobilization in support of Britain that eventually transitioned from vocal opposition to physical
action.

By January 17, 1776, they were ready. Just before sunset, they met at John Gedney's
tavern in New Rochelle, approximately twelve miles northeast of their target. The tavern
keeper provided drink along with the last tools needed for the mission: a pair of sledges.[88]
Between nine and ten o'clock, the group donned dark overcoats with caps and handker-
chiefs to hide their faces, and quietly departed the warm hearth of the tavern into the bitter
cold. Following the post-road, they made their way overland toward Kingsbridge and the
cannon. Arriving in the early hours of the morning, the group found the cannon lying in
two separate fields a few hundred meters apart.[89]

Seeing no movement and hearing no sounds from within the nearby houses, they split
into two groups and began to hammer home the steel files. Finding more cannon than expected, the men ran out of files. Undeterred, they filled the rest of the cannon "with stones
and other Rubbish."[90] Hands frozen and cannon disabled, they returned to John Gedney's
tavern just before daybreak. Content with their work, they parted ways in a successful mission, having struck a blow against the Patriots without being caught.[91]

By the time the sun rose on the morning of January 18, however, a handful of local
inhabitants had already alerted the Westchester Committee to the sabotage. Upon notification, the Westchester Committee sent a detachment of minutemen to guard the cannon,
and the New York Committee of Safety shortly thereafter established a permanent guard.
Assessing the damage, they determined to hire someone to un-spike the guns, a costly and
time-consuming, though necessary task. Next, the New York Committee instructed the
Westchester Committee to begin a manhunt. Spreading out across the countryside, they
drew on their established network of informants to provide information on any suspected
Loyalists, particularly anyone known to have recently made or sold steel files like those
used to disable the cannon. This led the committee directly to John Fowler.[92]

After receiving word from a local informant that Fowler "purchased a parcel of old
files the previous week," the committee dispatched a detachment of militia to Fowler's
home. Apprehending him on January 23, 1776, the committee dragged him before the New

---

*Chronicle of a border Town: History of Rye; Ernest Freeland Griffen, Westchester County and Its
People: A Record* (New York: Lewis Historical Publishing, 1946); Henry B. Dawson, *Westchester-
County, New York during the American Revolution* (Morrisania, NY, 1886); Robert Bolton Jr., *A
History of the County of Westchester, from Its First Settlement to the Present Time* (New York: Alex-
ander S. Gould, 1848); J. Thomas Scharf, *History of Westchester County*, New York (Philadelphia: L.
E. Preston, 1886); *Journal of the Provincial Congress*, 1:271–73.

88. *Journal of the Provincial Congress*, 1:272.
89. *Journal of the Provincial Congress*, 1:272–75, 280.
90. *Calendar of Historical Manuscripts*, 1:266.
91. *Journal of the Provincial Congress*, 2:139, 272–74.
92. *Journal of the Provincial Congress*, 1:256-57, 261, 274–75.

York Committee of Safety in the City. Fowler immediately confessed to having purchased the files but swore he was not involved in spiking the cannon. To prove his loyalty, he blamed William Lounsbury, claiming Lounsbury tricked him, and that he had no knowledge of Lounsbury's true intentions for using the steel files.[93]

Having gained Fowler's confession, the Committee ordered the New York City light-horse to "proceed immediately to Mamaroneck and take Wm. Lownsbury and his accomplices." Finding Lounsbury at home, they arrested him in the night and returned with him promptly by daylight on January 24. During his interrogation, Lounsbury admitted to contracting Fowler to purchase the files for him but claimed he still had the spikes as he intended to employ his neighbor Joseph Purdy, a poor blacksmith in need of work, to make some implements for his cart. Asked to produce the files, Lounsbury fell silent and refused to answer any further questions. Undeterred, the Committee passed along the information they obtained from their interrogation to Col. Joseph Drake of the Westchester Committee, ordering him to arrest and interrogate Joseph Purdy and Lounsbury's son James, along with "all other suspicious persons in that part of your country."[94]

After sending out a militia detachment to apprehend Purdy and James Lounsbury, the subcommittees diligently went door-to-door, questioning all the inhabitants in their precincts. One of these interactions proved fruitful. John Hains in New Rochelle informed the precinct committee that on January 17, he was walking along the post-road road when "he saw the said Wm. Lownsberry at the house of John Gidney, of New Rochelle, tavernkeeper, a little before sunset." Acting on this information, the committee made their way to the tavernkeeper's house. Finding Gedney at home, the committee apprehended and interrogated him. Gedney readily admitted that Lounsbury was at his tavern the night of the sabotage, along with five other men. While he claimed that he did not know most of them, he was sure that one was Joshua Gedney, the son of Isaac Gedney of Rye.[95]

With this new information, the local committee "despatched a company of men in quest of Joshua Gideny." During the night of January 26, 1776, the subcommittee, led by Colonel Drake, found, and apprehended him. Initially evasive and obstinate during his examination, Gedney eventually condemned William Lounsbury, placing full blame for the sabotage on his neighbor. Confronted with this information, Lounsbury confessed, but claimed Gedney "concerted the design of disarming the cannon." After reexamining both Lounsbury and Gedney, both men confessed to planning and executing the sabotage, identifying every detail of their operation along with the other participants.[96]

Over the course of the following week, the committee arrested and interrogated another eleven persons, and on the night of January 31, Colonel Drake and his militia found

---

93. *Journal of the Provincial Congress*, 1:262, 264.
94. *Journal of the Provincial Congress*, 1:262, 264, 266–67.
95. *Journal of the Provincial Congress*, 1:266–68; 2:139.
96. *Journal of the Provincial Congress*, 1:271–73; 2:139.

and apprehended Josiah Burrell and Thomas Hains—two of the other saboteurs—along with Isaac Gedney the blacksmith. Upon interrogation, the men broke down and confessed. Shortly thereafter, the committee found the remaining saboteurs, and sent all of them down to the make-shift jail at the Upper Barracks in New York City, "manacled and shackled, hands and feet, and strictly guarded."[97]

On March 15, 1776, William Lounsbury escaped from confinement and made his way to the warship *Asia*.[98] Once aboard, he waited for General Howe's invasion force and eventually received a commission from Robert Rogers to raise a company of men in his battalion of rangers.[99] Sometime after the British landed troops on Staten Island in July, Lounsbury "came to Mamaroneck to enlist a company of men for the royal cause."[100] Ensconced in the rocky woods of the Great Lots north of Mamaroneck, Lounsbury sent word through his wife to former neighbors to come to enlist for the Crown.[101] By the end of August, close to fifteen men had enlisted. Without weapons or uniforms, they remained in hiding, likely waiting to coordinate with Howe's invasion that began on August 22.

Seven days later though, Lounsbury was dead, four others captured, and the rest scattered. In examining his death, the Committee demonstrated two significant changes evident by August of 1776. The days of acting as a "community forum" or a school of revolution were over. In its place, the committees orchestrated the defense of the county with hundreds of militiamen deployed along the coast, organized, and supported a logistics and supply system to support them, oversaw the construction of extensive fortifications, and employed a specialized militia unit to find and stop Loyalists from enlisting and supporting British military forces.

The other meaningful change occurred in the mindset of the committee members regarding their Loyalist neighbors. Whether they were cognizant of their changed attitudes, the stark contrast is evident by the fall of 1776. Just days prior to killing Lounsbury, the committee members still acted in a restrained manner regarding the Loyalists. Five days prior to Lounsbury's death, John Thomas Jr., chairman of the Westchester Committee, advocated releasing many of the Loyalists in jail, stating that "these persons are chiefly considerable farmers, and this present season loudly calls upon them to attend the putting

---

97. *Journal of the Provincial Congress*, 1:264, 266–67, 270–74, 276, 279–80; 2:139.

98. "G. W. to John Beck, 16 March, 1776," CO 5/1107, 275–76; *Journal of the Provincial Congress*, 2:429.

99. *Calendar of Historical Manuscripts*, 1:465.

100. Stephen Hall, November 5, 1846, 396–97, MacDonald Papers.

101. While the exact location is unknown, it is likely they were hiding on the land leased by William Saxton, a Loyalist who operated a sawmill on "Lot No. 3" of the Great Lots. This lot is approximately three miles south-east of White Plains on the west side of the road leading to Mamaroneck. Scharf, History of Westchester County New York, 1:156, 657, 682; 1774 Heathcote Map, Westchester County Archives, Elmsford, NY; Journal of the Proceedings of the Commissioners in Partition of Lands, Lying in Mamaroneck, Scarsedale and Harrison's Purchase, 1774, Westchester County Archives, Elmsford, NY.

their seed in the ground."[102] Here were persons deemed "enemies of their country," who had tried to undermine the revolutionary movement, and yet the committee still offered them the chance at redemption.

After Lounsbury's death, that chance was gone. On September 18, 1776, Maj. Joseph Benedict of the Westchester militia announced this change in attitude. Whereas Thomas advocated on behalf of the Loyalists, still viewing them as his neighbors, less than one month later Benedict described the county's Loyalists as a "baneful herd," no longer "governed by principles of manhood or justice." He concluded that the only way to deal with them was their immediate removal "to some remote part of the country."[103] As for those actively resisting the committees and emerging states, the penalty was death.

In the ensuing weeks, full-scale war and widespread violence engulfed Westchester County. Even when Howe's and Washington's armies left, a brutal localized partisan war remained. By this point, the transformation of Westchester's committees—both the institutional transition to a war-making organization, as well as the transition in conduct from restraint to violence and terror—was largely complete.

As a new wave of scholarship emphasizes, the American Revolution was incredibly violent.[104] This effort to revise thinking about the committees and the centrality of war in the American Revolution is important, as anyone familiar with the partisan war in Westchester and other localities can confirm that enemy combatants were far less generous than many scholars have portrayed. But this new trend in scholarship focused on violence as well as on portraying Loyalists as nonthreatening or as victims at the hands of the Patriots, should not obscure the hesitancy, restraint, and leniency that rendered the move toward violence a prolonged process.[105]

While Westchester is just one locality, the development of its committees, political mobilization, and transition to war is representative of the wider movement across New York. As this county's experience makes clear, militant loyalism—demonstrated here by the actions of William Lounsbury—posed a serious threat to the revolutionary movement; especially when it was coordinated with the British military. In direct response to Loyalist actions and to outside British military activity, Westchester's committees adopted coercive

---

102. *Journal of the Provincial Congress*, 2:291.

103. *Journal of the Provincial Congress*, 2:218-219.

104. For an overview of recent scholarship emphasizing the importance of violence in the American Revolution, see review outlining the state of the field by Robert G. Parkinson, "Janus's Revolution," *William and Mary Quarterly* 76, no. 3 (July 2019), 545–61.

105. Ruma Chopra, *Unnatural Rebellion: Loyalists in New York City During the Revolution* (Charlottesville: University of Virginia Press, 2011); Maya Jasanoff, *Liberty's Exiles: American Loyalists in the Revolutionary World* (New York: A. A. Knopf, 2011); Robert M. Calhoon, "Civil, Revolutionary, or Partisan: The Loyalists and the Nature of the War for Independence," in *Tory Insurgents: The Loyalist Perception and other Essays*, ed. Robert M. Calhoon and Timothy M. Barnes (Columbia: University of South Carolina Press, 2012), 204–17.

tactics and violence. Notably, however, widespread coercion and violence were not adopted until after the war arrived. It took fifteen months from the time Westchester first organized a committee to get to that point (twenty-four months from when the first local committee formed at Rye), and the first death did not occur until after Howe's army had beaten the Americans at the battle of Long Island. When war arrived, the time for being generous was over—as the committees and militia demonstrated throughout the last quarter of 1776.

Overlooking or ignoring the transition to violence obscures another transformation. As shown in Westchester, the committees did not remain networks of political mobilization; instead, they changed and adapted. In New York, the institutional structures to wage war did not exist in 1776. Faced with invasion, New York's committees filled this wartime need by becoming war-making institutions.

As it turned out, the committees were not particularly good at waging war. Mobilizing thousands of soldiers, purchasing military supplies, preserving order, controlling Loyalists, handling refugees, and dealing with frequent British military incursions that brought widespread death and destruction overburdened the local committees. For local committee members "weary of being called together to deal with tories" as early as the summer of 1776, the arrival of the British invasion force and ensuing American retreat from New York City later that fall pushed many to the breaking point.[106] In December of 1778, William Miller, one-time chairman of the Westchester Committee and a man his neighbors "formerly Placed Some Confidence in," described the bleak situation in Westchester to Governor George Clinton. As Miller recounted, his fellow countrymen looked "with Gastly Countenances, Saying, what Shall wee Do [?]." The former committee member dejectedly admitted he had no solution, informing the Governor that the situation "Intirely Confounds me, I not knowing what to Advise."[107]

By 1778, Miller's plea for assistance was but one of many sent to Governor Clinton, underscoring the new state's wartime woes and the problems of the committee system. A handful of military leaders and members of the Provincial Congress had recognized these problems early on, and believed that to form a new state, they needed a better solution to organize and wage war against the most powerful military in the world. Commenting on the committee system's steady loss of "influence and authority," Governor Clinton believed the situation required establishing a "vigorous Government."[108]

By the end of the Revolution, the outcome of Clinton's prognosis was evident. The failure of war-making by committees pushed the state to create powerful and intrusive institutions that in turn played a significant role in New York's revolutionary process of state formation. What emerged in New York was a "strong revolutionary American state;" and it

---

106. *Journal of the Provincial Congress*, 2:204.
107. Hugh Hastings, ed., *The Public Papers of George Clinton*, 10 vols. (New York, 1899–1914), *Public Papers of George Clinton*, 4:320–21.
108. *Public Papers of George Clinton*, 2:876–79.

was that strong state that marched triumphantly into Westchester at the conclusion of the War.[109]

As armed conflict ended and word of a peace treaty arrived in America by the spring of 1783, Sir Guy Carleton, commander of the British Forces in New York, wrote to Governor Clinton on May 13, 1783, informing him "that the British troops shall be withdrawn from the County of West Chester this day," excluding a few "small Parties as may be employed to escort Supplies." Clinton hurriedly made preparations to move toward Kingsbridge, directing Richard Morris, the chief justice of the Supreme Court of New York to "repair to that County with all possible Dispatch" to "establish the Civil Authority."[110] Departing Poughkeepsie less than one week later, Morris and a detachment of New York's militia pushed toward Kingsbridge—the same place William Lounsbury had spiked Patriot cannon in January of 1776—where they watched the tail-end of the British vanguard withdraw onto Manhattan. For the first time since New York's revolutionary conception, Westchester was unequivocally under the "Jurisdiction of the State."[111]

---

109. This process was contingent and arduous, most obviously in Westchester, but also throughout the state. The creation of a "vigorous Government" was by no means guaranteed. Unable to control the rampant violence and destruction across Westchester for much of the War, many questioned their allegiance to a state unable to push out British forces. Yet the problems posed by wartime chaos in places such as Westchester played two important roles. First, it pushed the state to develop an impressive network of magistrates and state agents that formed the foundation of Clinton's "vigorous Government" to carry out intrusive and robust policies to deal with wartime disorder. Second, it convinced a vulnerable population to accept the centralized intrusion. See Dillon L. Streifeneder, "The Propriety of a Vigorous Government: State Formation in New York, 1740–1795" (Ph.D. diss., Ohio State University, 2022). Quote from William J. Novak and Steven Pincus, "Revolutionary State Formation: The Origins of the Strong American State," in *State Formations: Global Histories and Cultures of Statehood*, ed. John L. Brooke, Julia C. Strauss, and Greg Anderson (New York: Cambridge University Press, 2018), 148. See also Howard Pashman, *Building a Revolutionary State: The Legal Transformation of New York, 1776–1783* (Chicago: University of Chicago Press, 2018); Matthew P. Dziennik, "New York's Refugees and Political Authority in Revolutionary America," *William and Mary Quarterly* 77, no. 1 (January 2020), 66–72.
110. *Public Papers of George Clinton*, 8:182–83, 186.
111. *Public Papers of George Clinton*, 8:175–77, 182–83.

Working-Class Germans in the Salt City
Syracuse, New York, 1860–1916

Daniel Koch

The central city of the Empire State was once the home of thousands of Germans, the largest contingent in a multicultural, multilingual urban melting pot. Syracuse was one of the key industrial cities of the United States during the Civil War era and into the twentieth century. Like other American cities, its industrial might was built on immigrant labor, much of which was German. Yet, there has not been a historical study of German Syracuse since the editors of the German-language *Syracuse Union* newspaper produced a book called *Geschichte der Deutschen in Syracuse und Onondaga County* (The history of the Germans in Syracuse and Onondaga County) in 1897. Like the tomes of county history produced around the same time, the *Geschichte* focuses on the great and the good. Its subtitle gives its intention away—*Nebst Kurzen Biographien von Beamten and Hervorragenden Buergern* (With short biographies of officials and prominent citizens).

The book is handsomely illustrated with portraits of eminent German Americans who achieved great success in their careers, and who also gave back to their communities by supporting churches, schools, and charities. These leaders were a source of pride at a time when "great man" status was the aim to which young men were taught to aspire. But the men (and they are all men) whose portraits adorn the *Geschichte* were exceptions. Most German immigrants worked in industrial jobs, living in what urban accommodation they could afford. They clustered in immigrant neighborhoods with other Germans but also often in mixed communities with other groups of immigrants—Irish, particularly in the early decades, and Italian and Polish in the later part of the nineteenth and early twentieth centuries.

This article seeks to expose a little-studied German community, going beyond the limited great-man focused nineteenth-century sources that exist. Both the *Geschichte* and Dwight H. Bruce's *Memorial History of Syracuse* (1891), the two most detailed views of the city in the late nineteenth century, portray a highly positive view of a flourishing German

New York History, 103.2, Winter 2022–2023

American community that exemplified civic virtue.[1] Historians have maintained that Germans were widely accepted, even celebrated, in American society between the Civil War and the outbreak of World War I.[2] The purpose here is not to try to undermine this view; indeed, the records from Syracuse in this period clearly bear it out. Nor is it to write a labor history of Germans in Syracuse. It is rather to bring back to life some of what was left out or swept under the carpet in building this narrative of German success in America. This article seeks to answer why these omissions occurred and argues that it was at least partially related to pervasive racialist discourse in the nineteenth and early twentieth centuries. Furthermore, studying Syracuse's German community enables us to reconstruct the urban geography of a nineteenth-century industrial center and take a new look at a lost German neighborhood in a key American city.

Syracuse was a relatively late city to emerge in New York State. The land upon which it is built was part of the Onondaga Reservation, a 64,000-acre tract that was exempt from white settlement by the terms of the 1788 treaty between the State of New York and the Onondaga Nation.[3] Syracuse is still known as the salt city due to the briny waters that flow into Onondaga Lake, from which salt can be made using a boiling process. Water from Syracuse's salt springs, an 1834 map boasted, produced nearly seven times as much salt as the same quantity of sea water. "Solar salt" was also produced by allowing the water to evaporate in the sun and raking in the remaining salt.

Subsequent exploitative treaties with the state chipped away at the Onondaga Reservation (other Haudenosaunee people in New York experienced the same in the so-called treaty period between the 1790s and 1820s). The land upon which Syracuse was built was transferred first to the state and then sold off to private buyers. Settlers poured in, mainly from New England, in the early decades of the nineteenth century. The real impetus for Syracuse's growth was the Erie Canal, completed in 1825, which enabled salt to be shipped far more cheaply than before to all points west. As the frontier expanded and large cities started growing up on the Great Lakes in the 1850s and 1860s, Syracuse profited from a virtual monopoly on salt supply over a vast region. No other sources could produce such

1. The two main sources used in this article are Syracuse Union, *Geschichte der Deutschen in Syracuse* (Syracuse: J. P. Pinzer, 1897), and Dwight H. Bruce, *Memorial History of Syracuse: From Its Settlement to the Present Time* (Syracuse: H. P. Smith, 1891), hereafter abbreviated *Geschichte* and *Memorial History*, respectively.

2. Russell A. Kazal, *Becoming Old Stock: The Paradox of German-American Identity* (Princeton: Princeton University Press, 2004), 2; Katherine Neils Cozens, "Germans," in *Harvard Encyclopedia of American Ethnic Groups*, ed. Stephan Thernstrom (Cambridge, MA: Harvard University Press, 1980), 421–42; Don Heinrich Tolzmann, "German-American Studies: History and Development," *Monatshefte* 80, no. 3 (1988): 281–82; Vasiliki Ouka, "How Do Immigrants Respond to Discrimination? The Case of Germans in the US during World War I," *American Political Science Review* 113, no. 2 (2019): 405–22.

3. Alan Taylor, *The Divided Ground: Indians, Settlers, and the Northern Borderland of the American Revolution* (New York: Vintage, 2006), 181; Laurence Hauptman, *Conspiracy of Interests: Iroquois Dispossession and the Rise of New York State* (Syracuse: Syracuse University Press, 2001), 77–78.

great quantities at competitive prices. Demand skyrocketed in those decades, creating a need for laborers to boil, rake, package, carry, and ship bushels of salt onto canal boats and rail cars headed west.[4]

The growth in Syracuse's salt industry in the 1850s and 1860s coincided with a major wave of German and Irish immigration to the United States and was the main reason why large immigrant communities formed there. Early German immigrants to Syracuse from Baden and Württemberg (some of whom came from the region known as Swabia from its ancient inhabitants, the Suebi) settled around the corner of Butternut and Park Streets in an area that was called "Schwobenland." Another early German-speaking group of Swiss origin lived at the top of Seward Street on what was called "Schwitzerhill." In 1850, Syracuse's total population was 22,000. A small city, but still the twenty-eighth most populous in the United States (only marginally smaller than Chicago and larger than Detroit at the time). The *Memorial History* estimates that there were 6,000 Germans there by 1852. Between 1850 and 1860, Syracuse's population grew by 26 percent. In the next decade it grew a further 53 percent, to 43,051, even while most parts of New York saw a net decrease in population, partly due to losses in the Civil War.[5]

New York had over a quarter of a million German-born residents in 1860, far more than any other state. The overwhelming majority lived in one of seven cities: New York, Brooklyn (then a separate city), Troy, Albany, Syracuse, Rochester, and Buffalo.[6] Out of a total population of 90,000, Onondaga County, in which Syracuse is the central settlement, had roughly 20,000 residents who were born outside the United States.[7] Hundreds of Syracuse Germans fought in the Civil War. Some joined German-speaking units in the Onondaga regiments. Company B in the 12th New York Volunteer Infantry, Company H in the 101st and Company A in the 149th were composed almost entirely of young Germans from Syracuse. The German contribution to the Civil War is part of the reason why the political nativism that underwrote the successes of the Know Nothing Party—or, at least, the anti-German elements of it—during the 1850s faded away during the postwar Gilded Age.[8]

The 1875 New York State Census allows for a more granular view of Syracuse's German community. There were 5,401 German-born residents—the largest immigrant group

---

4. Map of the village of Syracuse and the village of Lodi, 1834 (Syracuse: W. Leavenworth & J.B. Clarke), 1834; Joseph Hawley Murphy, "The Salt Industry of Syracuse: A Brief Review," *New York History* 30, no. 3 (1949): 304–15; William B. Meyer, "Why Did Syracuse Manufacture Solar Salt?" *New York History* 86, no. 2 (2005): 195–209.

5. Syracuse Union, *Geschichte*, 195; Bruce, *Memorial History*, 343, 351.

6. Bruce Levine, *The Spirit of 1848: German Immigrants, Labor Conflict, and the Coming of the Civil War* (Urbana: University of Illinois Press, 1992), 59.

7. Census Office, *Population of the United States in 1860* (Washington, DC: Government Printing Office, 1864), 345.

8. Cozens, "Germans," 421; Tolzmann, "German-American Studies: History and Development," 282. Political nativism was already in decline in the years immediately preceding the Civil War. See Louis Dow Scisco, *Political Nativism in New York State* (New York: Columbia University Press, 1901), 224–45.

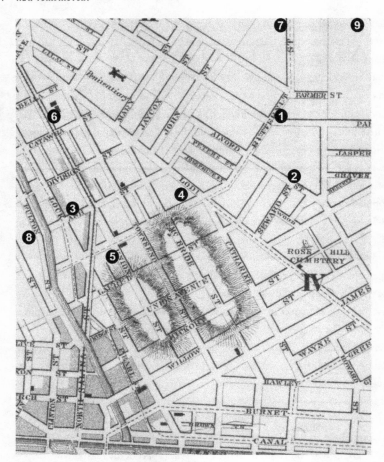

Detail from H. Wadsworth Clarke's Map of Syracuse in the Syracuse City Directory of 1871. CLARKE, H. WADSWORTH. MAP OF THE CITY OF SYRACUSE. [SYRACUSE, N.Y.?: ANDREW BOYD, 1871] Map. https://www.loc .gov/item/2011593657/. The Erie Canal stretches across the bottom and the Oswego Canal runs along the left side (now Routes 690 and I-81, respectively).

Approximate location of places: 1 "Schwobenland." Later the site of Woese's Theatre; 2 "Schwitzer Hill"; 3 Turn Hall. Nearby was the meeting place of the *Deutscher Handwerker Verein*; 4 Armbruster's Hall; 5 Site of St. Joseph's Evangelical Lutheran Church and the Lutheran Zion Church and Brummer's German School; 6 Church of the Assumption; 7 German Orphanage; 8 470 Fulton Street. Home of Martin and Theresa Zumkeller; 9 Schiller Park. The 1911 Goethe and Schiller Statue stands at the park's northwest corner.

in the city. In an age of large families, the number of children born in Syracuse growing up in German-speaking homes at the time was at least as large. More than half of Syracuse's Germans lived in the city's Fourth Ward, where they were by far the biggest immigrant group. 1,090 lived in the adjacent Second Ward, which also had a large Irish population. Syracuse was by no means the most heavily German city in America or even in New York State.[9] Buffalo (27,018), Rochester (11,987), and Albany (7,791) had larger German-born populations than Syracuse. But it was still a large and important community in a city that exploded in size and prominence, particularly during the Civil War years.[10]

Most German immigrants in Syracuse came from the southwestern part of what is now Germany—particularly the Grand Duchies of Hesse-Darmstadt and Baden, and the Kingdom of Württemberg. In the era before German unification in 1870–71, there were large disparities from one German kingdom or principality to the next, both economically and in style of rule. Baden and Württemberg had been particularly hard hit by the Napoleonic Wars early in the nineteenth century and were slow to recover. Rule there was arguably more despotic than in other parts of Germany, and there was a surplus of labor, particularly in the towns, which made earning a living there hard for small craftsmen. Many chose to leave after the failed revolutions of 1848—some for reasons that were directly political. Syracuse Germans remembered the spirit of 1848 for years to come. The meeting hall of the Syracuse Social Turn Verein on North Salina Street, just north of the intersection with Ash Street, was called by the *Memorial History* "an ornament to that part of the city, [and] at the same time . . . a monument to the liberty-loving sons of the revolution of 1848."[11]

German immigration to the United States peaked between 1880 and 1890. Many of the newcomers went directly to the rapidly developing west, but some settled in the more established cities of the east, including Syracuse. Although the city's salt industry was in

---

9. Some attention has been given by scholars to German communities in New York City and Buffalo. On Buffalo, see Andrew P. Yox, "Bonds of Community: Buffalo's German Element, 1853–1871," *New York History* 66, no. 2 (1985): 140–63 and David A. Gerber, "Language Maintenance, Ethnic Group Formation, and Public Schools: Changing Patterns of German Concern, Buffalo, 1837–1874," *Journal of American Ethnic History* 4, no. 1 (1984): 31–61. Buffalo's equivalent of the Geschichte is Buffalo und sein Deutschtum, published in Buffalo by the Deutsch-Amerikanische Historische und Biographische Gesellschaft in 1912. New York's German working class is studied in Dorothee Schneider's *Trade Unions and Community: The German Working Class in New York City, 1870–1900* (Urbana: University of Illinois Press, 1994); Stanley Nadel, *Little Germany: Ethnicity, Religion, and Class in New York City, 1845–80* (Urbana: University of Illinois Press, 1990); Christiane Harzig, "The Role of German Women in the German-American Working-Class Movement in Late Nineteenth-Century New York," *Journal of American Ethnic History* 8, no. 2 (1989), 87–107. The only significant resource on German Syracuse is Michelle Stone, "German Immigrant Ancestors to Syracuse and Onondaga County, New York," mstonegenealogy.org, accessed September 17, 2022, http://www.mstonegenealogy.org/.
10. New York State Secretary's Office, *Census of the State of New York for 1875* (Albany: Weed, Parsons and Company, 1877), 30–45.
11. Levine, *Spirit of 1848*, 32, 45–46, 54; Schneider, *Trade Unions and Community*, 3–4; Bruce, *Memorial History*, 337, 347; Jochen Krebber, *Württemberger in Nordamerika: Migration von der Schwäbischen Alb im 19. Jahrhundert* (Stuttgart: Steiner, 2014).

decline by the 1880s, other industries had grown up and were booming in Syracuse, where a growing number of factories were churning out everything from furniture to boilers to guns.[12] The city experienced another 70 percent growth spurt between 1880 and 1890, again fueled largely by immigration mainly from Germany and now Italy and Poland as well, bringing the population up to over 88,000. In 1900, Syracuse had a German-born population of 7,865.[13] Some German families were beginning to move out of the traditional German neighborhoods. A new church for German Catholics, St. Joseph's, was built in 1883 on Seymour Street, southwest of the city center over which the older German Church of the Assumption tried, unsuccessfully, to assert control.[14] The traditionally German area around North Salina Street would, in the first decades of the twentieth century, become the heart of Syracuse's Little Italy.

In Syracuse, Germans held a range of local public offices. Some of those who did were of working-class origin. Of those whose political affiliation is known, most were Republicans. Joseph Bondy, whose father was a German-speaking butcher from Prague, was a Republican who represented the New York 3rd District in Congress. Jacob Amos, son of a German miller in Baldwinsville and who went on to serve as Syracuse's mayor, was a firm and lifelong Republican. So too was Jakob Blixt, an upholster by trade who grew a successful business in North Salina Street. One prominent German, Carl Simon, who started working as a shoe smith as an immigrant boy, was a Democrat. He was elected to Congress in 1874, an unusual occurrence in central New York, which tended to elect Republicans.[15] A German-language newspaper, the *Syracuse Central Democrat*, ran from 1858 to 1899 as a rival to the Republican *Syracuse Union*, which ran until 1941.

A branch of the Sozialistische Arbeiter Partei (Socialist Workers' Party) was set up by Germans in Syracuse in 1877—a year when labor agitation reached a peak and led to large and sometimes violent strikes in cities across the United States. The *Geschichte* notes that the party was formed to advance the "Befreiung der Arbeiter-Klasse" (the liberation of the working class) and that they had done much to educate the workers of Syracuse by organizing meetings with expert speakers. But their political support was extremely limited, even among German workers in Syracuse. German socialists appeared in Syracuse newspapers on lists of candidates for local offices in the 1880s, 1890s, and 1900s, alongside (far longer) lists of Germans standing as Republicans and Democrats. From the lists of elected officers in Syracuse appearing in the *Memorial History* and in the political history of Syracuse in

12. William M. Beauchamp, *Past and Present of Syracuse and Onondaga County, New York* (New York: S. J. Clarke, 1908), 457.

13. Census Office, *Population of the United States in 1860*, 345; Census Office, *Abstract of the Twelfth Census of the United States, 1900*, 3rd ed. (Washington, DC: Government Printing Office, 1904), 102, 108.

14. "German Catholics at Odds: Trouble between Two Churches in Syracuse," *New York Times*, January 5, 1886.

15. Syracuse Union, *Geschichte*, 253, 257, 295.

William Beauchamp's *Past and Present of Syracuse and Onondaga County* (1908), there does not appear ever to have been a socialist alderman, let alone a mayor.[16] Thus, while there was some support for socialism among working-class Germans in Syracuse, it did not translate to significant electoral success at any point, even in ward-level local elections. In Joseph Bondy's 1896 election campaign, for example, he was opposed by Robert Berggren of the Socialist Workers' Party, who received only 19 votes compared to Bondy's 4,397.[17]

Syracuse did not experience the level of unrest that larger cities like Pittsburgh, St. Louis, and Chicago did, particularly in the violent railroad strikes of the summer of 1877 in which left-wing Germans played prominent roles. During those strikes the National Guard occupied Syracuse briefly, but the only significant action was by a group of strikers who briefly held up freight traffic by stopping a train at Dewitt. By the 27th of July, the situation had calmed, and the military occupation ended. The *Syracuse Daily Courier* wrote that peace was brought about "by the judicious action of the workmen themselves, who held a meeting, coolly discussed their position, and determined to resume work."[18] The *Syracuse Union* took a dim view of the rioters, calling those who did criminal damage during the strikes "Feind[e] unserer bürgerlichen Freiheit" (enemies of our civic freedom), and blaming the "sozailistischen Demagogen" (socialist demagogues) for inciting them.[19] Many German Americans reacted to labor agitation by actively trying to dissociate themselves from it, particularly after the Haymarket Affair in 1886, in which German agitators were suspected of murdering police officers in Chicago.[20]

In Syracuse, as in other cities around the country, many Germans joined bands and choirs, but membership in the more elite of these was limited to those who had leisure time and training sufficient to perform in them. The Gesangverein Syracuse Liederkranz choir's membership, for instance, consisted of Syracuse's "leading Germans," who performed at singing festivals throughout the country. It rehearsed at Armbruster's Hall on the corner of Butternut and Lodi Streets. In 1889, another choir called the Arbeiter Liedertafel formed, presumably (given its name) with a more working-class membership. It met in the same hall as the Liederkranz choir, but its goal was "durch Gesänge von sozialistischer Tendenz, die Emancipation der Arbeiter fördern zu helfen" (to help promote the emancipation of

---

16. See, for example, "Election Notice," *Syracuse Journal*, October 23, 1897; "Election Notice," *Syracuse Journal*, October 30, 1907; Bruce, *Memorial History*, 257-65; Beauchamp, *Past and Present of Syracuse and Onondaga County*, 552-7.

17. Syracuse Union, Geschichte, 258.

18. "The Strike," *The Daily Courier* (Syracuse), July 28, 1877.

19. "Über den Berg," *Syracuse Union*, August 4, 1877.

20. James M. Bergquist, "German Communities in American Cities," *Journal of American Ethnic History* 4, no. 1 (1984), 16; Levine, *Spirit of 1848*, 269–70; Schneider, *Trade Unions and Community*, 74–88; Christine Heiss, "German Radicals in Industrial America: The Lehr- and Wehr-Verein in Gilded Age Chicago," in *German Workers in Industrial Chicago: A Comparative Perspective, 1850–1910*, ed. Hartmut Keil and John B. Jentz (De Kalb: Northern Illinois University Press, 1983), 206–23.

the workers though socialist-leaning songs). Various charitable organizations such as the German Order of Harugari also existed in Syracuse as in other American cities, but again, membership in these was mainly limited to those who were able to give.[21]

The most prominent organization for working-class Germans in the 1860s was the Deutscher Handwerker Verein, which met on the corner of Ash and North Salina Streets. In an era before government social security benefits, unions such as these were funded by contributions from workers and were used to pay benefits to members' widows. At least seven similar German workers' unions existed by 1892. Membership fees were used to help members and families in trouble. German American unions, or *Veriene*, had their roots in Germany. They often served as social clubs, and sometimes they had political goals. In Germany, many of the *Vereine* challenged the established order, but in the United States, most did not advocate radicalism (though some in larger cities, including New York, did). The English and German-language histories do not comment on the unions' activities in Syracuse beyond their basic functions. They are hardly mentioned in the Syracuse newspapers of the time. The *Vereine* were an important part of working-class German culture but in Syracuse, but they do not seem to have played any significant role in politicizing working-class Germans.[22]

Churches were places where working-class and better-off Germans would gather under the same roof. The majority of Syracuse Germans were Protestant, a fact that was helpful to their acceptance by other Americans. The first German church in Syracuse, founded in 1840, was St. John's Evangelical Lutheran on Butternut Street and Prospect Avenue. Across from it at the same intersection was the Lutheran Zion's Church (1864). German Catholics worshipped in the Church of the Assumption on North Salina Street. It had been founded in 1841 and was housed in a grand brick building completed in 1867 (it is still standing). German Jews built synagogues south of the Erie Canal. The first was the Temple of Concord synagogue at Mulberry Street (now South State Street) and Harrison Street. In the 1890s, about five hundred worshipped there. Other Jewish congregations met in separate locations near Mulberry Street. The predominantly Jewish neighborhood of the Fifteenth Ward later became a center of African American life in Syracuse during the Great Migration period and before much of it was razed in the 1960s for the construction of Interstate 81.[23]

Most of Syracuse's German children attended public schools. Syracuse's system of free common schools was established in 1848. By the 1890s there were four schools in the Second and Fourth Wards, all headed by principals with English surnames. German-language

21. Syracuse Union, *Geschichte*, 160; Bruce, *Memorial History*, 345.
22. Schneider, *Trade Unions and Community*, 27–28; Bruce, *Memorial History*, 346–48, 367; Syracuse Union, *Geschichte*, 180–94.
23. Bruce, *Memorial History*, 516–17, 524–28, 358–59. On the Jewish community of Syracuse see B. G. Rudolph, *From a Minyan to a Community: A History of the Jews of Syracuse* (Syracuse: Syracuse University Press, 1970).

education was privately funded, and thus out of reach for the poorest. Those who could afford the 25 cents per week could attend a German-language independent school that was established in 1860 and taught by Adolph Brummel behind St. John's Lutheran Church on Butternut Street. As in other immigrant-heavy industrial cities, Syracuse's school system worked to assimilate immigrant children as quickly as possible. Middle-class Germans in Syracuse and in other cities worried about the loss of their language, particularly among their American-born children of German parents, and made efforts to preserve it. The charitable Order of the Harugari, for instance, insisted on the "exclusive use of the German language in its proceedings and ma[de] it a duty to do everything possible for the preservation of the language in other ways."[24]

But for working-class Germans, funding and motivating children to study literary German would have been a challenge, and there is little evidence that it was highly prioritized. In the 1890s, the *Memorial History* notes, "the younger German generations are laying aside the German customs and language and are becoming thoroughly Americanized in both language and spirit." The celebration of German poets and authors in Syracuse was related to a middle-class desire to vaunt German *Kultur*, just as the preservation of the German language in the community came under threat. Large-scale celebrations marked the centenaries of the birth of Johann Wolfgang von Goethe in 1849 and of Friedrich Schiller in 1859. In 1911, a statue of Goethe and Schiller was erected in what is now known as Schiller Park, previously a cemetery, in the heart of German Syracuse.[25]

The largest German festival of all—and one that illustrates the acceptance of the German community in Syracuse—was the Friedensfest, or Peace Festival, that was held on May 1, 1871. Prussia's resounding victory in the Franco-Prussian War and the news of Germany's unification was a cause of jubilation in German communities across America. Peace Festivals like the one in Syracuse took place in New York City, Pittsburgh, Detroit, Louisville, Madison, Buffalo, and other cities between April and May that year. The Syracuse Friedensfest organizers advertised the festival as being for all Germans in the city, "Ob Israelite oder Christ, Ob Katholik, ob Protestant, Für's einige deutsche Vaterland!" (whether Jewish or Christian; Catholic or Protestant; for the united German fatherland!) A two-mile-long parade started at the Turnhall and processed through German Syracuse's main streets: North Salina, Division, Lodi, and Butternut. Crowds lining the streets waved German and American flags and (as in other cities) held evergreens, a symbol of Germany.[26]

---

24. On Brummel's German school, see Syracuse Union, *Geschichte*, 141–43. For a comparison to Buffalo, see Maxine Seller, "The Education of Immigrant Children in Buffalo, New York 1890–1916," *New York History* 57, no. 2 (1976), 183–99. Quote from Bruce, *Memorial History*, 345.
25. Bruce, *Memorial History*, 351, 354; Heike Bungert, "Demonstrating the Values of 'Gemütlichkeit' and 'Cultur': The Festivals of German-Americans in Milwaukee, 1870-1910" in *Celebrating Ethnicity and Nation: American Festive Culture from the Revolution to the Early Twentieth Century*, ed Jürgen Heideking, Geneviève Fabre, and Kai Dreisbach (New York: Berghahn, 2001), 175–93. On German language in Syracuse and celebrations of Goethe and Schiller see Bruce, *Memorial History*, 350
26. Syracuse Union, *Geschichte*, 203.

The *Geschichte*, the *Memorial History*, and newspaper accounts from the time agree that non-German Syracusans enthusiastically supported the event. Bruce, in his *Memorial History*, states that "no celebration ever held in Syracuse equaled it in splendor, enthusiasm and magnitude." None of the commentary on the festival points to class divisions in the way German Syracusans celebrated. Leading Germans were given star roles in the parade, representing Kaiser Wilhelm, Otto von Bismarck, and other heroes of unification on a horse-drawn float. But ordinary Germans paraded too. German veterans of the Civil War marched carrying the bullet-hole ridden regimental flags they had taken into battle.[27] Smaller-scale German parades continued to feature in Syracuse and other upstate cities well into the early twentieth century.[28]

But there was a darker side to German life in Syracuse. While some Germans rose in prominence, others experienced downward mobility, alcoholism, violence, and crime. The *Geschichte* mentions German drinking saloons, notably Gallster's, and the aptly named Immerdurstig (Ever thirsty) or Schmidt's, near Henry Woese's Theatre at Butternut and Park Streets. Twenty German orphans lived on Spring Street near Butternut in an institution funded by wealthy donors and penny subscriptions from lowlier Germans.[29] The saga of the Zumkeller family of Syracuse provides a striking example of a working-class family that did not "make it" in America. Some of its members ended up in an urban underworld that the authors of the *Memorial History* and the *Geschichte* thought best to ignore.

When Martin Zumkeller signed up to fight in the Civil War in Syracuse in October 1861, he was twenty years old. He was placed in the B Company of the 101st New York Volunteer Infantry. We know little of his life before his enlistment. He was born in 1841 in Säge, near Herrischried, in the Grand Duchy of Baden, to Jost Zumkiller [*sic*] and his wife Perpetua. When he came to America is unclear. The 1855 New York Census captured Jost Zumkiller living with two children—Martin, aged 14, and a daughter, Catherina, in Buffalo's Sixth Ward in a community of Baden immigrants. They were all listed as "aliens" in their fourth year of residence in the city, suggesting that he may have arrived from Germany in 1851.[30] If Martin moved from Buffalo to Syracuse as he reached working age, it would most likely have been for better job prospects. This was the time of Syracuse's salt-making boom, which coincided with a dramatic rise in both its German-born and its overall population. Zumkeller's occupation in later life was a salt-boiler. He may well have got his start in the industry before the war changed his life.

---

27. Syracuse Union, *Geschichte*, 203–9; Bruce, *Memorial History*, 351–52; "Das deutsche Friedensfest in Syracuse," *Syracuse Union*, May 6, 1871; *Syracuse Daily Journal* (Evening edition), May 1, 1871.

28. See "Germans in Parade," *Syracuse Herald*, August 3, 1908; "Deutscher-Tag Tomorrow," *Syracuse Herald*, August 6, 1909. With thanks to Michelle Stone.

29. Bruce, *Memorial History*, 349.

30. New York State Census, 1855, County of Erie, Buffalo City, Ward 6, Household Number 1009, Line Number 10. ancestry.com

As a solider, his name was sometimes borne as Somkiller or Sumkiller. He transferred regiments twice—first to the 37th New York Volunteer Infantry, Company I, in December 1862, and then to the 40th New York, nicknamed the Mozart Regiment, Company I, in May 1863. He very likely fought at Gettysburg with his regiment in July 1863. His service record states he was wounded on May 5, 1864, at the Battle of the Wilderness, Virginia. His later pension records show that he had taken a gunshot wound to the hand. He remained with the Mozart Regiment until it was mustered out in 1865. Thus, by the age of twenty-five he had experienced nearly four years of war, been wounded, and had likely seen a great deal of death and suffering. His regiment's losses during the war were severe.[31]

Back in Syracuse, Zumkeller set about making a life for himself. He married a woman from Württemberg named Theresa in 1867 at Syracuse's Catholic Church of the Assumption. Theresa appears to have immigrated earlier that year. She learned to speak some English, but according to a later census report, could not read or write.[32] In 1872, Martin was working as a salt-boiler, and they were living at 344 North Salina Street, near the Turn-hall.[33] By 1880, the family had six children. The oldest three were daughters. Of them, two later married other German Syracusans. The younger three were boys: Martin (Junior), Joseph, and Frank. Their fates were far less happy.

At some point in the 1880s, the family moved to 470 Fulton Street, along the Oswego Canal that connected the Erie Canal to Lake Ontario. It was a working-class street, and conditions there were poor. A newspaper later called their house a "hovel." Most of the men on the street were classified as "laborers." Nearly all the adults had been born either in Germany or Ireland. Of the females on the street, many were employed as washerwomen, laundresses, or seamstresses in an era when women working outside the home often did so only due to poverty. There were two barkeepers (both Irish), and there was, at one time at least, a tavern on the street, suggesting that alcohol had a strong presence in the neighborhood. The city of Syracuse had 421 saloons in 1886.[34]

Although Martin was still employed as a salt-boiler in 1880, the salt industry was in decline. New sources of salt had been found farther west. Martin Zumkeller died in 1892 at the age of fifty. No obituary appeared in the English or German-language newspapers of Syracuse. A later document suggests that he may have been an alcoholic. His home on Fulton Street no longer exists. The I-81 highway now follows the route of the Oswego Canal. In Syracuse today, Genant Drive covers much of what was Fulton Street. All the homes on it have been razed.

31. Frederick C. Floyd, *History of the Fortieth (Mozart) Regiment, New York Volunteers* (Boston: F. H. Gilson, 1909), 468; United States Department of the Interior, Pension Office, *List of Pensioners on the Roll, January 1st, 1883*, vol. 2 (Washington, DC: Government Printing Office), 314.

32. 1900 U.S. Federal Census, State of New York, Onondaga County, City of Syracuse, Ward 7, District 0107, Sheet Number 11. ancestry.com

33. *Syracuse City Directory, 1872–73* (Syracuse, NY: Andrew Boyd, 1872), 312.

34. Beauchamp, *Past and Present of Syracuse and Onondaga County*, 457.

The oldest of Martin Zumkeller's sons, named for his father, was still living with his mother, Theresa, in 1894. The city directory listed him as a tailor. The census in 1900 records him at the age of twenty-five, working as a day laborer. By 1905, however, he was unemployed. Things were going badly for Martin. In 1904 he was "arrested for being drunk."[35] *The Syracuse Telegram* reported on June 13, 1905, that he violently beat his seventy-five-year-old mother. A committee of concerned G.A.R. (Grand Army of the Republic, a Civil War veterans' association) women requested that the city Health Inspector, James P. Maloney, visit the home at 470 Fulton Street. The reporter called Martin a "burly looking lad of about 30 years" who had administered "a sound thrashing" to his mother. He was charged with breach of the peace. The family home is described as "scarcely more than a hovel" with intolerable sanitary conditions. Martin, the report says, "does not work, but eats and drinks up [his mother's] pension money and then abuses her." He had already been arrested once for the same offense. When police found him, he was "in a Fulton Street saloon," where he was arrested.[36]

Theresa Zumkeller was sent to the Oxford Home for the Wives and Mothers of Dead Soldiers in Oxford, Chenango County. She died there in 1917. Martin, Junior appears to have succumbed completely to alcohol. He died a homeless "wanderer" on the 22nd of January 1913. He had been found soaking wet and suffering with severe pneumonia, but the cause of death, confirmed by an autopsy, was linked to cirrhosis of the liver.[37]

The middle son, Joseph, had moved out of Fulton Street by 1900. He was twenty-two years old, worked as a "picture frame gilter" and lived in a rented house at 309 Pond Street. He had also just married Nellie McCallum, an eighteen-year-old whose grandparents came from Tipperary, Ireland. Pond was another working-class German street, like the one on which he had grown up. Ten years later, he was still working in a picture frame factory. A daughter had been born, Genevieve, and Nellie's mother, Johanna, moved in. In 1913, just after his brother Martin died, he seems to have stopped supporting his family. A reporter for the *Syracuse Herald* evidently took some pleasure in reporting on his appearance before the police court alongside a few other "saddened derelicts." The report stated: "He hasn't, according to Friend Wife, been endowing [the family] to any considerable extent since October 1st, and as a result Mrs. Zumkeller and the Zumkellerettes had no fried cabbage."[38] The family later broke up after the death of their son Joseph Jr., at age eight.[39]

Martin Zumkeller's youngest son, Frank, was twenty years old in April 1900 when

35. "Minor Events in Police Courts," *Syracuse Herald*, Evening, February 22, 1904; New York State Census, 1905, City of Syracuse, Seventh Ward, First Election District, p. 5. ancestry.com.
36. "Martin Zumkeller Arrested—His Mother Makes Complaint," *Syracuse Post-Standard*, September 5, 1904; "Son Pounds Aged Woman," *The Telegraph* (Syracuse), June 13, 1905.
37. "Wanderer Dies from Pneumonia," *Syracuse Daily Journal*, January 23, 1913.
38. "Good Morning Judge," *Syracuse Herald*, October 30, 1913.
39. Joseph J. Zumkeller's death is reported in the *Syracuse Herald* of May 25, 1923, as resulting from a "brief illness." His death on May 23 is recorded in the New York State Department for Health's Death Index for 1923. Nellie Zumkeller later married Frank Paninski and died in Syracuse in 1942.

he was caught stealing coal from the West Shore Railroad freight yards and was fined $5 after a court appearance. He was living as a boarder at 111 North Clinton Street with thirty-three-year-old Emma Hurley, whose parents were immigrants from Scotland, and her two boys, aged fifteen and thirteen. The news report said he was a railway worker, and the 1900 census records his occupation as teamster but notes that he had been out of work for three months. Emma Hurley was listed as married (not widowed), but no husband was living at the residence.[40] By 1905, Zumkeller and Hurley had married and moved to 223 Spencer Street.[41] Frank is listed as the head of household in the 1905 state census, aged twenty-six. Emma appears on the census form as his wife, with her age reduced to twenty-six as well, though she was probably actually in her late thirties. Her teenaged son George Hurley still lived at home and was working as a day laborer.[42] Emma was arrested in 1902 for bursting into a saloon where George had been served liquor. She "raised a disturbance in the place" and pleaded in court that the saloon was selling alcohol on Sunday. Judge Thomson (the same who had fined Frank for coal theft) told her that she mustn't take the law in her own hands: "We don't want any Carrie Nations in Syracuse," he said, referring to the temperance advocate who was famous for destroying saloon bars with a hatchet.[43] Emma died in 1904.[44]

In 1915, Frank was slashed with a razor blade across his face in an attack, disfiguring him badly. He was living at 113 Orange (now South McBride) Street. He had married again, but the identity of his wife is not clear. The newspaper write-up of the attack reports that "Mrs. Zumkiller [sic], who also goes by the name of Anna Martin," was followed home from a trip to the shops by three men. When she reached home, the men demanded admittance and then smashed down the door. She ran to a neighbor's house, "where her husband was playing cards." Zumkeller and a friend returned to the house and began fighting with the three men, whom Mrs. Zumkeller identified as Italians in their early twenties. In the fight, Zumkeller was slashed across the nose and temple and behind the ear. The three assailants ran. Mrs. Zumkeller found her husband bleeding in the snow. He was rushed first to a doctor and then to St. Joseph's hospital.[45] In August 1916, Frank was interned in the Onondaga County Almshouse. His physical condition was marked as "very poor," and he was unable to perform any labor. He had tuberculosis and was also an alcoholic. His hospital internment card reads: "Habits: Intemp[erate]." It says his father, Martin Zumkeller, the Civil War veteran, had been intemperate as well. A few months later he was dead.[46]

40. 1905 New York State Census, City of Syracuse, Seventh Ward, District 107, Sheet 13.
41. Marriage notice in the *Syracuse Herald*, November 21, 1901.
42. Address also appears in 1908 directory.
43. "No Carrie Nations Here," *Syracuse Herald*, November 17, 1902.
44. Death notice of Emma Zumkeller, *Syracuse Herald*, January 17, 1904.
45. "Stabbed by men he attacked for assaulting wife," *Syracuse Herald*, January 10, 1915.
46. Census of Inmates in Almshouses and Poorhouses, 1875–1921, Series A1978, Reel A1978:157, Record Number: 7769, New York State Archives, Albany; Death notice in the *Syracuse Post-Standard*, October 18, 1916.

Naturally, events like these were not included in the great civic histories of Syracuse. Instances of alcoholism, domestic violence, petty theft, and assault among the poorest part of any society tend not to be given a place in its grand narratives. Stephen Therstrom, in his introduction to the *Harvard Encyclopedia of American Ethnic Groups*, warns that authors are often "eager to recount the achievements" of the communities about which they write, while the darker facts of life—disappointment, poverty, mental illness, along with others mentioned above—are frequently ignored. This was particularly the case in the period of "filiopietistic" writing about German America between the 1880s and World War I, most of which celebrates eminent German Americans and their public contributions.[47] In Syracuse, the narrative that the writers of the *Memorial History* and of the *Geschichte der Deutschen* wanted to convey was of a productive and successful German community that had contributed much to the making of a prosperous industrial city.

There was a view in Syracuse, and more widely held across America, that the Germans were a "model" immigrant group, in contrast to the Irish and, later, the Italians. Bruce, in his *Memorial History*, devotes an entire chapter to the Germans of Syracuse but does not do so for any other immigrant group. He begins it by saying, "It is a generally acknowledged fact that of the various nationalities of immigrants to this country, none surpass the Germans in all of the qualities of good citizenship." He lauds Germans for their "industry, frugality, honesty, and sobriety," calling them "a race of workers."[48]

Even German attitudes toward alcohol were often viewed as nonharmful or even exemplary. Although some temperance advocates took aim at German American brewers, particularly in a short period of anti-German hysteria during World War I, others looked to the Germans' beer and wine drinking as salubrious and "promotive of sociality," in contrast to the rum, brandy, and whiskey drinking preferred by Irish and American-born drinkers. The *New York Times* reported that Irish-born Americans in New York were arrested for drunkenness at rates far in excess of their German-born fellow immigrants.[49] Bruce reflects glowingly in his *Memorial History* on German festivities and convivial sociality, describing without a hint of disapproval the "old fashioned German saloons" of the Schwobenland neighborhood. By contrast, he describes the most degraded part of Syracuse as south of the Erie Canal, where few Germans lived. In the area around East Washington and Mulberry, he wrote, there were "drinking saloons, gambling dens, and houses of ill repute within a stone's throw in every direction."[50]

Some of the laudatory discourse about German Americans was intertwined with a form of racism, or racialism, that became increasingly prevalent in America, and in Europe, in the nineteenth and early twentieth centuries. Racial theorists in the 1850s propounded

---

47. Stephan Thernstrom, "Introduction," in *Harvard Encyclopedia of American Ethnic Groups*, ix; Tolzmann, "German-American Studies: History and Development," 281.
48. Bruce, *Memorial History*, 337.
49. "German-Americans and Drinking Habits," *New York Times*, May 3, 1871.
50. Bruce, *Memorial History*, 351, 528.

the inherent superiority of the Germanic and Nordic "races" over not only the native races of Asia, Africa, and the Americas but also the other "races" of Europeans. Germans were generally viewed as part of the same Germanic racial family as the English Anglo-Saxons. The widely read book *Races of Men* (1850) by the Scottish anatomist Robert Knox argued that the "pitiable state" of the Irish was not down to their Catholic religion (as other historians like Robert Macaulay had argued) but due to Celtic racial traits that compared unfavorably to those of Germanic whites.[51] Although Darwin himself did not advocate racial taxonomy in his *Origin of Species* (1859), others used his "survival of the fittest" argument to propose that the races that excelled did so because of an inherent superiority. Edward Z. Ripley's *Races of Europe* (1899) advanced the idea that the northern Germanic peoples were set apart from other European "races," such as southern European Italians, giving fuel to more strident racial theorists like Madison Grant. In *The Passing of the Great Race; or The Racial Basis of European History* (1916), Grant argued that in contrast to the earlier immigration of Germans, America was, in the early twentieth century, being infiltrated by "races drawn from the lowest stratum of the Mediterranean basin." Along with Poles and Slavs, it was a "human flotsam" that fill the nation's "jails, insane asylums and almshouses."[52]

The authors of the *Geschichte* and the *Memorial History* might or might not have been aware of these pseudoscientific theories of race, but the language of racial difference among immigrant groups was common in nineteenth and early twentieth-century discourse—even when it was not being used in an intentionally derogatory way. An 1897 article in the *Syracuse Journal* stated that the successful "immigrants from the northern races of Europe" were economical and thrifty in order to forward an argument for the establishment of Postal Savings Banks.[53] The *Syracuse Weekly Express* carried an article in 1887 about the "Italian Invasion" of America. The author described the growing "influx of the Italian race," and speculated about the way the "Latin element" might affect America's racial future, as he glanced at the "impoverished and ragged hordes" with their "dark-skinned faces."[54] In 1905, the *Journal* advertised a lecture by Professor Alexander Flick of Syracuse University (later the New York State historian) on the "Races of Europe" at the distinctly Anglo-Saxon Onaway Ladies' Club. Later lectures in the series focused on German

---

51. Robert Knox, *The Races of Men*, 2nd ed. (London: Henry Renshaw, 1862), 69. On wider racialist discourse see Silke Stroh, "Of Celts and Teutons: Racial Biology and Anti-Gaelic Discourse, ca. 1780–1860," in *Gaelic Scotland in the Colonial Imagination: Anglophone Writing from 1600 to 1900* (Evanston, IL: Northwestern University Press, 2017), 185–212. Kazal argues that among German Americans, racialist discourse was more prevalent among secular, middle-class groups, while German Catholics and Socialists tended to avoid speaking of a "German race" (*Becoming Old Stock*, 118–20).

52. Madison Grant, *The Passing of the Great Race; or The Racial Basis of European History*, 2nd ed. (1916; New York: Charles Scribner's Sons, 1919), 89–90.

53. "Postal Savings Banks," *Syracuse Journal*, December 28, 1897.

54. "An Italian Invasion," *Syracuse Weekly Press*, June 8, 1887.

culture, art, and education.[55] In *Memorial History*, Bruce lauds the German "Teutons," but the large ethnic Irish, Italians, Polish communities receive almost no attention.

Public discourse in Syracuse bears out the words of the historian John Higham—in America, up to World War I, "public opinion had come to accept the Germans as one of the most assimilable and reputable of immigrant groups. Repeatedly, older Americans praised them as law-abiding, speedily assimilated, and strongly patriotic."[56] The darker aspects of German Syracuse contrast with that narrative. The example of the Zumkellers, who mainly fell into the city's multicultural underclass, challenges the idea that German Syracuse was as homogenously successful as it is depicted in the *Geschichte* and the *Memorial History*. German Syracuse was in most ways typical of German neighborhoods in American cities. Each had their own Zumkeller-like families who struggled with similar forces and as a result have been forgotten, in contrast to the Germans who succeeded in America and whose history has been preserved. The significance of their story in German Syracuse, then, may be to awaken a memory of the thousands of German Americans who did not conform to the successful immigrant narrative and have been ignored within it.

Little remains of German Syracuse. As James Bergquist says of most of the once highly visible German enclaves in American cities, it is "now largely a matter of historical record." Its fate underscores Bergquist's argument that German enclaves were complex and changing structures—a "way station rather than a permanent home" in America—which were already in decline before the First World War delivered a final coup de grâce.[57] In the early twentieth century, successful Germans were moving out, and newly arrived immigrants, mainly non-German, were moving in. During World War I, many Germans changed their names or took other steps to identify themselves as American rather than as German Americans. The German neighborhood of Syracuse became its Little Italy, and now is home to new wave of immigrants: refugees from war-torn countries including Ethiopia and Somalia. Its Holy Trinity Church on Park Street, built by German Syracusans in 1904, has recently been converted into a mosque.[58]

All that remains to show that the area was once home to thousands of Germans is the Goethe and Schiller statue, erected in 1911 on a hilltop in Syracuse's North Side. From it—and from the civic histories of Syracuse in the English language as well as the German—one can extrapolate a story of an immigrant group that came to America, succeeded, and moved on. But digging deeper reveals that German life in the industrial city did not always conform to the narrative. It was far more complex than even its own historians let on.

---

55. "Onaway Club," *Syracuse Journal*, October 14, 1905.
56. John Higham, *Strangers in the Land: Patterns of American Nativism, 1860–1925* (New Brunswick: Rutgers University Press, 2002), 196.
57. Bergquist, "German Communities in American Cities," 10, 17 (quoted), 23. Kazal reaches a similar conclusion in his study of German Philadelphia, *Becoming Old Stock*.
58. "Plans to Turn a Church into a Mosque Bring Pain and Hope to Changing Neighborhood," Syracuse.com, April 6, 2014; "From Church to Mosque: Syracuse Islamic Group Cuts Crosses, Tries to Connect to Neighborhood," Syracuse.com, March 22, 2015.

Artifact NY
Marion Weeber's Flatware of the Future

Jennifer Lemak

For centuries, cutlery was made from mixtures of silver, gold, pewter, or other hard metals. Silver, often purchased by wealthier families was the most common material for flatware. As a result, "silverware" was the general term used for flatware whether it was made from silver or not. Prior to the mid-nineteenth century, spoons were the only utensil used at the dining table. Knives were treated as tools and were not to be used at the table. Forks were considered "coarse and ungraceful."[1] Matching flatware place settings became common in the mid-nineteenth century, around the same time the new technology of electroplating was developed. Electroplating, or silver-plating, is a process in which a thin coating of silver is chemically adhered to a cheaper metal item. The resulting "silverware" was almost indistinguishable from flatware made from silver.

Silver and silver-plated utensils remained the household norm well into the mid-twentieth century. However, new technologies were being developed. Stainless steel was first produced in Sheffield, England, in 1913 by Harry Brearley, a chemist and metallurgist working to improve armor plates.[2] By the 1920s, stainless steel was used for medical equipment and small tools, which soon transitioned into military uses and engines during World War II; but it was not until the 1960s and 1970s that the material made its way into household items such as flatware.

Industrial designer Marion Weeber took advantage of this new medium for flatware. Weeber's Classic Column tableware was promoted as the future in 1967 when it was selected for the U.S. Commission for Design Excellence at the International and Universal Exposition in Montreal, Canada. Used in the American Pavilion at the Exposition, this tableware was made of highly polished stainless steel and featured futuristic geometric shapes that were rooted in classical forms. The design promoted specific American ideas

---

1. Donald L. Fenimore, *The Knopf Collectors' Guides to American Antiques Silver and Pewter* (Knopf: New York, 1984).
2. Harold M. Cobb, *The History of Stainless Steel* (Materials Park, OH: ASM International, 2010).

CLASSIC COLUMN

Figure 1. Classic Column flatware designed by Marion Weeber, 1967. COURTESY OF THE NEW YORK STATE MUSEUM, ALBANY, H-1986.59.39.

to the world: precision, polish, and forward thought, with an elegant nod to its classical past. Weeber designed several flatware sets and tableware lines in stainless steel for EKCO Products International Company. Working with stainless steel allowed her unlimited design possibilities resulting in a durable and affordable end-product.[3]

Like her flatware designs, Marion Weeber was ahead of her time. Born in Albany, New York in 1905, she was the daughter of Christian Weeber, an automotive pioneer and aeronautical inventor. She attended the Art Students League of New York City and became a lifetime member. At the age of twenty-three, her father encouraged her to postpone her art studies and work with him in his Albany shop as an apprentice on a helicopter rescue craft. During this time with her father and until his death in 1932, Weeber learned how to create industrial designs by producing mechanical drawings and drafts and work with patent lawyers—skills she would employ for the rest of her career.[4] By the mid-1930s, Weeber returned to New York City to work for design and advertising firms, and by 1938, she started her own industrial design company, Marion Weeber, Inc., which lasted until the early 1990s.

3. The "Classic Column flatware 52-piece service for 8" retailed in 1967 for $60. Press release, EKCO Products International Company, New York, Chicago, Japan, 1967. New York State Museum, Albany, H-1986.59.
4. "Marion Weeber: Industrial Designer," *Antiques and the Arts Weekly*, March 6, 1998.

Figure 2. Marion Weeber models her tulip buttons and clip designs, ca. 1945. Polished silver plate with copper tulips. Designed for La Mode. COURTESY OF THE NEW YORK STATE MUSEUM, ALBANY, H-1986.59.40.

As an independent industrial designer and business owner, Weeber designed and pro-duced thousands of items—jewelry, buttons, scarves, housewares, kitchen items, lamps, and picture frames—that were sold in finer department stores.[5] Additionally, she patented dozens of her designs over her long career. In the last decade of her life and still thinking about the future, Weeber donated several of her designs and finished pieces to museums all over New York State—to the Metropolitan Museum of Art, the Cooper Hewitt Design Museum, the New York State Museum, and the Albany Institute of History & Art. Each

---

5. Marion Weeber Collection, Albany Institute of History & Art.

donation was accompanied by newspaper clippings, product press releases, production drawings, and information written on her business letterhead. When she passed away in 2000, her will also included instructions for the disposition of specific collections at these museums.[6] Weeber's business and design archive, which went to the Albany Institute of History & Art, depicts a prolific designer who was constantly pitching ideas to manufacturing companies around the globe and churning out the designs of tomorrow.

6. Marion Weeber will, January 13, 1993, New York State Museum, Albany, H-2000.39.

Teach NY
Engaging with the NYS Regents Exam's Civic Engagement Essay

Zachary Deibel

In January 2020, the New York State Education Department's (NYSED) Civic Readiness Task Force presented a series of recommendations to its Board of Regents. Formed two years prior as a committee of practitioners, scholars, state officials, and experts to enhance student engagement with civic education, the Task Force published a comprehensive curriculum that was to enable students to earn a "seal of civic readiness" on their high school diplomas. Since 2020, the Education Department has developed a variety of student project templates, teaching resources, and classroom materials that integrate civic agency into the daily academic explorations of students across the state. "Civic readiness," the Task Force's initiative states, "is the ability to make a positive difference in the public life of our communities through the combination of civic knowledge, skills and actions, mindsets, and experiences." By emphasizing the importance of civic understanding as an essential learning outcome, NYSED has asserted its prioritization of meaningful historical, political, and social studies education that students can apply in the context of their own communities.[1]

Importantly, the initiative focuses on equipping teachers with adequate preparation and training to implement such an expansive pursuit. While many of the projects, classroom activities, and other long-term programs provide space for innovation and adaptation, some of the initiative's elements are more directly applicable to the everyday classroom. In particular, assessment of student learning is a critical component in measuring civic development. As part of the redesigned Regents Examination in United States History, students are required to complete a "Civic Literacy Document-Based Essay." Combining civic readiness with academic historical practice, students explore a series of primary sources to develop a historically informed argument about a significant moment of public

---

1. "Civic Readiness Initiative," New York State Education Department, January 2020, accessed May 2022, http://www.nysed.gov/curriculum-instruction/civic-readiness-initiative.

engagement in American history. According to the state's framework, "The Civic Literacy Essay is designed to test a student's ability to work with historical documents within the context of constitutional and civic issues."[2] As a key component of the open-response portion of the exam, the Civic Literacy Essay serves to assess student understanding of pivotal moments in a particular and meaningful context. By integrating issues that relate students' knowledge to historically applicable situations into the state's culminating final assessment of American history, the Education Department has further solidified the importance of civic readiness to the learning outcomes of New York's high school students.

Teachers, then, will find themselves preparing students throughout the year for a sizable assessment that combines both civic understanding and historical knowledge—a daunting task that the state's educators are surely eager to pursue. In an effort to provide teachers with resources for classroom application, *New York History* has developed a lesson plan aligned to the outcomes of the Civic Readiness Task Force. The lesson plan engages students with primary source analysis, guides them through complex questions of historical inquiry, and prepares them to compose a well-crafted document-based essay. Using materials acquired from the New York State Archives and in conjunction with professionals at the NYSED, the following lesson offers students a unique study of the state's history and an opportunity to authentically apply the skills, test the standards, and assess the outcomes related to the Civic Readiness Initiative.[3]

In September 1935, New Yorkers were ready to celebrate. Six years into the worst economic depression in U.S. history, Americans witnessed some of the first results of New Deal initiatives within their communities—and New York was no exception. Since 1933, members of the Civilian Conservation Corps (CCC) spearheaded many diverse infrastructure and development projects. New dams, reservoirs, and renovations across the Empire State affirmed the New Deal's effort to rebuild and preserve the nation following the onset of the Great Depression. When state officials gathered in Lake Placid in 1935 to celebrated "Fifty Years of Conservation," the CCC occupied a central position in the honorifics alongside the organization's founder, the former governor of New York and first-term president of the United States Franklin Delano Roosevelt. Revving up for a critical campaign for reelection to the presidency in 1936, Roosevelt addressed the crowd, encouraging New Yorkers—and the nation—to stay the course of social and economic reconstruction: "The people in the last two years have become more and more conscious of the practical economic effect of what we are doing. They are becoming more and more conscious of the value to

---

2. "United States History and Government Framework," New York State Education Department, 2020, http://www.nysed.gov/state-assessment/united-states-history-and-government-framework.
3. Summarized and excerpted below, this article presents an analysis of the activity with samples of the sources used. The entire resource, which includes a student-facing activity packet and a teacher-facing guided lesson plan, can be found at https://www.cornellpress.cornell.edu/new-york-history/.

themselves—city dwellers and country dwellers—in protecting these great assets of nature that God has given us." The CCC not only preserved the natural resources that abounded in places like Lake Placid; it also sustained the economic well-being of a recovering nation.[4]

At its core, the New Deal constituted a massive civic engagement enterprise aimed to address an immediate and unprecedented national crisis. As Roosevelt commented in his 1935 address, "We have a long way to go." However, Roosevelt also underscored the usefulness of these initiatives in addressing problems that faced places like New York. "There is enough work in sight right in this State . . . to continue the work of the CCC camps for a whole generation to come."[5] As a result, national, state, and local governments coordinated massive efforts at economic expansion, while communities across the nation supplied labor, resources, and political capital to facilitate the most expansive government intervention program in American history. In New York, programs like the CCC and the Works Progress Administration (WPA) oversaw thousands of diverse infrastructure projects like the construction of the Loudonville Reservoir or the renovation of the Buffalo Zoo.[6] In the Susquehanna Valley, WPA workers could be found "improving school grounds . . . filling in roads . . . clearing out creek beds . . . and building rip-rap bulwarks against subsequent floods."[7] Workers also coordinated orchestral rehearsals at schools and community centers, led safety instructions at workplaces, led sewing projects, and founded nursery schools.[8] Murals became widespread across the state as the WPA employed artists and painters to beautify New Deal projects across the state. By the end of the decade, Roosevelt's prescription proved prescient: a whole generation of workers, citizens, and residents became integrated into the state's public rehabilitation.

However, issues of civic significance are rarely one-dimensional, and the New Deal was no exception. Despite the seemingly overwhelming support that Roosevelt's initiatives enjoyed during the 1930s, a closer look at a localized historic moment reveals that the debates surrounding New York's New Deal projects were often contentious, disputed, and contingent. Projects sometimes stalled amid rancorous political feuds, and Roosevelt's national strategies of court-packing and expansive government intervention raised the eyebrows—and objections—of conservative officials, politicians, and judges. Former secretary of the treasury Ogden Mills spoke out against the excessive spending associated with the New Deal, voicing Republican critiques that would persist throughout the period. Fellow Democrats also opposed certain dynamics of the plan. For example, in a baffling political development, former New York governor, presidential candidate, and avid reformer

---

4. Franklin Roosevelt, excerpts from his speech at the Fifty Years of Conservation in New York celebration (1935), New York State Museum Archive.

5. Roosevelt, excerpts from Fifty Years of Conservation in New York.

6. Benjamin J. Smith, "A WPA Epic: Loudonville Reservoir," Works Progress Administration (1937). "WPA in the Empire State," Works Progress Administration (1938).

7. "WPA in the Susquehanna Valley," Works Progress Administration, 1937.

8. "WPA in the Susquehanna Valley.".

Al Smith voiced heated criticisms of Roosevelt's New Deal. Conservative Democrats like Lewis Douglas, a former administration official, warned the public of the projects' excessive costs. New York senator Royal Copeland ran for both the Republican and Democratic nominations in the New York City Mayoral Race of 1937, largely on a platform of opposition to the New Deal and Roosevelt's court-packing proposal to preserve his policies from judicial review.

Other Democrats critiqued the plan for not going far enough to address larger social and political concerns. First Lady Eleanor Roosevelt pushed the administration to make public displays of support for civil rights and women's rights by hosting the world-renowned singer Marian Anderson to perform on the steps of the Lincoln Memorial.

Civil rights activists like A. Philip Randolph noted the ways the New Deal fell short of assisting some of society's most vulnerable groups. As the nation inched closer to war, liberal activists aimed to hold Roosevelt accountable for the program's oversights that limited opportunities for some Americans to engage in the civic project that constituted the New Deal. Thus, the New Deal presents a compelling lens for assessing civic dynamics of political action. As both a political project and a contested government action, the New Deal constituted a civic experiment that tested American willingness to participate in recovery from crisis, to deliberate on the proper role of government in addressing the needs of its citizens, and to petition the state for fairer treatment and progressive reform.

In assessing the New Deal as a historical, civic issue, the Civic Engagement Activity asks students to reflect on both the historical context of the New Deal in New York and the assigned three-part task: to describe the historical circumstances surrounding this civic issue, to explain efforts by individuals or groups to confront this constitutional or civic issue, and to discuss the extent to which these efforts were successful. Before engaging with the sources or outlining their essays, students should begin by reflecting on the directions with the instructor. By summarizing what they are being asked to do, students will then internalize the task at hand and begin considering the steps necessary to complete the assignment. Additionally, by summarizing their understanding of the directions, students will glean a clearer understanding of their essay's direction. Once students have discussed what they already know through a review of their background knowledge and thorough engagement with the directions, they can then begin engaging with the sources.

The documents of this activity present a series of events, publications, and debates that characterized the New Deal's development in New York. For each document, students can work with a partner or individually to identify three key elements of the source that could be relevant to the essay they will craft; they can then compose a brief response to the Analysis Question presented after each source. This activity can be done piecemeal, asking students to regroup and discuss their observations, or students can work through the source analysis phase on their own. The critical component of this portion of the activity is that students are engaging in deep analysis of the sources and identifying ways they might be able to integrate each source into their essay on the civic issues relevant to the history of the New Deal. The documents present a variety of perspectives. Roosevelt's speech to the 1935 Conservation in New York celebration, artwork commissioned by the WPA in the mid-1930s, promotional literature highlighting WPA projects in New York, and testimonies about the efficacy of the Loudonville Reservoir all attest to the multifaceted, dynamic, and expansive nature of the New Deal projects across New York. Additionally, a 1936 speech by Al Smith criticizing the New Deal's efforts in New York, a letter from A. Philip Randolph to Fiorello LaGuardia criticizing the lack of employment opportunities for African Americans, and Roosevelt's Executive Order 8066 that "ended discrimination in the employment of public workers in defense industries or government" demonstrate the contested nature of the New Deal's initiatives throughout the period. By engaging with these sources, students will begin to assess the extent to which Great Depression presented opportunities for public investment and civic discourse.

After exploring the sources and assessing the key points relevant to each document or image, students will then begin to collect the evidence they want to use to support their arguments in their responses to the essay prompt. They can begin by grouping documents according to themes.

For example, students might sort documents that demonstrate the programs' successes into one category, while relegating documents that illustrate the programs' shortcomings to another. Alternatively, students might group documents according to the civic impact of each initiative—focusing on assessing the New Deal's social, political, and economic impacts. Within small discussion groups or individually, students can group documents according to the ideas they want to argue related to the civic impact of the New Deal in New York. Once they have identified their main arguments around each group of documents, students can then craft a thesis that answers the prompt: "The New Deal presented significant civic issues in American history because . . ." This allows students to engage in historical argumentation, assessment of policy initiatives, and evaluation of civic institutions through analysis of primary sources.

Armed with a clear thesis, students can then proceed to outlining their essays. They should adopt a method of analysis that requires students to answer the prompt with a clear statement of argument, cite specific evidence and aspects of the sources to support their claim, and explanation of how the sources support the overarching argument—otherwise known as the "ACE" method. For each source, students can develop a brief summary of how they will incorporate the information into the larger argument using the template provided in the supplementary materials that accompany this article. Upon finalizing the outline, students can then compose their individual essays. After composition, students can either engage with an individualized reflection question or they can exchange papers with a partner and conduct a peer review of each other's essays. The instructor can facilitate a class discussion on both the historical content explored in the activity and the composition

Part 3 – Collecting the Evidence and Composing the Argument

Let's revisit the essay prompt. Recall that you've been tasked to read and analyze the documents. Then, using information from the documents and your knowledge of United States history, write an essay in which you:
- Describe the historical circumstances surrounding this civic issue.
- Explain efforts by individuals or groups to confront this civic issue concerning government's role in Americans' social and economic lives.
- Discuss the extent to which these efforts were successful.

You've reviewed the documents. Is there any way we can group the documents based on what information they provide?

Group	1	2	3
Documents			
Document Group Claim			

Figure 1. Document Analysis Guide. When students work through the lesson, they will have interactive guides built into the activity that allow them to engage further with the sources and to structure their argument. Here, students group documents according to the larger claim they aim to make in answering the essay prompt. Sample material courtesy of the author.

process to enhance students' engagement with the practice of refining written communication skills. As a final reflection exercise, teachers can ask students to consider the New Deal's relevance to our understanding of civic society in contemporary America. It may be difficult for students to imagine a time when such a massive civic undertaking became a national touchpoint. However, asking students to consider what aspects of the United States' past and present contribute to that disconnect might also encourage them to consider the dynamic meaning of civic engagement throughout the nation's history.

Part 5: Reflection & Revision

1. Place a check next to each item that your essay accomplishes.

    __ A clear thesis that answers the question

    __ Citation of specific evidence from two documents in Paragraph 1
    __ Analysis of how the evidence cited supports the claim

    __ Citation of specific evidence from two documents in Paragraph 2
    __ Analysis of how the evidence cited supports the claim

    __ Citation of specific evidence from two documents in Paragraph 3
    __ Analysis of how the evidence cited supports the claim

    __ Conclusion that offers contextualization, refutation, or concession

2. What is one aspect of your essay that you think is particularly strong?

3. If you could change one aspect of your essay, what would you change?

1. For your final reflection question, consider the New Deal within our contemporary political context. As you compare what you know about the New Deal as it existed in the 1930s, think about how it could (or could not) exist as a political project today. Here are some guiding questions:

    a. How does the legacy of the New Deal as a civic project inform your thinking about the role of government today?
    b. Would the New Deal be possible in today's civic climate? Why or why not?
    c. What might the political debate look like if a modern president proposed a program similar to the New Deal?

Figure 2. Student Reflection Activity. At the end of the lesson, students will be able to conduct individual or peer review of the essays composed. They will also be prompted to consider areas in which their work particularly exceeded expectations, and they will be asked to think about an aspect they might wish to improve for the next time. Finally, the reflection ends with a contextual consideration, asking students to consider the New Deal from a contemporary political perspective. SAMPLE MATERIAL COURTESY OF THE AUTHOR.

The New York Education Department's Civic Readiness Initiative is a profoundly worthwhile pursuit because it asks students to apply lessons from the past as a means of engaging with the ongoing project that is American democracy. No era exhibits a "more perfect" model for civic participation; the United States has always grappled with the complexities inherent in building a democratic society. Perhaps more than most, 1941 proved a trying year for Americans' civic resolve in this effort. By December of that year, the United States would be mobilizing for war against Nazi Germany and imperial Japan, and workers who had dug trenches in Loudonville or spearheaded industrial projects in Schenectady would either take up arms against the nation's enemies or convert businesses across New York to weapons production enterprises. In the months before Pearl Harbor, though, the nation had already begun arming its allies in the struggle against fascism. A. Philip Randolph, a prominent civil rights activist, petitioned New York City's mayor Fiorello LaGuardia to "address a delegation of Negro citizens who will march to the City Hall . . . [to petition] President Roosevelt to issue an executive order to abolish discrimination in all departments of the Federal Government and national defense." On behalf of African Americans across the country, Randolph demanded "equal opportunity" to access the federal employment in New Deal programs and wartime mobilization industries. Randolph further insisted that this demand be extended beyond the immediate needs of employment or income. As citizens, he maintained, African Americans were entitled to "equal opportunity to share in the benefits and responsibilities and duties and sacrifices incident to this great and tremendous national effort . . . to safeguard the cause of democracy."[9] Only a few generations prior, Randolph and other African Americans would have been denied citizenship and, in fact, many were still enslaved. Now, individuals who had suffered under the yoke of slavery and who endured ongoing segregation and second-class treatment, demanded the right to defend the "cause of democracy." A few weeks later, Franklin Roosevelt signed Executive Order 8066, which asserted, "there shall be no discrimination in the employment of workers in defense industries or government because of race, creed, color, or national origin."[10] Demanding the ability to defend an imperfect nation from calamity, Randolph and millions of Americans proved their civic readiness to repair, rehabilitate, and remake a democracy shaken to its core.

"United States History and Government Framework," New York State Education Department, 2020, http://www.nysed.gov/state-assessmentunited-states-history-and-government -framework.

---

9. A. Philip Randolph, Letter to New York City Mayor Fiorello LaGuardia, June 5, 1941, New York State Archives, Albany.
10. Franklin Roosevelt, Executive Order 8066, June 25, 1941, New York State Archives, Albany.

BOOK REVIEWS

New York's War of 1812: Politics, Society, and Combat

By Richard V. Barbuto. Norman: University of Oklahoma Press, 2021. 364 pages, 6" × 9", 10 b&w illus., 6 maps, 1 table. $39.95 cloth, $24.95 paperback, $32.95 e-book.

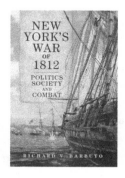

Richard Barbuto's *New York's War of 1812* presents a fascinating account of the military history of New York during the War of 1812 and can be considered the definitive work on the war. We needed a full-length account since we previously had only several regional studies, like Harry Landon's *Bugles on the Border: The Story of the War of 1812 in Northern New York*, Allan Everest's *The War of 1812 in the Champlain Valley*, or David Fitz-Enz's *Final Invasion: Plattsburgh, the War of 1812's Most Decisive Battle*. Richard V. Barbuto fills the need for a comprehensive analysis of the war's military events that has not been provided by any other historians. While the War of 1812, as Barbuto emphasizes, was New York's war, the state's government, unlike Maryland's, has done virtually nothing to commemorate these important historical events.

Governor Daniel Tompkins emerges during the war as the best wartime executive. Tompkins succeeded in mobilizing the manpower and resources of the state. He did his best to arm, equip, feed, and shelter the militia called up for service. Tompkins's leadership led to the successful fortification of the approaches to New York City, preventing a repeat of the British occupation of the city during the Revolution. Throughout the war, Tompkins marshaled the resources to send to the frontiers of the state. Barbuto criticizes President Madison and War Department leaders for repeatedly failing to adequately supply and provide effective leadership for the regulars and the militia. In addition, Barbuto blames the Federalists in 1812 and 1813 for their unwillingness to support the governor in his efforts to provide the necessary financial resources to sustain the war effort. An important point raised in this study is the need for cooperation between the state and federal governments to wage the war, and Barbuto gives Governor Tompkins high marks for his consistent actions to foster state-federal cooperation, which President Madison eventually recognized. Tompkins took the initiative because the federal government failed to do its part, crippling the ability of the governor to fully mobilize the state's resources. One of the strengths of

Barbuto's analysis is his emphasis of the relationship between the federal government and state leadership, an issue not necessarily stressed in other military histories of the war.

Barbuto evaluates the barriers to military success. Citing Lt. Joseph Hawley Dwight, Barbuto highlights one of the ongoing internal problems—the willingness of younger officers to fight and go on the offensive and the reluctance of senior officers "who appeared cautious to a fault" (135). This occurred during the failed 1812 Niagara campaign and in 1813, too; but this division within the ranks of both the regulars and the militia reappeared throughout the war. The reluctance of senior officers to lead demoralized troops contributed to the unwillingness of the soldiers to risk their lives when they had no faith in their senior officers, like General Smyth. Some of the officers of the regulars, like Smyth, detested the militia, and this prevented effective military cohesion in both offensive and defensive operations. If effective and heroic militia officers, like Jacob Brown and Peter Porter, led their men, the militia performed well. At the opposite end of the spectrum was Brig. Gen. George McClure, who "entered the annals of infamy" (177) by ordering the destruction of Newark, Canada, which led to the British retaliation along the Niagara Frontier. Barbuto also explores the problems of logistics, offering a careful and sophisticated analysis of the difficulties faced by the militia and the regulars, issues often underemphasized in other studies.

Divided into eighteen chapters covering every significant battle, raid, and military operation in the state, this study addresses every military campaign and all significant failures and successes. Six chapters concentrate on the Niagara Front, both in western New York and Canada; seven chapters focus on the North Country campaigns; and two chapters deal with the efforts to build fortifications around New York City. This study devotes one chapter each to background, preparation, and peace. Included in the text are several illustrations and maps, but more detailed maps would have been helpful in following the battles. Barbuto includes several accounts from individuals during the war, including those from average militiamen and from a forgotten female hero of the war, Betsy Doyle, a laundress in the First U.S. Artillery, who fired a six pounder at Fort Niagara during the fierce British cannonading from Fort George. When Fort Niagara fell to the British, Betsy took her four children and marched "320 miles across the state to Greenbush." (181).

Barbuto also looks at the off and on efforts to coordinate military and naval operations. Naval leadership on Lake Ontario gave priority to defeating the British naval forces based in Kingston and at times refused to support military operations by the regulars and militia, thus preventing the achievement of American military goals. Commodore Isaac Chauncey worked well with military forces during the 1813 campaigns, but in 1814 he refused to cooperate until his naval forces achieved superiority by defeating the British naval squadron under the command of Commodore Sir James Yeo. Because militia and regulars needed naval support for offensive operations, Chauncey thus crippled several American military plans in 1814.

Barbuto researched the major military records at the New York State Archives, the New York State Library, the Buffalo History Museum, and the National Archives as well as the resources at Brock University and the National Library in Canada and National Archives of the United Kingdom. These records provided the information Barbuto weaves into his compelling and majestic study of the war. Resources at the New-York Historical Society Museum and Library and at the New York Public Library might have added to the account of the economic and social impact of the war on New York City, since Raymond Mohl's *Poverty in New York, 1783–1825* mentions the devastating impact of the war on the poor of the city. Historians teaching classes on American military history, New York history, or the early national period will welcome Barbuto's work. Public libraries and historical societies should purchase *New York's War of 1812* since this study will appeal to both amateur historians and the general public.

Reviewed by Harvey Strum, Professor of History, Political Science, and Film at Russell Sage College. He is the author of "New York Militia and Opposition to the War of 1812," which appeared in New York History *in 2020, and "Impact of Foreign Policy on New York Politics, 1806–1815," which appeared in* Community College Humanities Review *in 2021.*

Palisades: The People's Park, 20th Anniversary Edition

By Robert O. Binnewies. New York: Fordham University Press, 2021. 424 pages, 6" × 9", 30 b&w illus. $150.00 cloth, $43.95 paperback, $38.99 e-book.

Fordham University Press has republished Robert O. Binnewies's comprehensive history of the many varied parks and natural areas that comprise the Palisades Interstate Parks near the New York–New Jersey border.

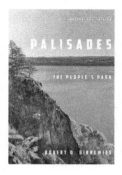

The Palisades Interstate Parks and its governing body, the Palisades Interstate Parks Commission (PIPC), are unique and creative land management entities that have had international influence on land conservation. In the early chapters, Binnewies tells the stories of the Rockefellers, the Harrimans, the Perkinses, and others with roles in preserving this land—a "who's who" of wealthy American families with conservationist legacies. Binnewies makes a strong case that the preservation of these natural areas, so close to New York City, influenced conservation strategies of the National Park Service.

Binnewies tasks himself with telling the whole story of these many parks: what was there before they were parks, how they were made into parks, and how they were managed.

This is a lot to bite off in one book. Because of that, the narrative is sometimes disjointed, and some chapters can be difficult to follow. There are just so many actors and Binnewies packs in so much information that the chronology can be confusing. For instance, he jumps from nineteenth-century preservation efforts to seventeenth-century background on the Revolutionary War, and then back to the twentieth-century preservation of Nyack Beach (all in a chapter titled "Welch," a man he does not introduce until the second-to-last page of that chapter).

This account is ultimately an insiders' account, since Binnewies led PIPC for many years. Binnewies is not a historian, which is evident when he makes big claims (for example, that the Storm King controversy was the foundation for modern environmental movement, and that PIPC parks set the precedent for the National Park Service) but fails to cite any secondary sources to contextualize his points.

But because Binnewies was an insider and the people who fought to protect these lands were some of the richest in New York City and the world, his account shines when he talks about the insider deals from the era when he was personally present. The "Minnewaska" and "Sterling Forest" chapters are especially good. These chapters can stand alone as case studies for historians of land management or for environmentalists thinking through how best to creatively protect land through partnerships.

The new edition lacks some of the illustrations of the first, but it has some textual updates. The most significant addition is a new chapter, "Honor and Electronics," about the creation of the National Purple Heart Hall of Honor in New Windsor, New York, and the fight against the LG towers in Englewood Cliffs, New Jersey.

When he wraps up the conclusion of the LG controversy, Binnewies wants to spin it like a victory, as PIPC did, and which follows the storyline of so much of PIPC's legacy. But in reading the paragraph on page 347 that discusses the resulting low-lying building and how employees can enjoy nature from it, I could not help but feel like he was employing the same rhetoric as that used by the Sterling Forest Corporation and against which the PIPC fought a hard battle. How much more ecosystem was disrupted to make way for this long, flat building, and was it more than would have been damaged if the towers had been built instead? This conflict ultimately gets to the question of what matters more: viewshed protection or ecosystem protection? But Binnewies does not really grapple with that issue. Would ending with a critical look at the outcome be a more effective call to action than pretending a huge office park built in a forest was a win for conservation and the environment?

That said, PIPC is a unique, interstate, quasi-governmental entity that has had many successes. In an era of environmental catastrophe, we need all the creative solutions we can find. Binnewies's book is a handbook for activists, an encyclopedia for people who love and enjoy these lands, and an ode to the wealthy families who have dedicated generations to protecting greenspace around New York City.

Reviewed by Jackie Gonzales, PhD. Gonzales is a historian with Historical Research Associates, Inc. (HRA), in Albany, New York. She has written numerous administrative histories and other history studies for the National Park Service (NPS). Before HRA, Jackie worked for the NPS at several different sites and at several environmental policy organizations in Albany.

Commemoration: The American Association for State and Local History Guide

Edited by Seth C. Bruggeman. New York: Rowman & Littlefield, 2017. 180 pages, 6" × 9⅔". $88.00 cloth, $41.00 paperback, $39.00 e-book.

Despite the fact that the COVID-19 pandemic has set planning back, the calendar continues to march toward 2026 and the 250th anniversary of the Declaration of Independence and the American Revolution. Planning is ramping up at the national level, where the America250 organization is coordinating efforts to establish state commissions or otherwise duly designated nonprofit partners in all fifty states. In New York, the state legislature unanimously passed legislation creating a 250th Commemoration Commission, and Governor Hochul signed it into law in December 2021. State agencies such as the Office of Cultural Education, the Office of Parks, Recreation and Historic Preservation, and the Empire State Development (I Love NY) are coordinating efforts with the state's National Park Service sites and Heritage Areas, while planning is also underway at the local and regional level. As such, now is an important time to consider the American Association of State and Local History's (AASLH) guidebook on facilitating a successful commemoration.

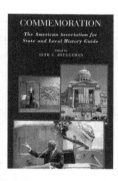

There is no doubt that the planning currently underway with relation to the 250th is being done at a time of great cultural and political conflict, and the history of the United States remains a focal point of contention. Ideas related to what, and whose, history is privileged both in educational curricula and at sites of public history remain hotly debated. Seth C. Bruggeman, the editor of the book, notes in his introductory essay that there remain many pitfalls in relation to the role of history in commemoration and that history and commemoration are not necessarily the same. "Unlike history, which is concerned primarily with circumstance," Bruggeman writes, "commemoration dwells almost entirely on feeling," which is why it can be both so powerful and so contentious" (1). Past commemorations erred on the side of feeling and, as such, relegated the complex and difficult aspects of history to the fine print, if mentioned at all.

We are presented today with the opportunity to do better. Bruggeman suggests that the way to do so is to introduce nuance into every part of the planning and programming for any type of historical commemoration. This can be done in a variety of ways, including understanding that any commemoration is a reflection not so much of the times it is commemorating, but of the times in which the commemoration is taking place. As such, commemorations should be, as Erika Doss suggests in her chapter "Commemoration, Conversation, and Public Feeling in America Today," "discursive—a kind of conversation, an act of speech or performance, a form of communication—that occurs when publics come together to remember, to honor, to celebrate, and/or to mourn people or events deemed significant, or exceptional, at particular moments" (137). Engaging with the public in the planning of the commemoration, rather than simply presenting a select committee's viewpoint, ensures that what is being prioritized within the context of the commemoration is informed by the current priorities of the community.

There is much of value in this book for current commemorative planners, whether working on the 250th or on another type of historical commemoration. Essays on festivals and their role in commemoration (William S. Walker), the complex and disputed role of reenactors and reenactments throughout the commemorative past (Cathy Stanton), and pieces that highlight the pitfalls and opportunities inherent in local (Anne C. Reilly), state-wide (Janet L. Gallimore), cross-border (Adam Hjorthén), diverse (Kenneth C. Turino), and difficult (George W. McDaniel) commemorations provide both cautionary tales and pragmatic guideposts for planners across genres. Jean-Pierre Morin, meanwhile, challenges us to consider how commemorations engage with the idea of the "Great Men" of history by outlining the political realities and missed opportunities in how Canada commemorated one of its "founders," Sir John A. Macdonald, during its 150th commemoration in 2017. By overfocusing on Macdonald as THE founder of Canada, the commemoration missed out on the opportunity to talk about other, lesser known but still important, players in the founding of the nation.

There is a lesson to learn in this failure, particularly in relation to the commemoration of the United States' 250th. There is perhaps a natural inclination for commemorations to focus on the positive aspects of a nation's founders without analyzing too closely their flaws, which can be seen as representative of overfocusing on the positive aspects of a nation's history while ignoring or downplaying its negative realties. With regard to the commemoration of the Declaration of Independence and American Revolution, there has long been a cult of personality surrounding the likes of George Washington, Thomas Jefferson, Benjamin Franklin, and Alexander Hamilton, among others, that portrays them as heroic figures. Past commemorations have emphasized this version of "founders chic" in a largely uncritical way. There is an opportunity today to examine these revolutionary leaders and to acknowledge both their accomplishments and their flaws, just as there is an opportunity to commemorate the many positive aspects of the founding of our nation and the subsequent struggle to realize its ideals while fully examining the negative impacts of the Revolution and who was harmed by it. By accepting this fuller and more accurate account of the nation's founding and founders, the 250th commemoration can remove mythology and replace it with history.

Reviewed by Devin R. Lander, New York State Historian, New York State Museum, Albany.

United University Professions: Pioneering in Higher Education Unionism

By Nuala McGann Drescher, William E. Scheuerman, and Ivan D. Steen. Albany: State University of New York Press, 2019. 307 pages, 6" × 9". $95.00 cloth, $33.95 paperback, $25.49 e-book.

Nuala McGann Drescher, William E. Scheuerman, and Ivan D. Steen have coauthored a seminal book in labor history by chronicling the countervailing forces that led to the emergence and growth of the largest higher education union in the nation— United University Professions (UUP). The coauthors' insights are especially credible given their respective roles as long-standing professors in the State University of New York system and as prominent union leaders of the UUP. Moreover, historiography provides little treatment of the union movement in higher education. The coauthors had exhaustive primary sources at their 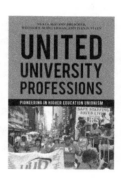 disposal, which they fully utilized to craft an extremely comprehensive history of the formation, growth, and maturation of UUP.

To understand the emergence of the union, it is critical to set the stage with the unique circumstances surrounding the formation of public higher education in New York State, which culminated with the creation of the State University of New York system (SUNY). The history of higher education is steeped in its support of New York's private institutions. In fact, New York used resources available through the Morrill Land Grant Act (1862) to establish Cornell University. Normal schools (teachers colleges) were scattered across the state with the mission to train teachers. Up until the post–World War II era, matriculation into private institutions was the only other viable option for postsecondary education in New York State. With the advent of the GI Bill, the state was forced to establish a statewide public higher education system to accommodate the burgeoning enrollment of soldiers returning from the war. In 1947, President Truman called for the expansion of higher education with greater access for socioeconomically disadvantaged populations. With his own presidential aspirations, Governor Thomas Dewey wasted no time responding by signing the bill in 1948 that established SUNY. With thirty-two institutions, which included the teachers colleges, it was clear that the private schools were still sacrosanct. Indeed, funding continued to pour into the state's private institutions. The mission of the public system was simply to complement not to replace the state's private institutions.

In 1957, Governor Nelson Rockefeller changed the entire complexion of public higher education in New York State with his vision for SUNY. His administration poured billions into SUNY's infrastructure and the "Higher Education Act of 1961 provided the legal framework for SUNY's emergence as a giant public university" (10). By 1970, SUNY boasted an enrollment of 300,000 students. While governance for SUNY switched from Regents to Trustees, local campus presidents wielded tremendous, unilateral control and power over individual campuses and salaries; they also served as the final arbiters of grievances. As one can imagine, the size and complexity of SUNY naturally resulted in an escalation of grievances. Moreover, nonteaching professionals (NTPs) had no job security, much less any leverage over workload issues, a real problem that would not be resolved for some time. Disparities also existed in the salaries for women. "Growth brought bureaucratization," and SUNY quickly became a managed, paternalistic university system (25). These circumstances combined with and end of SUNY growth and shrinking state budgets created the perfect storm for unionization.

The Taylor Law in 1967 (Public Employees Fair Employment Act) provided the enabling legislation for SUNY to unionize with the Public Employment Relations Board (PERB) serving as the administrative agency charged with administering the collective bargaining statutes. Despite the abhorrence to the notion of being associated with blue-collar workers and trade unionists, faculty and NTPs had no choice but to find a mechanism through which to voice and exert a measure of control over their own professional destinies. Professional organizations quickly moved into the fray to earn the right to represent SUNY faculty and NTPs. Throughout the SUNY system, there were pockets of allegiances to the more prominent national organizations like the National Education Association (NEA), the American Association of University Professors (AAUP) and the American Federation of Teachers (AFT/AFL-CIO) through the State University Federation of Teachers (SUFT). NTPs were loyal to the State University Professional Association (SUPA). Of course, the Faculty Senate and the Faculty Association of the State University of New York (FASCUY) were very active in vying to represent SUNY faculty and NTPs. The Civil Service Employees Association (CSEA), an affiliate with the American Federation of State, County and Municipal Employees (AFSCME), an AFL-CIO affiliate, also became a player as representation activity increased leading to collective bargaining unit determination.

All these organizations had ideological differences toward unionism. Moreover, there were issues with representing both professors and NTPs and questions about whether there would be multiple bargaining units or a single unit. The University Medical Centers and NTPs wanted to split from the very beginning. Amid this labyrinth of differences among these organizations, the Senate Professional Association (SPA) emerged from a merger of the Faculty Senate and the SUPA as a pragmatic solution to stave-off pure trade unionism and to preserve the idyllic integrity of its knowledge workers as well as represent the NTPs under the umbrella of one organization. The PERB ruled that a single bargaining unit would represent SUNY faculty and NTPs, and SPA won the certification election on January 29, 1971. "SUNY faculty and professionals were the last state employees to enter collective bargaining after the passage of the Taylor Law" (35). Despite the initial success, SPA was ill-equipped in terms of the resources and expertise needed to engage in collective bargaining, much less to address the diverse needs of a university system that consisted of 15,000 faculty and NTPs from twenty-six campuses that included teachers colleges, agricultural and technical colleges, and university and medical centers. The SPA negotiated its first contract in August 1971 with resources and support through its affiliation with the NEA. The contract provided a 9 percent salary increase through 1973, "guaranteed academic freedom," arbitration procedures, and job security for NTPs (59). While SPA's leadership was delighted with the results, not all constituents shared that sentiment, given the loss of longevity. Shortly thereafter, SPA changed its name to SUNY/United then United University Professions (UUP) in 1973 after its merger with SUFT. Lawrence DeLucia (SUNY Oswego) became UUPs first president, succeeding Robert Granger, SPA's first president. It quickly became apparent "that in merger there would be survival" (73).

As soon as the first contract and its corresponding salary reopeners (mutual agreement to revisit salaries) ended, it was time to begin anew, a recurring theme throughout UUP's history. DeLucia served only one term amid efforts to impeach him. Samuel Wakshull (College at Buffalo) was elected in 1975 to serve as UUP's president. Initially, UUP's office—which consisted of Wakshull and Evelyn Hartman—was hit with state fiscal shortfalls, retrenchment, representation challenges, competition for state funding from the private institutions, and internal conflict. Wakshull and Hartman stood strong and moved UUP forward. Union membership and advocating for SUNY were the priorities. Legislation in 1977 provided secure resources through an agency fee (union dues). Membership increased, lobbying, and picketing through the SAVE SUNY campaign resulted in legislative budget restorations, a fourth rank for librarians was established, and a definition of retrenchment (notification) was included in the contract ratified in 1977. Despite some criticism regarding the contracts negotiated during UUP's first eight years, UUP's membership overwhelmingly voted to keep the union as its bargaining agent and supported the contracts with ratification percentages that ranged from 69 to 93.2 percent. With salary increases in the contracts, rank and file membership clearly voted their pocketbooks.

The early 1980s ushered in Nuala McGann Drescher's (College at Buffalo) presidency, boasting a membership of 13,000. Challenges included ongoing "philosophical differences" between the United and Reform caucuses within UUP, but the "evenly split" delegates between the two caucuses promoted cooperation (109). The United Caucus focused on "bread-and-butter" unionism, whereas the Reform Caucus "saw itself as the more democratic and idealistic element in the organization, committed to using the union's power to uphold social ideals of reform and change" and "check the establishment" (110). The United

Caucus "was by no means opposed to supporting broader social-justice issues," when such initiatives "were in harmony with the basic agenda" of "promoting the welfare" of its members, "collectively and individually, through contract negotiations and enforcement to advance that welfare" (109).

The impact of Reaganomics during Drescher's tenure led to the closure of SUNY's demonstration schools (K12), and Governor Mario Cuomo's proposed budget cuts were so deep that UUP reignited the SAVE SUNY campaign, which resulted in campus demonstrations (picketing) and lobbying by members as well as by thousands of students. President Drescher was a master tactician and enlisted the support of SUNY's trustees and chancellor, who had historically been somewhat passive advocates for funding. She also enjoyed greater cooperation from the Governor's Office of Employee Relations (GOER). John "Tim" Reilly (SUNY Albany) would succeed her on May 2, 1987, and inherit many victories that helped propel the union forward that included a workload agreement, professional development resources, a disparity fund, a tax shelter, successful adjudication of grievances, affirmative action initiatives, an AIDS committee, and the (federal) Pepper Bill, which negated the mandatory retirement at age seventy. Drescher's administration also won job equity for NTPs, an Employee Assistance Program (EAP), two full-time vice presidents, health insurance through the Empire Plan, and greater labor-management cooperation, which in part led to the restoration of SUNY's budgets and contracts with salary increases during her presidency.

For President Reilly, the priority included ramping-up legislative and political activities to positively impact salaries, benefits, and working conditions. The contracts negotiated saw increases for 1988–91 and 1991–95. Health insurance for part-timers with a two-course criterion was a major victory, as was the elimination of the mandatory retirement age of seventy. The state increased its contribution to the UUP Benefit Fund by 43 percent. Funding was increased for affirmative action and daycare. Unfortunately, the state's fiscal shortfalls during this same period and Governor Cuomo's subsequent cuts to SUNY could not be restored, and retrenchments followed on many campuses. UUP and the New York State United Teachers (NYSUT), UUP's long-standing K12 affiliate, rallied its members, lobbied, and picketed, but it was all to no avail. When the governor released his 1992 budget for SUNY—although a $50.5 million increase over the preceding year—it was noted that SUNY's state allocation was at an all-time low of 34 percent. During these tumultuous fiscal periods, SUNY was saved by UUP's legislative and political activism. User fees for certain campus services, natural personnel attrition, state tax hikes and, ultimately, tuition increases helped offset the cuts, and UUP's effective legislative campaigns motivated the legislature to restore the SUNY budget in numerous instances. These contractual and financial battles took their toll on the union and depleted its treasury. Moving forward into the 1990s, William Scheuerman—who had served as UUP's chief negotiator—would quickly return UUP to financial solvency, but like his predecessors, he would have to lead them through a myriad of financial challenges and help the union adapt to the realities of shrinking state resources, more part-time faculty, fiscally conservative political leadership, and trustees who were not interested in supporting SUNY's growth.

Thanks to an elimination of term limits for UUP officers (2001), William Scheuerman (SUNY Oswego) served as UUP's president through 2007. He was also the Reform Caucus's nominee, which signaled a capstone in the evolving unity of the union, one that had been fostered by Scheuerman's predecessors through cross-caucus appointments and increased social and political activism. President Scheuerman's honeymoon was short-lived, however, when he faced the exigencies of Governor George Pataki's budget cuts, threats of downsizing, support for outsourcing, and trustees who supported neither SUNY nor UUP and instead promoted privatizing SUNY, and a state that coveted the millions of dollars generated by the University Medical Centers through the Clinical Practice Plans that UUP had fought to establish in the early 1970s.

During Schererman's tenure, UUP's membership grew to 27,000. Scheuerman's longevity, his role at the national level as an AFT committee member, and his effective leadership and commitment to legislative action equaled credibility that resulted in the union wielding tremendous influence. The UUP's voluntary member contributions steadily increased to support pro–public education and pro-labor candidates through NYSUT's nonpartisan political action committee VOTE-COPE (Voice of Teachers in Education). The 1999 contract provided a 19.83 percent increase in salaries with a 96.15 percent approval of the membership. It was the only union to provide health insurance coverage for part-timers during the summer months. Highlighting UUP's political acumen, Scheuerman shared with delegates at the Winter 2000 Assembly that "chancellor Robert King, the former director of the Division of Budget [state], conceded that any plan SUNY would bring to the legislature without clearing it with UUP was dead on arrival" (200). There was also much greater cooperation from the Faculty Senate. Academicians who viewed the union as their bête noir, were now cooperating and supporting UUP, including SUNY's provost Peter Salins. The good rapport and collaboration continued with Scheuerman and Chancellor John Ryan, which led SUNY trustee Candace deRussy to remark that Ryan was in the "back pocket of the big union" (227).

The UUP had matured during Scheuerman's tenure. He stepped aside in 2007 to pursue other professional interests and Phillip Smith (Upstate Medical University, Syracuse), the former vice president for academics, was elected to serve as UUP's next president. His presidency can best be characterized as abysmal, according to the authors. Smith's administration faced the state's financial crisis in 2008 that was projected to be a $10 billion deficit by 2010. By Smith's own admission, the 2011–16 contract negotiated under his watch was "the worst contract in UUP history" (250). When his constituents needed him the most to fight against SUNY cuts, he and other UUP officers were at a conference in Hawaii. In 2013, Fred Kowal (SUNY Cobleskill) stepped into the presidency and began the process of restoring UUP to its rightful place as the largest and most powerful higher education union in the nation that grew from 3,500 in 1973 to 35,000 members at sixty-four campuses with an enrollment of 193,824 in 2018–19.

The story and journey of UUP can best be characterized as an authentic grassroots movement, conceived and propagated by its own leaders, faculty, and professional staff who recognized the need for collective action and were willing to make the sacrifices to preserve their self-determination. The postwar era ushered in this new breed of academic unionists who became professional unionists amid the backdrop of the social and political movements of the 1960s and 1970s, and "the changing economic realities and declining political support for higher education," (29). "Austerity budgets endowed collective bargaining with added appeal" (30). For nearly fifty years, UUP grew its base membership and strengthened its relationships and coalitions with affiliate unions and political leaders. UUP has always fought to preserve academic freedom and negotiated contracts that included salary increases and enhanced membership benefits and working conditions. UUP has been the single, most powerful advocate for SUNY, which has prevented massive retrenchments and campus closings over the years. Despite its successes, fiscal challenges continue, and SUNY has also faced declining enrollment over the past decade. In 2018, in the "case of *Janus v. American Federation of State, County and Municipal Employees*," only those who join the union are required to pay the agency fee. As a result of the Janus ruling, "UUP's reaction to a negative decision will now determine its future well-being and, more importantly, that of almost 40,000 members of the SUNY family that UUP represents" (250).

Reviewed by Will Kayatin. Kayatin holds a PhD from the State University of New York, University at Albany. His dissertation, "Higher Education Unions and Social Responsibility: UUP's Response to Social and Political Change in New York State, 1973–1993," was completed in 2004. He is currently and Educational Consultant for Transition and Higher Education at the Kentucky Valley Educational Cooperative. He is the author (with Joseph "Rocky" Wallace and Joe Blackbourn) of Rise$_2$ to Deeper Learning, Model: Real World Innovations = Systemic Enduring Engagement (2020), Equity and Access Pre K-12, accessed September 19, 2022, https://ace-ed.org/wp-content/uploads/2020/06/RISE-2-Deeper -Learning-2.pdf

Rescue Board: The Untold Story of America's Efforts to Save the Jews of Europe

By Rebecca Erbelding. New York: Anchor Books, 2018. 400 pages, 5 ³⁄₁₆" × 8", 19 b&w illus. $17.00 paperback; $12.99 e-book.

In *Rescue Board: The Untold Story of American Efforts to Save the Jews of Europe*, Rebecca Erbelding, a historian and archivist at the United States Holocaust Memorial and Museum (USHMM), provides the first book-length treatment of the War Rescue Board (WRB), the government agency created by President Franklin Roosevelt in 1944 to attempt to rescue European Jews from Nazi extermination. In this book, Erbelding seeks to address a divide in the historiography that has existed for nearly a half century. She argues that historians have staked out two camps regarding American inaction between 1939 and 1945 toward the Holocaust.  The first camp argues that possibilities for wartime rescue were extremely limited, particularly in the context of an isolationist and oftentimes anti-Semitic American society. The second camp, led by the late David Wyman, have countered that much more could have been done to save the Jews and who see such contextualization as excuses that pardon inaction (285). In her focus on the WRB, Erbelding argues that both schools have treated America's most significant effort toward rescue as an aberrant afterthought, "the one bright spot, however 'little and late'" (285).

In many respects, Erbelding sides with the former school of thought, asserting that "people who point to the 1930s and 1940s with outrage that the United States did not do more to save the Jews of Europe neglect the context of the period" (273). She points to the pervasiveness of racism and anti-Semitism in the United States, the crippling effects of the Great Depression, and the grip of isolationism on a large swath of the American population. Erbelding argues that "No one knew the word 'genocide' until 1944" (273) and that few contemporaries could have imagined the evolution of Nazi persecution of the Jews from the 1930s to the mass extermination of the Final Solution during the war. She convincingly shows that the nation's struggles to intervene or prevent genocide in the intervening decades—when the shadow of the Holocaust loomed in American consciousness—should give at least some historians pause in their willingness to condemn American inaction. While not pulling punches over Americans' antipathy and inaction toward the plight of Europe's Jews during World War II, Erbelding instead offers a nuanced examination of the lone example of America's determination to act. The War Refugee Board, as the author points out, remains "the only time in American history that the U.S. government founded a government agency to save the lives of non-Americans," (273), and that the WRB's "importance is in its sheer existence and its actions, not in pithy summaries of quantifiable 'results'" (277).

Throughout *Rescue Board*, Breckinridge Long and other obstructionist and, often-times, anti-Semitic officials within the U.S. State Department emerge as the antagonists to the noble efforts of John Pehle and the WRB. In presenting the context in this manner, Erbelding can be faulted for treating the failures of inaction on the part of President Roosevelt too lightly. On more than one occasion, FDR's caution or lack of action is summarily dismissed as the consequence of election year politics. These failings have been debated in several histories of the subject, and Erbelding in no way lets Roosevelt completely off the hook for his decisions, so this is but a minor criticism of the importance of the larger work.

The book is structured around twenty-one short chapters, often only 10 to 12 pages each. In this format, Erbelding's ability to craft her narrative into a compelling story truly shines. In fact, the fast pace of the narrative at times resulted in somewhat abrupt transitions where, as a reader, one is so engrossed in the story Erbelding is telling that one almost feels deflated as yet another WRB effort falls short, and a new chapter begins. It is hardly a criticism that Erbelding's ability to draw her readers into a gripping story occasionally runs afoul of the fact that the actual history being told is frequently so heartbreakingly unsatisfying.

The first six chapters examine the struggle to create the War Refugee Board amid State Department obstruction and willful inaction. Chapters 7 to 19 explore numerous rescue efforts pursued by the WRB. In these chapters, Erbelding highlights the challenges to analyzing the success of the Refugee Board. Quantifying the numbers of Jews rescued in any given effort is oftentimes nearly impossible. In many instances, the WRB succeeded simply by ensuring that bureaucratic hurdles to operations by other, nongovernmental relief organizations did not impede rescue efforts (77). In describing the WRB's efforts to save Jews, Erbelding writes, "none of it was certain. All was intangible; all were guesses." What John Pehle and the staff of the WRB sought to do was to promise "that the War Refugee Board was trying everything" (129). The book's final chapters follow the war's final days as WRB tackled its largest bureaucratic and logistic challenges in delivering aid packages to survivors in Nazi concentration camps as Allied armies closed in. Erbelding also provides a tantalizing glimpse at the efforts of Florence Hodel, the only female on the Board's executive staff and "the only WRB staff member whose work spanned the entirety of the board's existence" (236).

The book evolved from Erbelding's doctoral thesis, and her notes on sources provides a wonderful glimpse into her exciting dive into unmined archival sources at the USHMM, the FDR Presidential Library in Hyde Park, New York, and other repositories to flesh out this heretofore untold story. Her research endeavors, many of which have been provided to the FDR Library, provide future scholars with a building block with which to continue to explore this fascinating period in American and world history, a time in which the forces of government action and inaction waged a tumultuous battle that, in many respects, redefined America's role in the post–World War II world. Erbelding is to be commended for crafting a thoroughly engaging and fast-paced narrative history of the WRB and America's most ardent effort to save Europe's Jews from the Holocaust.

Rescue Board offers a lot to engage scholars of New York history because many of the most prominent figures, from Franklin Roosevelt and Henry Morgenthau to Stephen Wise, Samuel Dickstein, Emmanuel Celler, Donald O'Toole, Robert Wagner, Ira Hirschmann, and *New York Post* columnist Samuel Grafton all hailed from the Empire State. The efforts of many of the Jewish relief organizations in the book were headquartered in New York City, and the story of the 982 refugees brought to Oswego, New York, in August 1944 also feature prominently in the book. The book should engage scholars of the Holocaust and of U.S. immigration and political history. Thanks to Erbelding's compelling storytelling, the book should also prove appealing to undergraduates and a more general readership.

Reviewed by Aaron Noble. Noble is Senior Historian for Political, Military, and Governmental History at the New York State Museum in Albany.

A Traitor to His Species: Henry Bergh and the Birth of the Animal Rights Movement

By Ernest Freeberg. New York: Basic Books, 2020. 336 pages, 6" × 9". $30.00 cloth, $17.99 e-book.

Ernest Freeberg has produced a splendid study of the nascent animal rights movement in Gilded Age America, centered on that movement's most recognizable and polarizing figure: ASPCA founding president Henry Bergh. While the book offers gripping accounts of pivotal episodes throughout Bergh's public life, it is not a biography; rather, Freeberg's exploration of Henry Bergh's career is a vehicle for interrogating broader trends in industrial America, uncovering surprising histories of the centrality of animals to the Gilded Age city, and inviting profound philosophical reflection. This carefully crafted, wonderfully readable work is 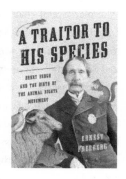 bursting with fascinating anecdotes and poignant insights, all animated by masterful storytelling. *A Traitor to His Species* is a magnificent achievement that will inform, surprise, entertain, and challenge anyone interested in Gilded Age America or curious about the complex relationships between people and animals.

It is easy for modern city-dwellers to forget the timeless, "ubiquitous and seemingly inevitable" role of animals in urban life through most of human history. Freeberg reminds us that as cities grew in the nineteenth-century United States, so too did urban Americans' reliance on animals "for energy and food, companionship and entertainment" (2). At that moment, some Americans began pondering the ethical dilemmas of anthrozoological relations and sought "to untangle animal rights from human privileges" (8). While a dramatic shift in the role of animals in Gilded Age society was thus "provoked by technological revolution," it was "mediated by men and women who organized for the first time to protect animals from the worst abuses of human exploitation" (3). In all of this, New York State took the national lead, incorporating the American Society for the Prevention of Cruelty to Animals in the spring of 1866 and then swiftly passing a trailblazing anti-cruelty statute—enforceable by ASPCA agents with police powers—that "became a model for similar legislation across the country" (4). Henry Bergh, the dynamic figure behind the law and founding president of the ASPCA, immediately emerged as "the highest lightning rod in every stormy clash over animal rights" (5). While centered on Bergh's influential and controversial career, this compelling study transcends its main character to furnish fascinating insights and nuanced analyses of a diverse array of issues arising from the countless roles of animals in Gilded Age life.

One of the many commendable features of this book is its structure. A series of thematic chapters are arranged around a specific controversy, allowing the author to use each example to build multiple stories at once: the centrality of animals to urban life; the often spectacularly brutal results of human use of animals in an industrial metropolis; the response to such abuses by a growing anti-cruelty movement; the place of Henry Bergh as the recognized leader of this movement; and the evolving relationship between activists, industry, the state, and the public, when it came to moderating cruelty and modifying social attitudes.

From the perspective of content alone, these chapters are delightfully informative. For example, several chapters remind readers that Gilded Age New York was very much an equestrian city. Yet these "vital partners in building the Gilded Age city" were "pushed to the limits of their strength by the demands of a rapidly growing industrial economy," and so "many became interchangeable parts, worked intensely and therefore briefly, recycled in just a few years to the market for broken horses or the rendering plant" (52). From the eleven thousand horses pulling New York's streetcars in the late 1860s to the aging horses of the city's impoverished hawkers or carters, the "brutal excess" involved in coercing these animals across the metropolis "was a common and demoralizing sight on city streets" (47, 48, 52). Although Bergh and his agents routinely monitored and occasionally arrested working-class teamsters, and although the aristocratic Bergh condescendingly lectured Irish immigrant drivers, the plot became more complicated when Bergh's "struggle to end horse-car abuse soon led him to agree that the real culprits were ... ultimately, the wealthy corporate owners and their stockholders" (53). Thus does Freeberg's exploration of the brutalities involved in the horse-drawn city reveal a fresh angle on Gilded Age class privileges: "Feeling patronized by Vanderbilt and the other railroad owners who voiced their support but took no action, Henry Bergh, the snob and nativist, felt the burn of class-conscious anger," denouncing corporate tycoons as "the real criminals" by 1868 (55).

Another fascinating horse-centric chapter explores the 1872 virus that ravaged the nation's horse and mule population. Titled "America's First Energy Crisis," this chapter is one of several that could easily be incorporated into an undergraduate course on Gilded Age America, and it reveals the centrality of horses to the nineteenth-century economy. As the disease swept from city to city and as veterinarians and editorialists debated an endless array of proposed names and cures for the mysterious epizootic, urban transit networks ground to a halt; the coal supply dwindled; canal traffic stalled; harvests were "significantly disrupted"; food rotted on docks; ox teams, goats, donkeys, dogs, or manpower were employed by flailing businesses; and cities were left prone to catastrophic fires for lack of horses to pull fire engines (91–103). While providing such fascinating historical insights, Freeberg does not stray from his central theme, for "the epidemic forced many Americans to notice that these engines of commerce were, in fact, suffering creatures" (104). While Bergh called on Americans to recognize the "'moral as well as material aspect' to the crisis," the great lesson for the public was ultimately not humans' debt to their equine partners, but rather that "the city was far too dependent on the health of horses" (105, 108). Horsepower would remain preeminent for decades more, but the search for alternatives was on. In the meantime, Bergh and his associates sought to make city life more humane for horses—monitoring overloaded streetcars, lobbying for improved pavements, and constructing ornate stone watering troughs at major intersections in cities nationwide (114).

These are but two examples of Freeberg's highly effective narrative approach. Other chapters contend with Bergh's battle to ban blood sports in New York among the working-class immigrants who attended dog fights and ratting contests in the bloody pits of Kit Burns' Sportsman's Hall (a victory for Bergh that drew the ire of Tammany and led to a movement in Albany that nearly stripped the ASPCA of its power to prosecute) as well as among "genteel ruffians" like the publisher James Gordon Bennet Jr., who enjoyed congregating with fellow aristocrats for ostentatious trap-shooting tournaments, including an 1881 "Coney Island pigeon massacre" that obliterated more than sixteen thousand birds in a single weekend, when "feathers of dead birds covered the Brighton Beach shooting ground 'like snow' " (175–76). These chapters again allow Freeberg to cast a critical light on the imbalances of class and power in Gilded Age New York while maintaining a clear focus on how such inequalities affected animal rights and informed responses to human cruelty.

Another chapter explores both the rise of the pet shop trade and the violent and brutal responses to the summerly "hydrophobia" scares that left terrified city-dwellers fearful of dog bites and led New York to offer bounties to children and street toughs to slaughter "ungoverned" dogs in an annual extermination campaign (194). This hysterical violence collided with growing pet ownership in New York (where the first Westminster Kennel Club show was held in 1877 with opening remarks from Henry Bergh), as well as with Bergh and the ASPCA's protests against the spectacle of this annual street slaughter; these contradictory forces led to licensing laws and professional city dog-catchers in 1877. This meant the institutionalization of pet ownership but also of dog-killing—in New York, where Bergh promoted a "humane" death by drowning; or in Philadelphia, where genteel women calling for merciful treatment became advocates of the gas chamber (207).

Freeberg's analysis of this "War on Dogs" is another shining example of the author's nuanced presentation. Activists repeatedly argued that one reason to prevent cruelty was to develop empathy among humans, especially children, contending that constant exposure to violence against animals could, in fact, cultivate sinful tendencies among people. Yet Bergh and his allies also understood that "the surest path to rousing the public's sympathy for the plight of animals was to have them see the suffering for themselves" (159). Thus, one paradox of relative success: at the very moment when human reliance on companionship, power, and protein from animals was made more acute and more visible by the dynamism of the Gilded Age city, the earliest American anti-cruelty advocates were laboring to make the suffering involved in such relationships less visible to the metropolitan populous. When it came to stray dogs, the battle against public bounties and brutal street killings led to urban shelters and "methods of merciful killing"; the "removal of this dog-killing process from public view" effectively "*sheltered* the public from the harsh reality that this could only be accomplished by every year putting many thousands of dogs to death" (210–11). Likewise with meat: SPCAs had protested both the long train rides of live cattle and the violent urban spectacle involved in droving these animals to local slaughterhouses. Such excesses were moderated not so much out of compassion but out of corporate innovations (centralized meat processing and distribution in refrigerated rail cars). Anti-cruelty activists hailed this as an improvement, but therein lay another paradox: while "the new dressed meat corporations reduced some of the worst excesses of livestock suffering," the "brutal nature of this business" was "reduced, but never eliminated"; what had unquestionably changed, however, was that "the bellowing and blood of the stockyard and slaughterhouse" were "an increasingly distant abstraction," so that "for American meat eaters, the benefits of cheap beef became obvious, while the suffering inherent in the system became obscure" (158–59).

Each of these stories reveals much about the Gilded Age city and is tied elegantly back to the author's overarching analytical framework. Others are just as fascinating—chapter 13 on Bergh's battle with operators on the Erie Canal will be of particular interest to readers of this journal. With all this rich storytelling, the work is also deeply analytical and philosophically stimulating—it asks profound questions about ethics, expertise, the role of the state, class privilege, the humanity of the marginalized, and of course, animal rights. Moreover, it addresses these issues while revealing the history of numerous systems and concepts that contemporary readers likely take for granted—for example, noting that "worrying about our obligations to other species" seems like "a very modern development" (5).

Simultaneously, Freeberg never loses touch with his protagonist. He states, from the opening, that "no person in nineteenth-century America pushed the bounds of this public debate over animal rights as far as Henry Bergh" (4); and Freeberg repeatedly demonstrates why this was so: "Bergh concluded that it was better to provoke the press's ridicule than to wither under its apathy" (15), leading to a "theatrical defense of animals" (26) that was often "so sweeping and provocative that he even surprised his followers" (5).

Freeberg offers a useful foil in two chapters chronicling a series of showdowns between Bergh and P. T. Barnum, allowing readers to recognize the anti-cruelty crusader as just as much the showman. But rather than money-getting, Bergh was fueled by indignation: "He was usually more outraged than sad, his contempt for cruel men providing an adrenaline surge that drove him in the work" (27). Freeberg aptly remarks that Bergh had a "keen nose for human sin" (142) and concludes several times that Bergh "hated human cruelty more than he loved dogs" and other animals (8, 82). This near-misanthropy led Bergh to curate a "museum" of instruments of human cruelty, to promote public floggings of those guilty of violence, and to call for the invention of a steam-powered corporal punishment machine (28–30).

Bergh's headline-grabbing antics and radical priorities are also contrasted with the tactics of notable contemporaries: George Angell of Boston and Caroline Earle White of Philadelphia. The comparison with Angell, "steadier, less inclined to provoke," shows an alternative approach of "moral persuasion" that led to prolific publication of propaganda materials (33). White's story, strategically woven throughout the narrative, allows Freeburg to explore the important complications layered onto this activism by Victorian notions of gender roles.

Freeberg has produced a fascinating and engaging study—it is highly recommended for scholars but also for undergraduate classrooms and general readers. Informative and entertaining, *A Traitor to His Species* provides a unique perspective on the Gilded Age city and a compelling contemplation of the relationships between humans and animals—in Bergh's time as well as our own.

Reviewed by Robert Chiles, University of Maryland. Chiles is a senior lecturer at the University of Maryland with a focus on U.S. politics and society from the Gilded Age to World War II. He is coeditor of the journal New York History *and author of* The Revolution of '28: Al Smith, American Progressivism, and the Coming of the New Deal *(Cornell University Press, 2018).*

Exhibitions for Social Justice

By Elena Gonzales. New York: Routledge, 2019. 212 pages, 6" × 9", 45 b&w illus. $128.00 cloth, $37.56 paperback, $37.56 e-book.

Elena Gonzales's *Exhibitions for Social Justice* is a valuable handbook on museums that mount exhibitions explicitly engaged with social justice. Not intending to rationalize the need for this kind of work, Gonzales instead seeks to provide support and evidence-based examples for people working in this field. By drawing a bit on neuroscience, Gonzales focuses on how best to engage viewers; what leaves the most lasting impression with them; and how that can lead to an array of impact and actions over time. Although the book was published in 2019, it remains as relevant as ever, as museums and their employees have grappled with their content, collections, and in some cases their very existence during the COVID-19 pandemic. Gonzales presents an optimistic take on the importance of museums, arguing that socially engaged work is both doable and meaningful.

A range of scholars and readers may find Gonzales's work compelling. The book is directed at people who study or work in museums, with worksheets and checklists at the back of the book. The introduction offers a useful engagement with literature in the field, but overall, the book is accessible and readable to practitioners with a range of backgrounds and training. It is also valuable to public historians and to historians who want to think about how the narratives they craft are received by broad audiences. That said, there is not much specific to New York history or institutions—other than a brief mention of the early iteration of the Museum of Chinese in America—as a deliberate choice on the author's part. Gonzales focuses on inland and international institutions, with Chicago museums (art museums, history museums, zoos, and aquariums) at the heart of the book. Still, the case studies, of which there are a lot, both speak to, and transcend, place and allow Gonzales to make the larger points that animate her work.

Chapter 1, "From Empathy to Solidarity," introduces foundational terminology for the book. As someone who has written about solidarity and social movements, I was fascinated to see this term being used in the museum context. Gonzales argues that before we reach solidarity between museum staff and visitors, we must work to propagate empathy in museums. To do that, we must challenge "groupness"—through bringing in those historically considered outsiders to museums or to a particular museum's community—and engage in hospitality. Hospitality initially sounded like a for-profit consumer model, but the example Gonzales gives, of the historic house museum Hull-House serving tea to visitors in what was activist and Hull-House founder Jane Addams's bedroom, makes a powerful case for the application of this concept (30).

The crux of the first chapter shows how exhibition content that emphasizes individual narratives can engender empathy. Gonzales gives several examples, but dwells on the children's exhibition at the Verzetsmuseum Amsterdam, dedicated to Dutch resistance to Nazi occupation during World War II. Gonzales discusses Holocaust museums throughout the book with admirable nuance, and here shows how the exhibition provides glimpses into Dutch experiences by physically building house-like structures for four people who were children during the war. She moves toward solidarity using her own experience as a curator on the show *Roots, Resistance, and Recognition: Who Are We Now?* (2006) at the National Museum of Mexican Art, which explored Mexican and African Americans solidarity in the United States and Mexico and created an institutional priority to extend solidarity to African American museum goers. She also shows how solidarity can function between institutions themselves, through networks such as the International Coalition of Sites of Conscience, which left me curious for more examples of employee and institutional solidarity and how that can shape content.

The second chapter argues that physical experiences, in addition to "resonant content," imparts visitors with lasting memories of their museum visits (58). In addition to touching on Stephen Greenblatt's classic essay "Resonance and Wonder" (1990), on the power of museum objects, Gonzales dips into brain science to explain what physical experiences may stick best with audiences; she then provides several examples of museum exhibitions that viewers may remember for their interactivity. Using a swing at the Jane Addams Hull-House Museum, sitting on a couch to view content, or learning dance moves from instructions on the floor all provide a useful reminder that this interactivity need not be digital.

The third chapter, "Inspiring Action," presents a range of ways exhibitions physically engage visitors with the goal of having them take concrete action. This could mean issuing an open call for people to knit welcome blankets for refugees that total the length of the border wall advocated for by Trump and displaying the growing stacks in a gallery before passing them along, as the Smart Museum at the University of Chicago did in 2017. It could also mean putting on an exhibition about colonization at the Museum of Anthropology at the University of British Columbia in Vancouver by centering living Native people and their stories rather than their objects, and by encouraging individuals and institutions to repatriate objects that they have found and taken (some actually did). Gonzales also provides anecdotes about a range of figures who have written about the long-term impact museums had on them in childhood and adulthood, including Oliver Sacks. Gonzales takes care to take a broad approach to what it means to take action, and with a gentle push to keep going, reminds the reader that this is a long game.

Chapter 4, "Welcome, Inclusion, and Sharing Authority," examines ways that museums involve stakeholders and visitors in creating exhibitions. This can comprise crowdsourcing labels, including oral histories of community members, convening working groups, and more. She also categorizes internal museum work that is not always known to the public, such as updating problematic labels, as part of decolonizing museums. Here would have been an interesting place to add more about other internal museum initiatives. During the pandemic and the anti-racist uprisings of 2020 (after the publication of this book), museums grappled with labor organizing, mobilizations around board member investments, and Diversity Equity Access Inclusion work (DEAI). In New York City, the Department of Cultural Affairs mandated DEAI analysis at institutions that are on city-owned land in 2019, prompting a range of internal processes that are still unfolding.

Given this extended moment of unexpected precarity and possibility for museums, Gonzales's book is as important as ever. During the pandemic in New York in 2020 and 2021, museums served as hospital storage sites, polling sites, and vaccination sites. How do we move forward while acknowledging this period of unprecedented loss, economic hardship, and for many and to varying degrees, trauma? *Exhibitions for Social Justice* gives examples of museums seeking to be more "hospitable, equitable, and sustainable" by addressing equity and redressing past inequity. The worksheets at the end of the book provide concrete steps for museum professionals; but as a whole, the book affirms the work of museums as trusted sites of learning and experience and serves less a call for complete reinvention than a gentle prod to keep going.

Reviewed by Sarah J. Seidman. Seidman is Puffin Foundation Curator of Social Activism at the Museum of the City of New York.

The Kidnapping Club: Wall Street, Slavery, and Resistance on the Eve of the Civil War

By Jonathan Daniel Wells. New York: Bold Type Books, 2020. 300 pages, 6" × 9". $30.00 cloth, $19.99 paperback, $17.99 e-book.

The Last Slave Ships: New York and the End of the Middle Passage

By John Harris. New Haven, CT: Yale University Press, 2020. 312 pages, 5 ½" × 8 ½", 21 b&w illus. $22.00 paperback, $30.00 e-book.

From Frederick Douglass and Harriet Tubman to Marcus Garvey and Malcolm X, the state of New York has a long history of serving as a home base for Black freedom fighters. However, despite its prohibition of slavery in 1827, New York City was never a stronghold of abolition or anti-racism. Historians have long explored the links between southern slavery, the urban north, and international markets. Two recent books advance this historiography by putting nineteenth century New York City at the center of stories of human trafficking, espionage, bribery, and transatlantic crime schemes. *The Kidnapping Club: Wall Street, Slavery, and Resistance on the Eve of the Civil War* by Jonathan Daniel Wells and *The Last Slave Ships: New York and the End of the Middle Passage* by John Harris work together to demonstrate the complex cooperation of northern capitalists, southern and Caribbean slavers, and transatlantic traffickers. In doing so, both books reveal the roots of structural oppression and lucrative ruthlessness in America's most dominant megalopolis.

In *The Kidnapping Club*, Wells draws from antebellum newspapers, court documents, maps, illustrations, and speeches to explain the ways in which New York City was indispensable in maintaining the southern slave regime that fed international markets with slave-produced raw materials. The author foregrounds the personal stories of Black New Yorkers who openly resisted a powerful slave trading syndicate that specialized in abducting African Americans and delivering them into the hands of southern enslavers. Wells also describes the ventures of New York's law enforcement officials, policy makers, judges, and brutal opportunists who made life difficult for African Americans before and after the Fugitive Slave Law of 1850. Rather than depicting New York's role in the domestic slave trading system abstractly, Wells directly indicts individuals and institutions involved in the corrupt practice of seizing and enslaving African Americans within the city. Wells identifies men like Governor William Marcy, City Recorder Richard Riker, and police officers Tobias Boudinot and Daniel Nash as part of a "reverse underground railroad" that carried Black people southward to the plantations that served as the U.S. economy's engine in the nineteenth century (20). The Black radical abolitionist David Ruggles, a central figure in Wells's narrative, invented the name "New York Kidnapping Club" to describe the "powerful and far-reaching collection of police officers, political authorities, judges, lawyers, and slave traders who terrorized the city's Black residents throughout the early nineteenth century" (9).

Aside from the threat of abduction into the world of chattel slavery, Black New Yorkers also experienced everyday indignities at the hands of racist local police and policy makers. Wells scatters several condensed biographies throughout the book to exemplify the daily distresses Black New Yorkers suffered as a result of systemic discrimination and mistreatment. For example, a prominent businessman named Thomas Downing was beaten for riding in the Whites-only car on the Harlem Railroad, and a jury refused to bring his assailants to justice. Segregation in public transportation would continue until Elizabeth Jennings, a Black woman from an influential abolitionist family, refused to sit in the "colored" railcar on her way to church. Her case led to the desegregation of New York City public transit and helped to begin the lengthy process of unraveling state-sanctioned racism in the city (228).

Readers will anxiously brace themselves as the details of abductions, escapes, and court judgments emerge. The author's glimmering prose offers readers the literary flair of a crime drama while highlighting the humanity of the historical actors—protagonists and antagonists alike. Although significant portions of the book bypass the direct topic of kidnapping, these portions are by no means tangential. For example, though certain sections of the book that address the illegal transatlantic slave trade in New York City do not fully adhere to the central theme of the metropolitan collective of kidnappers, these portions serve as an apt introduction to John Harris's more comprehensive work on the same subject. Moreover, every chapter works to illuminate the precariousness of Black freedom in the antebellum North. The author even caps his study with a call to action for modern reparations based on the evidence presented throughout his text.

In *The Last Slave Ships*, Harris fills in some of the gaps in Wells's narrative of New York City's centrality in the illegal transatlantic slave trade in the decades leading up to the Civil War. According to Harris, about one-third of all African captives crossed the Atlantic between 1800 and 1860, despite the United States' official closure of the transatlantic traffic in 1808. The lack of American enforcement of the slave trade prohibition was due to American administrators' being "more interested in facilitating commerce than suppressing the slave trade" (26). Lax enforcement on the docks and the high seas allowed the illegal slave trade to rely on American-built ships while enjoying the protection of the stars and stripes against British patrollers. After the United States. had proven its ability to resist British military might by winning independence, the American government maintained an unwillingness to concede to Britain's "right of search" for their vessels at sea. Aside from the United States' material contributions to the illegal slave trade, Harris highlights the New York capitalists who facilitated the profitable practice of human trafficking. The book focuses chiefly on "The Portuguese Company"—a collective of traffickers that conducted business in the merchant and shipping district of Lower Manhattan. Though the company's slave dealers came from all over the Atlantic world, they operated out of New York City because, by the mid-nineteenth century, it had become second only to London as a major hub of global trade. Legal trades in guns and powder with West African societies bolstered the illegal trade in captives because it gave shippers legitimate reasons to travel to slave-trading regions of the African coast. Similarly, legal trades with Brazil and Cuba for coffee and sugar kept American ships in their proximity as well. After examining the origins of New York's role in the illegal slave trade in the introduction and first two chapters of the book, Harris's evocative narrative intensifies in the second half.

A chapter titled "Aboard an Illegal American Slaver" offers one of the book's most somber highlights. Here, the author describes the ways in which the absence of legal regulation on slave ships led to riskier, less humane, but more profitable shipments of captives. Ship captains like James Smith of the slave ship *Julia Moulton* could remove shackles to pack upward of four hundred Africans (with ever-increasing numbers of children) on their sides. Captives like Cujdo Lewis—a source interviewed by the famous writer Zora Neale Hurston—suffered starvation, diseases, and longer confinement in African barracoons. Mortality rates were substantially higher than they had been during the period of legal slave trafficking. When American or British patrols intercepted the illegal slave ships, the British sent the captives to Sierra Leone or to West Indian colonies to serve as apprentices or indentured servants, while the Americans often sent captives to Liberia to earn their freedom as apprentices. Most Africans caught in the politics of slave trade suppression never returned home.

Chapter 4 focuses on the lives of antislavery spies like Edward Archibald and Emilio Sanchez, who used coded correspondences to sabotage shipments of captives across the Atlantic world. Under the pseudonym "South Street," Sanchez published the names of slave vessels and their owners in the *New York Evening Post* (178). Ultimately, the rise of the Republican Party, widespread resentment of the southern slaveocracy, and the advances of the abolitionist movement contributed to the decline of the domestic and transatlantic slave trade. Around the start of the Civil War, both the Union and Confederate states hoped to maintain their respective relationships with the British Empire by demonstrating their compliance with Atlantic slave trade suppression. Consequently, the United States acquiesced to British pressures for right of search and later entered into the Lyons-Seward Treaty with Great Britain to suppress the slave trade more completely.

Harris's historical narrative relies heavily on legal, economic, and social analyses of primary sources such as ship logs, diaries, political speeches, legal doctrine, commerce ledgers, and newspapers like the *New York Herald*. The result is an unimpeachably persuasive argument. Although only a fraction of African captives ever set foot in the United States,

Harris adeptly confirms the outsized contribution of New York capitalists and opportunists in maintaining slavery throughout the Western hemisphere.

Harris's and Wells's analyses fit neatly into the developing history of global capitalism while magnifying New York's place in the already rich field of Atlantic history. Despite many of the historical actors involved in the illicit trades going to great lengths to conceal their crimes, both books are replete with examples to support the authors' theses. Taken together, these two books show that New York City's economy, justice apparatus, and social hierarchy grew parasitically alongside the displacement, subjugation, and continued oppression of Black people. At the same time, the authors inform readers of the assiduous efforts by activists and insurgents like David Ruggles and Emilio Sanchez that undermined the intermingled systems of global capitalism and chattel slavery to bring an end to an era. New Yorkers may find particular value in reading the works of Harris and Wells as they trace the sobering history of scandalous slave trading and cruel capitalism along the familiar avenues of Lower Manhattan. Overall, the smooth readability both these works makes them not only remarkable within their scholastic genre but also ideal for anyone curious about slavery, capitalism, and the heritage of anti-Black racism in New York City.

Reviewed by Thomas B. Blakeslee, Harvard University. Blakeslee studies the social histories of the African Diaspora in the United States and Black resistance movements.

No Useless Mouth: Waging War and Fighting Hunger in the American Revolution

By Rachel B. Herrmann. Ithaca, NY: Cornell University Press, 2019. 308 pages, 6" × 9", 5 b&w illus. $27.95 paperback, open access e-book.

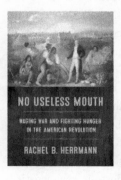

Rachel B. Herrmann's *No Useless Mouth* explores perceptions of hunger in the years preceding, during, and after the American Revolution. She provides us with a new understanding of hunger and power, specifically the power of Native Americans and the formerly enslaved. Herrmann pushes back against the traditional idea that the Revolutionary era was a time of declining power for both populations. She begins with a geographic focus on the United States while also taking an Atlantic approach to include experiences of hunger in Canadian Nova Scotia and African Sierra Leone. Herrmann "[takes] a long view of the revolutionary period" (5) beginning with the Seven Years' War and concluding with the 1810s to better incorporate the experiences of these groups.

Hermann argues that Native Americans actually gained power throughout the war due to conflicting white understandings of Native hunger and traditions. After the Revolution, Native Americans began to lose this power, and state and federal governments gained the upper hand. Herrmann has a different understanding of Black hunger. Her analysis covers the experiences of freemen, formerly enslaved, and the enslaved. These groups started out in a very limited position and gained a small amount of power due to the limited freedom of movement granted by the Dunmore Proclamation. Following the war, Black Loyalists who migrated to Sierra Leone and Nova Scotia experienced an initial increase in power, acquiring control over food prices and production, but they soon lost that power to government oversight and legislation.

Herrmann divides her book into three parts; Power Rising, Power in Flux, and Power Waning. These sections track changes in power and the characteristics of hunger practices that accompanied these transitions. To better follow the power dynamics, she introduces readers to three behaviors: food diplomacy, victual warfare, and victual imperialism. Food diplomacy is "the sharing of or collective abstention from [food]…to create or maintain alliances" (9). Both the British and the American military strategically provided food to Native Americans to cement military aid. Victual warfare "entails stealing, withholding, or destroying grain or animals…to create hunger, instability, and chaos" (10). The Sullivan-Clinton Campaign is a key example of victual warfare. The final behavior is victual imperialism, or "the use of hunger prevention policies…to seize land or to disrupt and transform trade" (10). To illustrate this behavior Herrmann includes information about federal land grabs and price fixing, particularly in Sierra Leone.

Those interested in New York history will find chapter 2 the most valuable. This chapter focuses primarily on British and American relationships with the Iroquois, particularly in relation to the destructive Sullivan-Clinton Campaign. Herrmann examines the consequences of the campaign on British forts. Displaced Iroquois sought refuge with British allies and expected to be fed by the British. The risk of not providing refuge was the loss of their Native allies, so the British complied with this expectation. The Iroquois were thus able to increase the food aid they received and the power they held in the sphere of food diplomacy. The book is full of other New York–centric contributions, including from the Genesee, Hudson, and Mohawk Valleys, as well as from Niagara, New York City, and the North Country. Herrmann opens with, and frequently revisits, an account of the Seneca leader, Cornplanter, being told a false history of Native hunger and European success by Timothy Pickering while in New York.

What is most impressive about this work is Herrmann's ability to utilize the available archives to tell the story of those who historically have been left out. She masterfully puts Native American and enslaved men and women front and center by reading between the lines of the archival records. She acknowledges that "times of confusion were difficult times to preserve accurate records of the past" (85), particularly when it comes to the demographic this book focuses on. Thanks to her reinterpretation, our understanding of hunger in the Revolutionary era is more than just a passing reference to the struggle at Valley Forge.

Reviewed by Lauren Lyons, New York State Museum. Lyons is Assistant to the New York State Historian and Coordinator of Museum Chartering for the Office of State History.

Resisting Independence: Popular Loyalism in the Revolutionary British Atlantic

By Brad A. Jones. Ithaca, NY: Cornell University Press, 2021. 314 pages, 6" × 9", 15 b&w illus., 1 map. $49.95 cloth, $32.99 e-book.

Significant scholarship exists covering the Patriots and their cause during the American Revolution. While this scholarship is important, it tells only part of the story. Much of the historiography's focus remains on the Patriots of the thirteen British North American colonies, providing much less insight on the Loyalist population within these colonies and on the rest of the British Atlantic. Brad A. Jones's monograph, *Resisting Independence: Popular Loyalism in the Revolutionary British Atlantic,* seeks to address this gap by expanding upon the research of historians who have looked at the role Loyalists played in the colonies and their experiences during the American Revolution and throughout the twenty-six British Atlantic colonies. Jones's work broadens the scope and understandings of the American Revolution and continues the narrative to consider the effects it had on colonies and citizens within the larger British Atlantic.

Focusing his study on four cities within the British Atlantic—New York, Halifax, Kingston, and Glasgow—Jones shines light on the conversations and sentiments within those cities before and during the American Revolution. Previous scholarship often focuses on the ideology and messages of the Patriots, which narrows the geographic focus to the thirteen North American British colonies and leaves the voices of Loyalists throughout the British Atlantic on the periphery. Jones brings those voices to the forefront, analyzing the politics behind their loyalty. Through his use of newspapers and letters, Jones shows how information and news of larger events spread throughout the British Atlantic. In doing so, he shows how Loyalist thought developed in places like Jamaica, where the idea of representation was similar to places like Philadelphia; but he also shows how the decision to stay loyal to the Crown was driven by the fear of slave revolts, making necessary British military protection. Similarly, in Halifax, despite concerns over funding and defense against the Mi'kmaq, Haligonians became tacit supporters of the Patriot cause. Local Haligonian leaders, however, attempted to suppress Patriot support by controlling the information that flowed into and out of the colony. Again, relying on newspapers, Jones shows how the policing of information in Halifax suppressed a rise in support for the Patriot cause and prevented both material and intellectual support from leaving Halifax. Local leaders in Glasgow were also far more concerned about their economic interests, particularly in places like the Chesapeake, and were thus more outwardly supportive of the Crown. By looking at print shops and the proliferation of pro-British news articles, Jones demonstrates how Glasgow's economic success took precedence over support for the Patriot cause. The print shops of New York City also proved to be a significant source for Jones, and he utilizes the work of prominent printers such as James Rivington. Rivington was an ardent Loyalist, and his paper spread throughout the British Atlantic, proliferating Loyalist sentiment and ideology out of New York.

A major strength of Jones's work is his ability to demonstrate how, despite having similar Whiggish ideals, Patriots and Loyalists ended up on opposite sides of the Revolutionary conflict. Similar to Linda Colley's *Britons*, which Jones cites, he shows how the development of British identity in the seventeenth and eighteenth centuries influenced the development of Patriot and Loyalist ideologies. The concept of creating a common identity through the construction of a common enemy put forth by Colley is reinforced by Jones's analysis of Loyalist and Patriot identity. On the one hand, Jones makes the claim that Loyalists reinforced their defense of their Britishness once the Catholic French became involved. On the other hand, he also shows how Patriots reinforced their identity as British through their opposition to Parliament's perceived assaults on British natural rights. Jones thus attempts to paint a comprehensive picture of how the two sides developed and interacted during the Revolution.

By using these four cities, Jones allows modern readers to see how the complex decisions by people in power and by average citizens alike influenced their support of either the Loyalist or Patriot causes. Jones's contribution to the historiography surrounding the American Revolution broadens the narrative to include new voices and perspectives, including Loyalists from throughout the British Atlantic. His work shows that it was not simple to choose whether to identify as a Patriot or a Loyalist, but that identities and loyalties were nuanced and went far beyond concepts of representation and repression. These decisions were, ultimately, tied to concerns over economics, defense, and competing understandings of British identity throughout the colonies.

Reviewed by Nicholas Truax, State University of New York, University at Albany. Truax is a PhD student focusing on eighteenth-century American history, economic history, and social class development.

Overcoming Niagara: Canals, Commerce, and Tourism in the Niagara–Great Lakes Borderland Region, 1792–1837

By Janet Dorothy Larkin. Albany: SUNY Press, 2019. 300 pages, 6" × 9". $95.00 cloth, $32.95 paper.

Janet Dorothy Larkin's *Overcoming Niagara* examines the impact of the Erie, Oswego, and Welland Canals on the economic, social, and cultural growth of the Niagara–Great Lakes borderland region during the late eighteenth and early nineteenth centuries. While a significant portion of Larkin's analysis is focused on the development of the canals as a method for overcoming the cataract of Niagara, the regional transnational cooperation that facilitated the planning, financing, and construction of each canal is addressed in this well-written and thoroughly researched book. The emergence of Niagara Falls as a tourist destination in the early nineteenth century is also well-covered and linked with the emergence of the transportation revolution of the canal age. Canal systems, Larkin argues, "promoted commerce, market development, tourism, and progress" for the Niagara–Great Lakes region and economically and culturally linked peoples from Upper Canada and Western New York (7).

Larkin begins with the development of the Niagara–Great Lakes borderland region during post–Revolutionary War period when settlers first migrated into Western New York and Upper Canada. Throughout the book, Larkin's focus centers around the impact of the canals and the broader market revolution "from a borderland and transnational perspective" (4). During this time, both Americans and Canadians used commerce, transportation, and tourism to overcome Niagara's barriers and develop an integrated, transnational network linking the two peoples together. The post–Revolutionary War construction of roads, bridges, and ferries, Larkin argues, improved access around Niagara Falls, which helped to forge cross-border social, commercial, and recreational ties.

Post–Revolutionary War disputes between the United States and Great Britain eventually led to the War of 1812, which is discussed throughout the early part of the book. Despite the passage of the Embargo Act of 1807 and the Non-Intercourse Act of 1809 (which effectively cut off trade between the United States and Great Britain), Larkin demonstrates how commerce and smuggling between Upper Canada and New York further strengthened regional ties during the lead-up to the war. Interestingly enough, the War of 1812 and the tensions between Britain and the former colonies also directly impacted the decision to construct the Erie Canal. To be sure, deliberations surrounding the viability of a canal linking the Hudson River with the Niagara region and also a canal traversing Niagara Falls originated in the 1790s, when New York State began investigating various canal scenarios to facilitate regional trade. Fears of competition with Montréal and the Saint Lawrence region heightened the need for internal improvements to open up the Mohawk River valley and connect it with Lake Ontario.

One of the many strengths of this book is Larkin's assessment of the deliberations over the construction of the Erie, Oswego, and Welland Canals. Each canal has its own chapter, and Larkin examines each canal from both the Canadian and American perspectives, weaving in personal stories, newspaper accounts, and legislative debates. The debate over the route of what eventually became the Erie Canal is covered in great detail, including accounts of the competing factions who supported a different route to link the Niagara region with the Hudson River. While Treasury Secretary Albert Gallatin, Canal Commissioner Peter Porter, and several western New York business interests supported the Ontario route (with canals at Oswego and around Niagara Falls), Governor De Witt Clinton ultimately sided with New York business leaders who pushed for an inland route, bypassing Lake Ontario altogether. The 363-mile-long "highway of commerce and navigation" was opened in 1825 with great fanfare; it linked the Atlantic with the Great Lakes and opened up the state's interior to commerce, settlement, and numerous social and economic changes.

Larkin's study does not end with the "wedding of the waters." While the Erie Canal ushered in a transportation revolution, Larkin gives plenty of attention to the Oswego and the Welland Canals, the latter which bypassed Niagara Falls through Canada and allowed larger vessels to travel through the region, connecting midwestern cities like Cleveland and Detroit with the Eastern Seaboard. Both canals utilized engineers and laborers from the Erie Canal. Canadians invested in the New York canals, and Americans provided most of the financing for the Welland Canal. Larkin breaks new ground here as many canal histories have overlooked the significance of both the Oswego and Welland Canals. Larkin also argues that the social and cultural reform movements of the 1830s, in particular the temperance and spiritual awakenings, were influenced in part by the migration of people into the region.

The last chapter examines the impact of the canals on tourism in the Niagara–Great Lakes borderland region. While most readers are familiar with Niagara Falls and its status as a tourist destination, Larkin acknowledges that while the canals transformed the cataracts into a "fashionable tourist resort" in the 1830s, scholars have overlooked their impact on the cross-border tourist experience (143). Larkin argues that the canals helped visitors overcome Niagara's natural and artificial barriers, which then also helped to make the region a "premier tourist destination" and strengthened the borderland economy and relations (144). The canals were also tourist attractions themselves, revolutionizing travel and popularizing the Northern Tour as a transnational experience. As visitors flocked to witness the spectacles at Niagara Falls, enjoy a barge tour, or see the Salina Salt Works near Syracuse, the canals helped to promoted cross-border commerce, friendship, and interdependence

Overcoming Niagara is an important book that addresses an often-overlooked part of New York State history. While hundreds of books have been written about the Erie Canal and Niagara Falls, very few have addressed the interconnection of the Niagara–Great Lakes region. Readers and scholars interested in New York history will find this study valuable and worthy of their attention.

Reviewed by Terry Hamblin, Professor of History, State University of New York, College at Delhi.

Dagger John: Archbishop John Hughes and the Making of Irish America

By John Loughery. Ithaca, NY: Three Hills, 2018. 407 pages, 6" × 9", 16 b&w illus., 1 map. $32.95 cloth, $15.99 e-book.

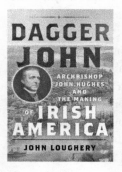

Biographer John Loughery has written an engaging and meticulously researched biography of a man who "wanted to be a cardinal, not a saint," and who had the personality to match his ambition. Forty years since Richard Shaw's famous work on the archbishop, Loughery received access to diocesan records that were previously available only to religious scholars, which has resulted in a richer understanding of the role of the church in American history. This biography not only traces the life and work of "Dagger" John but also shows the path his flock took during the tumultuous years of anti-Catholic and anti-Irish prejudice. Hughes's life ensured he interacted with most of the public figures of his day, and the biography details his many dealings with, and reactions to his many critics and his admirers. Among the former are Walt Whitman, James Gordon Bennett, and Horace Greeley; the latter include Henry Clay, Stephen Douglas, and Abraham Lincoln.

Loughery starts with John Hughes's early life, noting the isolation and prejudice the family experienced in Northern Ireland, which led to his father and older brother immigrating to the United States before being joined by the rest of the family. This prejudice continued in young Hughes's life as a groundskeeper in Mount St. Mary's Seminary in Emmitsburg, particularly at the hands of Father John Dubois, the rector. It is apparent that the sense of inadequacy the young man felt in his early days never quite left him and perhaps drove some of his obstinacy and determination in his later years. He spent much of his life battling his superiors in the church or unruly parish councils; anti-Catholic sentiment in Philadelphia and New York; and politicians who were quick to score points against the Catholic leader.

Hughes focused on three areas to ensure that his flock would be more welcomed in their new homeland—assimilation, education, and church building. He walked a fine line between encouraging his parishioners to retain some link with and pride in their ancestry, while urging them to become loyal and patriotic Americans, especially as the Civil War approached. While Hughes was initially sure that slavery would inevitably end without a war, once that was no longer likely, he strongly encouraged Catholic men to enlist in the Union army, and he carried on a significant correspondence with his unlikely friend William Seward, New York's Whig governor and later secretary of state. Seward shared Hughes's thoughts on politics and the military with Abraham Lincoln, and in fact, at Seward's urging, Hughes sailed to France to try to persuade Emperor Napoleon III to stay neutral in the war. Although the emperor remained evasive in their meetings, Hughes's diplomacy may have helped ensure France's refusal to recognize the Confederacy.

Perhaps because it had been true for himself, Hughes believed that education was the surest way to escape poverty, and he insisted that schools be built for the children of immigrants. He abhorred New York's public school system, believing it to be anti-Catholic, and he fundraised tirelessly to promote a parochial school system. He firmly believed that more and better schools, with properly trained, and perhaps sympathetic, teachers, would make the Irish more employable and allow Catholic Irish Americans to live a more prosperous but also a more faithful life. This was where his friendship with Seward was solidified as the then-governor supported Hughes in his unsuccessful efforts to secure public funding for parochial schools. Undaunted, he founded Fordham University, and his sister (a nun) founded the College of St. Vincent.

Hughes consecrated more than one hundred churches in New York State and New Jersey in his twenty-five years as head of the archdiocese. Many of the Great Hunger–era Irish were fundamentally not catechized, and he worked tirelessly to ensure that his flock attended mass and were properly instructed by clerics. He traveled to Europe several times, twice with Whig politician Thurlow Weed, to fundraise and to recruit personnel. He believed that a glorious new St. Patrick's Cathedral would not only serve as his greatest legacy but also allow his parishioners to feel pride in their own culture and identity. It is not surprising, perhaps, that he chose an Irish saint as its namesake—as much a nod to his own ethnic background as it may have been a final taunt to his old co-adjutor and the man who had first rejected him in the seminary, Father Dubois. The Irish were finally on top.

While the Civil War brought construction of the cathedral to a standstill, it also brought the largest crisis of "Dagger" John's career and almost ended his life. For so many years, he had defended the church and his parishioners from Nativist taunts and violence, but the violence of the Draft Riots in 1863 seemed certain to undo all the progress he thought had been made on behalf of Irish immigrants. The Irish were, once again, condemned as barbarians and as violent, not capable of becoming respectable American citizens. A feeble and almost incoherent archbishop made his final public appearance outside his residence where he pleaded with rioters to go home in peace.

When he died six months later, his funeral was one of the largest the city had seen.

Devotees and critics alike came together to acknowledge the former groundskeeper who had risen to the top of New York's powerful circles.

Loughery has a written a lively and balanced portrait of an ambitious, stubborn, and often unlikeable man. Hughes worked passionately for what he believed in and was a tireless advocate for his people. The symbol next to his signature might have been a crucifix, not a dagger, but Loughery's portrayal of "Dagger" John, depicts a complicated man who was not afraid to fight when it was called for, who defended immigrants against religious bigotry, and who believed in the promise of America.

Reviewed by Elizabeth Stack. Stack is Executive Director of the Irish American Heritage Museum in Albany. She joined the museum from Fordham University, where she taught Irish and Irish American History and was Associate Director of the Institute of Irish Studies. She completed her PhD at Fordham, writing about Irish and German immigrants in New York at the turn of the twentieth century.

Dogopolis: How Dogs and Humans Made Modern New York, London, and Paris

By Chris Pearson. Chicago: University of Chicago Press, 2021. 248 pages, 6" × 9", 21 b&w illus. $95.00 cloth, $24.00 paper, $23.99 e-book.

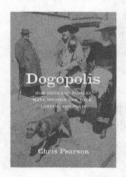

Writing in the June 2021 *American Historical Review*, Jessica Lang describes how for much of the twentieth century, historians neglected the history of animals, regarding them as merely "part of the background noise of daily life."[1] The first two decades of the twenty-first century, however, have seen animal history evolve into a "thriving academic enterprise" that takes seriously the ways in which animals have shaped American cities.[2] Scholars writing on New York have made significant contributions to this recent "animal turn," notably Catherine McNeur (*Taming Manhattan*, 2014), Lang herself (*Mad Dogs and Other New Yorkers*, 2019), and now Chris Pearson, with *Dogopolis*. Pearson's book is unique in that he situates New York's historical experience with dogs within a transnational framework that also includes Paris and London. In all three cities during the nineteenth and early twentieth centuries, the

---

1. Jessica Lang, Review of *Animal City: The Domestication of America,* by Andrew Robichaud, *American Historical Review* 126, no. 2 (June 2021), 726.
2. Lang, 726.

middle classes strove to create an urban environment where dogs and humans could coexist in a "civilized, healthy, and safe way" (2). This model for human-dog interaction is what Pearson calls "dogopolis."

Before the advent of dogopolis, stray dogs had been ubiquitous in Paris, London, and New York. For middle-class commentators, their presence represented the worst of modern cities, namely "disease, dirt, and disorder" (15). Rabid dogs, especially, were feared because their bites could spread one of the era's most terrifying diseases: rabies. So, to combat strays, the three cities enlisted policemen, dog catchers, and citizens to kill or impound them. Paris had the oldest official pound, dating from the late eighteenth century, and New York established their first pound in 1851.

Rabies fears eased toward the end of the century when the French scientist Louis Pasteur produced a viable vaccine in his Paris lab. Administered first to French dog-bite victims, the vaccine's reach quickly became transnational. In a widely reported case, a group of boys from Newark, New Jersey, having been attacked by a rabid dog, traveled to Pasteur's institute in December 1885. The boys survived, and upon their return home, they were exhibited at a Bowery dime museum, "allowing New Yorkers a firsthand encounter with Pasteur's miraculous treatment" (68). The New York Pasteur Institute, located on Central Park West, opened fewer than ten years later. Although Pasteur's treatment ultimately gained widespread support, it was not uncontroversial. Anti-vivisectionists in all three cities drew attention to the agony of the dogs that Pasteur experimented on, portraying the Pasteur Institutes as canine "torture chambers" (71).

The success of Pasteur's treatment did not entirely eliminate middle-class anxieties, however, and there remained a strong desire to see strays killed. Prior to Pasteur, whenever a loose dog exhibited signs of being rabid, citizens took matters into their own hands—which resulted in wild scenes of street fighting between working-class men, boys, and dogs. Urban authorities viewed such mob violence as a threat to public order. The preferred site for the culling of strays thus became the more respectable and less-visible pound. In the mid-nineteenth century, the Paris pound executed dogs by hanging, and in New York, the preferred method was drowning. As concerns over the suffering of animals emerged over the course of the nineteenth century, humanitarians deemed these methods "crude and retrograde" and sought more efficient and merciful ways to put dogs to sleep (89). London's Battersea Dogs' Home was the pioneer in this regard, installing a lethal chamber in 1884 that exposed dogs to chloroform and carbonic acid. The Paris and New York pounds soon followed suit, though they chose to use gas, which was cheaper than chloroform. Paris executed tens of thousands of dogs in 1892 alone and over a million and a half dogs were killed in New York between 1894 and 1908.

The destruction of undesirable dogs brings to mind eugenics. In his chapter on strays, Pearson highlights how scientific racism and pedigree dog breeding "fed off each other to admonish the mixing of races in humans and breeds in dogs" (33). I was expecting Pearson to also make connections between nineteenth-century experiments in animal execution and later Nazi methods of human extermination. Gas chambers used on animals bear a striking similarity to those developed during World War II. One wonders to what extent Nazis drew from the work of the humanitarians whom Pearson writes about.

While strays were ostracized from dogopolis, "thinking dogs" were embraced. First in Europe and then in the United States, police departments experimented with training dogs to "direct their biting instinct toward criminals" (118). In 1908, the New York Police Department began operating a canine unit in Flatbush, Brooklyn. Pearson describes these dogs as "participants in the policing of race in the Jim Crow era" (140). Pearson is probably correct in this regard but only provides one example of a dog used to track down a Black man. The history of police dogs and racial terror in the New York is a topic worth exploring in greater depth than Pearson does here.

With strays being killed in large numbers, the threat of rabies mostly contained, and the training of police dogs underway, a middle-class dogopolis was evolving. One pressing issue remained to be tackled: how to handle dog mess. Public health authorities, journalists, and reformist groups all led campaigns that frequently targeted the upper classes (instead of the working class), who were portrayed as negligent for letting their pet dogs defecate anywhere except for in their expensive homes. Of the three cities, New York passed the strictest sanitary code in 1918, which called for dog owners to ensure that their pets did not commit "any nuisance upon any sidewalk of any public street, avenue, park, public square, or place" (172). Notably, it never crossed anyone's mind to ask owners to pick up their dogs' excrement themselves. This came later with the introduction of New York's famous "poop scoop law" in 1978.

The book's coda takes the reader up to the present. New York is now home to numerous dog parks and a host of dog-sitting and dog-walking businesses. People continue to have strong feelings for lost dogs in shelters and animals subjected to testing in labs. However, neutering, instead of killing, has become the preferred method for limiting the urban dog population. "Dogopolis has changed," Pearson concludes, "but for better or worse, Western urbanites are still living within it" (181).

Reviewed by Eric C. Cimino. Cimino is Associate Professor and Chair of the History and Political Science Department, Molloy University, Rockville Centre, New York.

Thomas Cole's Refrain: The Paintings of Catskill Creek

By H. Daniel Peck. Ithaca, NY: Three Hills Press, 2019. 200 pages, 8" × 10", 93 color illus., 7 maps. $34.95 paperback.

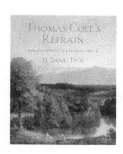

The Hudson River valley can be a study in contrasts, and like many contrasts there is often mutual dependence. In *Thomas Cole's Refrain: The Paintings of Catskill Creek*, author H. Daniel Peck offers a new way to look at Cole's work that captures the tensions in the American landscape during the Industrial Revolution and Cole's response to them. Peck's unique approach argues that Cole's ten paintings of Catskill Creek between 1827 and 1845 should be seen as a series, even though the artist did not explicitly conceive of them that way, contra the paintings of his series "The Course of Empire and The Voyage of Life." Thus, while no one painting illuminates Cole's complex feelings about Catskill Creek, when examined together, they are the best source of understanding the emotional impact of industrial change to the landscape that Cole cherished. Although published to accompany an exhibition, *Thomas Cole's Refrain* stands on its own as an important addition to scholarship on Cole, and it draws liberally on a wide variety of scholarly work to support the author's novel interpretation of paintings never before studied as a series.

Divided into five chapters, and with a prologue and epilogue, Peck moves chronologically through Cole's career. He provides a relevant background narrative to make connections between the ideas and motifs in Cole's work and to highlight important points in the artist's life. The prologue, titled "Catskill Creek and a Sense of Place," names its central theme, and through it Peck examines the notion of "contrast" in the natural, industrial, and painted landscape. There is the Hudson River itself, fed by numerous streams such as Catskill Creek, contending with the tidal forces of the Atlantic Ocean at the River's mouth that push deep into its length. The waters of the "river that flows both ways" move with breakneck speed compared to the geologic time of the Valley's landscape, that is, until the forces of nature met the forces of civilization—the most significant contrast that Peck explores. But even here there are contrasts within contrasts.

Just west of the village of Catskill, along its namesake creek, the English-born American transplant Thomas Cole found a place he could visit repeatedly and paint in different ways. First, Cole regularly altered his vantage point, as he had done in several versions of Kaaterskill Falls, which gives the paintings a verse-like quality, with the refrain the location itself. The author includes some clever, aerial-view maps that show Cole's various perspectives; Peck even included a few drone photographs for comparison. Second, there is repetition among the figures that Cole portrayed in each picture, though each figure's specific activities vary somewhat. And third, the paintings chronicle changes to the landscape with some subtle hints of industrial progress and others more overt, such as the addition of a railroad. For Peck, the Catskill Creek paintings are the most sustained sequence of landscapes Cole ever produced, and Peck suggests that the specific location reveals "universal concerns."

The natural landscape and the incursion of human activity presented a measure of ambiguity to Cole. In both painting and writing, Cole could express disdain and resignation as well as appreciation for the "hand of man" in a landscape where he often preferred the "hand of God." Writing was a significant part of Cole's life (if a picture is worth a thousand words, he often provided both), and Peck frequently quotes letters, journals, poetry, and essays to explain those deep-seated ambiguities. Peck interprets Cole's work through the language of the sublime, beautiful, and picturesque—the same language used by the artist and his contemporaries. Whisps of smoke from farmhouses and small mills along with small plots of cleared pasture in picturesque scenery (*View Near the Village of Catskill*, 1827) are favorable elements of progress to Cole, while the heaving smoke of a locomotive symbolized the needless destruction of nature's beauty (*River in the Catskills*, 1843). Whatever benefits might come from industry, the costs to picturesque beauty could be too steep.

Painting the human form did not come as naturally to Cole as did landscape, but each painting has figures that contribute to a narrative. Peck argues that they complicate, contradict, or even obfuscate the theme, because some of the faces are blank or turned away from the viewer. Additionally, the placement of fences and hedgerows separates rather than connects their activities. In the creek, the rowers or fishermen ply the crosscurrents either in the foreground or less perceptibly off to one side, while women, children, hunters, husbandmen, and animals round out the cast. In Peck's interpretation, the figures almost compete with the landscape to tell a story.

But not always. Several paintings have personal meaning for Cole. Peck indicates that Cole likely used his wife, Maria, as a model for *View on the Catskill—Early Autumn* (1836–37); and the man rowing vigorously to meet a woman coming down a hill in *Settler's Home in the Catskills*, could represent Cole's longing to return home—he worked on this painting in 1842 while on a second trip to Europe. The confluence of his personal and professional life makes the paintings a type of refuge from the social and industrial forces that threatened a landscape so close to his home in Catskill.

Thomas Cole's Refrain: The Paintings of Catskill Creek by H. Daniel Peck has a nice balance of scholarly thinking and concise history, and in it the author explores his subject the same way that Cole explored the Catskill Creek. Various vantage points over many years reveal that which changes and that which remains the same—a kind of serial, staged performance where we are never quite sure of the outcome. The Catskill Creek paintings resonate with that narrative and its locus holds the pictures together like the refrain of a song. From them, H. Daniel Peck gives us a welcome chapter in the study of Thomas Cole.

Reviewed by Anthony Anadio, State University of New York, University at Albany. Anadio is a cultural historian with an interest in art, architecture, music, and literature.

Co-conspirator for Justice: The Revolutionary Life of Dr. Alan Berkman

By Susan M. Reverby. Chapel Hill: University of North Carolina Press, 2020. 408 pages, 6 ⅛" × 9 ¼", 19 b&w illus. $32.50 cloth, $22.99 e-book.

What makes someone a revolutionary? And how is that label influenced by the historic moment? Thanks to the work of the 1619 Project, we are finally coming to grips with the results of the struggle of enslaved Africans seeking human rights and, ultimately, freedom in the New World. The Founding Fathers are considered to be revolutionary because they led the effort to overthrow English rule and cohere a democratic form of government. Militant abolitionist John Brown was a revolutionary who took up arms to overthrow the slave system in the mid-1800s. And then we arrive in the 1960s and 1970s, when the Black Freedom Struggle moved from nonviolent civil rights protest to become an armed Black liberation struggle, while at the same time, the United States was fighting a genocidal antiliberation war in Vietnam. It was a post–World War II moment, now some fifty years past, that still reverberates in today's definitional conflict between democratic rights for all and white supremacist authoritarianism.

In *Co-conspirator for Justice: The Revolutionary Life of Dr. Alan Berkman*, author Susan Reverby addresses the question of who is, or what makes someone, a *revolutionary*. Her book, published in 2020, tells the story of a New Yorker who grew up in Middletown, became a people's doctor, underground bomber, and political prisoner, who served nearly a decade in maximum security prisons before emerging to play a truly significant national and global role in the fight to overcome the deadly AIDS epidemic. Alan Berkman's story, along with that of his partner, Dr. Barbara Zeller, and other colleagues and comrades near and far, not only puts his life forward with the respect it deserves but provides important insights as we contemplate the coming stage in our nation's political development.

Reverby and Berkman knew each other as children, and as students at Cornell University. But their paths crossed dramatically in 1971. Both were living in New York City, Berkman in the last year of medical school, Reverby working for a left policy think tank. Black Panther Party leader Bobby Seale was on trial for murder in New Haven, Connecticut, and Alan wanted to know if Reverby would be willing to "take up arms if Bobby is convicted?"

Although a yes answer was unlikely at the time, it became moot when Seale was acquitted. But I know from personal experience that it was a question many were asking in those days as the police and government killings of Black revolutionary leaders escalated under orders from FBI head J. Edgar Hoover. For me, it was the police killing of admired colleague Fred Hampton in Chicago on December 4, 1969, that propelled me into the armed underground.

It is a benefit for readers that Reverby knew Berkman as she unfolds his story. Recognized by his family and classmates from his years growing up as the smartest kid around, she follows the course of his life with the care and analysis it deserves. Ultimately, the essence of his life's work is not so much revolution, in the sense of overthrowing a corrupt government, as fighting for a system of health care that provides for the poorest, least advantaged, and most oppressed among us. The story describes how Berkman, Zeller, and other medical radicals strove to provide high quality, unbiased health care while also confronting the white supremacist polices that they understood to be the foundation of the capitalist system.

But it was not enough to provide thoughtful health care. The system responsible had to be confronted, challenged, and changed. Much of Reverby's narrative describes this in detail. In October 1981, for example, following the Black Liberation Army–led robbery of a Brinks truck in Nanuet, New York, in which a Brinks Guard and two Nyack police officers were killed, Berkman was asked to treat Marilyn Buck in a Mt. Vernon safe house for wounds sustained during her escape from police capture. Subsequently working as part of the woman-led May 19th Communist Organization, Berkman participated more directly in unspecified armed activities. Along with several others, he was ultimately arrested, convicted, and jailed.

And then the narrative turns to Berkman's story of overcoming the lack of medical care in prison as he diagnoses his own cancer. In a Pennsylvania jail he met revered political prisoner Mumia Abu-Jamal, who became a guide and inspiration for how to do meaningful work as a person in prison. And this coincided with a new stage of personal struggle, focused on his fight to survive brutal prison conditions while facing a potentially fatal illness. With the support of family, friends, and political allies, he emerged nearly a decade later. There was much to sort out. Reverby spends time on the story of how his family was rebuilt, including relations with two daughters—Sarah and Harriet—and with Zeller and longtime companion Dana Biberman. Of particular note is the interaction with the daughters in a now-familiar discussion—at least to those who have listened to the podcast *Mother Country Radicals* (written and narrated by Zayd Ayers Dohrn)—which ends with a discussion among some of the generation of kids born underground about the impacts on them of their parents' risky political decisions.

Having survived cancer and prison, the final portion of the book is focused on how Berkman rebuilt his life and integrated his politics. He was welcomed shortly after his release at a public gathering of hundreds at a Manhattan school. His release was called a "miracle" by some. His lawyer Ron Kuby compared his prison ordeals to enduring "slavery's middle passage, the trail of tears, and the Holocaust." A Puerto Rican *independentista* credited him with saving lives in that movement. He was praised for demonstrating "revolutionary love" by the woman who held Malcolm X in her arms as he lay dying. But what was Berkman going to do next?

Guided by Zeller and her work in a community AIDS clinic, Alan made his way back into a medical practice. Recognizing society's response to the AIDS crisis as more about isolating those with the disease than about doing what was necessary for treatment and to stop the spread, his attention turned to Africa, where he saw the legacies of colonialism and racism as exacerbating the epidemic, especially for women and children. Over time, as his parole requirements relaxed, he was able to travel. Drawing on the political analysis that guided his life, he became both a leader in the United States and then globally, involved in crafting a meaningful response to the crisis. He eventually founded Health GAP, an AIDS response organization.

Berkman's and Zeller's work in the AIDS fight, while told in great detail by Reverby, is validated in *To End a Plague: America's Fight to Defeat AIDS in Africa,* an important new book by Emily Bass, released in late 2021. By 1994, Berkman had become a staff physician at the Highbridge Woodycrest Center, a residential health facility for people dealing with drug addiction and HIV. In 1998, Berkman and Zeller attended an International AIDS Conference in Geneva, Switzerland. Meeting under the slogan "Bridging the Gap," they came to understand that failures to address the AIDS/HIV crisis in the United States were also mirrored globally. Bass reports how, upon returning home, they began to partner with others to demand affordable medicine—a criticism of big pharma similar to those we hear today of the pharmaceutical industry's profit-focused response to the COVID pandemic—and meaningful global action by the Clinton administration. Health GAP and other militant groups went on to play a major national and international role. Their actions helped lead to the announcement in January 2003 by President George W. Bush that the United States would launch and fund a multimillion-dollar effort to confront AIDS in Africa. Acknowledging that nearly thirty million people in Africa, including some three million children under the age of fifteen, had the AIDS virus, while only 50,000 victims had access to existing drug treatment, the president pledged a major initiative that became known as the President's Emergency Plan for AIDS Relief (PEPFAR).

Several years earlier, Berkman had been a primary author of a Global Manifesto that laid out demands for governments, pharmaceutical companies, and world health bureaucracies: "We demand ACTION and not statistics and press releases," it said. Ultimately, according to Bass, "more than 5,000 scientists, researchers, activists, and public health professionals signed on to the *Durban Declaration.*"

As a doctor and a self-described dialectical materialist, Berkman had no illusions when his cancer subsequently reasserted itself. He saw the end coming. Asked why he never wrote a memoir of his life, he answered that he "enjoyed living it rather than writing about it." In her account, Reverby admires Berkman's choices "as it reflects a willingness to act on deeply held beliefs in the face of danger." She even compares Berkman to Che Guevara, who gave up his dream of being "a famous medical research scientist to instead be part of revolutionary struggle."

That is high praise for a kid from Middletown, New York

Reviewed by Jeff Jones. Jones is an environmental and climate justice activist and political strategist living in Upstate New York.

EXHIBIT REVIEWS

Black Experience in Saratoga County 1750–1950

Saratoga County History Center at Brookside Museum, Ballston Spa, NY

Temporary exhibit. February through November 2022

Exhibit team: Jim Richmond, Saratoga County History Roundtable; Kendall Hicks, Exalted Ruler, Frederick Allen Lodge No. 609; Lauren Roberts, Saratoga County Historian; Mary Ann Fitzgerald, Saratoga Springs City Historian; Lorie Wies, Saratoga Springs Public Library; Anne Clothier, Education Director, Brookside Museum

Through the combined efforts of the Saratoga County History Center and the Saratoga County Roundtable, the *Black Experience in Saratoga County 1750–1950* exhibit at the Brookside Museum in Ballston Spa, NY, opened to the public in February 2022. The purpose of the exbibit is to show the presence and activities of African Americans county-wide, beginning in the colonial period and ending just before the modern Civil Rights Movement. At the exhibition entrance visitors are informed that the exhibit "is not comprehensive, but rather snapshots of experiences shared by many people of color, designed to help us all better understand an important aspect of our complex American story." In this way, the exhibit shines light on interesting and important information about African American organizations and individuals who, for far too long, have been overlooked or easily dismissed in histories of the area. But at the same time, telling the story of the Black presence as a "shared" experience across such a long span of time lends to the traditional nostalgic trope that racism inevitably waned, which in turn obfuscates the presence, impact, and evolution of racial injustice that permeated Saratoga County in the post–Civil War period. Despite this, the exhibit showcases not only some of the achievements of African American residents in Saratoga County but also the remarkable research conducted to make the exhibition possible.

Overall, two hundred years of African American experiences are confined to several panels and a handful of feature boards and display cases in a decidedly small space. But the rarity of the documents, artifacts, and other objects that are featured in the exhibit deliver probing content that will appeal to a broad audience, regardless of education level or profession. Some of the earliest dated artifacts on display introduce vital information that allows the community at-large to begin to reckon with the history of enslavement in Saratoga County. Late-eighteenth and early-nineteenth-century newspaper clippings advertising the sale of enslaved African Americans, a bill of sale documenting the financial

Figure 1. View of the gallery for *Black Experiences in Saratoga County* during the exhibit opening. PHOTOGRAPH BY DAVE WAITE.

transaction of an enslaved woman and her infant purchased by a Clifton Park (lower Saratoga County) resident from an Albany County enslaver, and a Saratoga enslaver's inventory records documenting his ownership of four people and their financial value attest to the conflicting realities of white residents and enslaved people of African descent. These documents juxtapose the ideals of the American Revolution and the battles for independence in Saratoga with the institution of human bondage practiced before, during, and after the Revolution (until 1827, when slavery was abolished in New York). This irony is underscored further through the stories of featured figures, such as Agrippa Hull, who highlight the military participation of African American men (some who were free-born and others who were enslaved) who fought for both sides during the war to obtain their freedom, literally and figuratively.

A refreshing feature of the exhibit is that it does not make the Underground Railroad the central focus of free African American residents' lives before the Civil War. Instead, the occupations, involvements in legal proceedings, and economic pursuits of free African American residents are presented, encouraging visitors to appreciate the daily lives, aspirations, actions, concerns, and challenges of those men and women, some of whom assisted freedom seekers when periodically called upon to do so. This provides a strong historical context for visitors to better understand the way race trumped legal status during the

Figure 2. Visitors to the *Black Experiences in Saratoga County* exhibit at Saratoga County History Center during the exhibit opening. PHOTOGRAPH BY DAVE WAITE.

antebellum era, making for the kidnapping of free African Americans like Solomon Northup a constant threat and lucrative practice in the North.[1] (Northrup was kidnapped from Saratoga Springs in 1841 and spent twelve years in bondage before his rescue. His account of the experience, *Twelve Years a Slave: Narrative of Solomon Northrup*, was first published in 1855. A copy of the first edition is on display at the exhibit.)

A strong theme across the exhibit's two-hundred-year time span focuses on the military service of African American men. This steady drumbeat helps lift African American veterans out of the shadow cast by President Ulysses S. Grant's Wilton cottage by reminding visitors that African American men not only served in the American Revolution but also fought in the Civil War and World Wars I and II, as was the case of Captain Clarence Dart, a Tuskegee Airman, who passed away in 2012.

One of the best displays in the exhibit is of materials related to African American benevolent efforts in the early twentieth century. These fraternal orders and women's

1. Jonathan Daniel Wells, *The Kidnapping Club: Wall Street, Slavery, and Resistance on the Eve of the Civil War* (New York: Boyd Type Books, 2020); Richard Bell, *Stolen: Five Free Boys Kidnapped into Slavery and Their Astonishing Odyssey* (New York: 37 Ink, 2019).

auxiliaries, such as the Frederick Allen Lodge No. 699, the Mary A. Carter Temple No. 362, and others, were the bulwark of social reform and community self-help during the Jim Crow era. In addition to hosting lavish banquets and designing parades that demonstrated Black respectability at that time, these associations organized Black youth group activities and supported Black business, which provided the Spa City with African American performers and music during the Jazz Age. It is important to point out that history buffs and folks familiar with Myra B. Young Armstead's work, *Lord, Please Don't Take Me in August*, will find that the exhibit goes beyond the scope of her work by displaying more community facets and new discoveries since that book's publication.[2]

Since the items on exhibit do not speak directly to local-level racial injustice in the post–Civil War sections, and as the exhibit concludes on the eve of the modern Civil Rights Era, visitors should see Armstead's work or rely on a museum docent for that content.[3] And although the exhibit does not specifically speak to or connect with the recent racial justice movement in Saratoga County, it is worth a visit as it both lays the groundwork for future community conversations and supports the call for further inquiry into race relations and the African American experience in Saratoga County.

Reviewed by Jennifer J. Thompson Burns, Lecturer, Department of Africana Studies, State University of New York, University at Albany.

Crafted in Schenectady: The Building of a Community

Schenectady County Historical Society, Mabee Farm Historic Site, Rotterdam Junction, NY

Temporary exhibit. November 2021 through April 2023

Exhibit team: Susanna Fout, curator; and John Ackner, installation

---

Craft—in its most basic definition, the creation of objects by hand—has experienced a resurgence and revival of interest in the last decade. This has happened for many reasons, among them the desire to slow down and reconnect with the world, a need to combat the boredom of the early stages of the pandemic, a method for expressing political ideas, and

---

2. Myra B. Young Armstead, *Lord, Please Don't Take Me in August: African Americans in Newport and Saratoga Springs, 1870-1930* (Urbana: University of Illinois Press, 1999).
3. Armstead, 83–87, 109–13. At the Brookside Museum, Museum Docent Fred Sober Jr. provides a deeply insightful historical context for the entire exhibit, but especially for the period from 1900 to 1950.

Figure 1. A blacksmith's forge. COURTESY OF A PRIVATE COLLECTION; ON LOAN.
PHOTOGRAPH BY THE AUTHOR.

a means to support local people in our communities working under ethical circumstances.
The new exhibit, *Crafted in Schenectady: the Building of a Community*, at the Schenectady
County Historical Society's Mabee Farm Historic Site places our current craft obsession
within the context of the history of craft in Schenectady County, NY—who made it, who
used it, what materials they worked with, and what it meant against the growing tide of
factory-made goods.

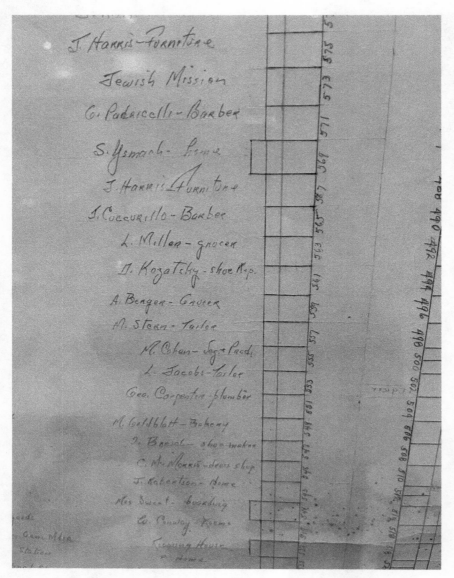

Figure 2. Detail of a map of Center Street, ca. 1912, hand drawn by Francis McCartin. COURTESY OF THE SCHENECTADY COUNTY HISTORICAL SOCIETY. PHOTOGRAPH BY THE AUTHOR.

The exhibit is organized thematically, although there is also a chronological progression of focus. The main text panels of the exhibition explore themes impacting craft—"landscape," "industry," "process," "community," "colonization," and "creativity." Each is treated across time, with local examples from Schenectady County from the eighteenth century to the present. The text refers to crafts that would have been vital to an eighteenth-century farm like the Mabee Farm, and one panel references a contemporary craft event held at the site, helping the visitor understand, "why this exhibition at this site?"

Artifacts presented in the exhibition comprise a mixture of finished goods—such as hats, shoes, furniture, textiles, and a sleigh—and tools used for making—such as a forge, a loom, and a carpenter's toolbox. A hands-on shelf also allows visitors to touch a variety of materials and to consider the difference between raw materials and processed materials and their roles in craft. With a focus on the big questions pertaining to the history of craft in the area, there is, of course, neither room to consider all the specifics of how each of the various tools is used nor to detail the processes for making different categories of craft. However, getting this glimpse into early crafts, many of which are not widely practiced to-day, leaves the viewer with many questions about the tools and techniques entailed in their use. One case, which displays a variety of hand tools used by diverse craftsmen, provides a short description of how each was used and asks the visitor to try to identify which is which. This was a great vehicle for promoting conversation and thought about form and function; but I also wish there had been some kind of a key, or even images of the tools in use to assist in this process. A hands-on station featuring a table-top loom allows the visitor to engage with the materials and process of weaving in the gallery.

One particularly effective artifact is a map of Center Street (now Broadway) in the city of Schenectady, drawn circa 1912 (see Figure 2). With its listing of individual businesses lo-cated along the street, the map invites viewers to think about "the communities and neigh-borhoods built around craft and trade." This provides the visitor with an invitation to delve into the type of archival evidence that historians use to put this type of exhibit together in the first place. For locals (and to anyone familiar with small upstate New York cities), it is an opportunity to think about the craftspeople and trades that once inhabited our commu-nities, and how our neighborhoods have changed over time.

Presented on text panels are several examples of craft in the present or recent past, which are very effective in allowing the visitor to connect with craft as they may know it. For example, in "community," which focuses on the development of the artisan middle class and the formation of trade fraternities in Schenectady, the story is carried to the pres-ent through craft-based communities online via social media, blogs, and YouTube. While the examples on the text panels include recent crafts, the artifacts displayed are all from the eighteenth and nineteenth centuries. Here, the story on the walls may have been better carried out through the inclusion of some later artifact examples as well.

In the final panel of the exhibition, the text focuses on a shift to the politicization of craft as well as its functions in fighting both shortages and boredom during the COVID-19 pandemic. Recent scholarship has focused on the ways in which the rise of "craftivism" is not altogether new but connected to a history of craft and politics together, especially in the realms of traditional women's crafts (textile work, knitting, cross-stitch, etc.).[1] This through

---

1. Some helpful and related glimpses into this history can be found in Hinda Mandell, ed., *Crafting Dissent: Handicraft as Protest from the American Revolution to the Pussyhats* (London: Rowman & Littlefield, 2019).

line of craft and politics is not apparent in this exhibition. Additionally, a euphemistic reference to the pussyhat, a national example of the use of "craftivism," as "those knitted pink hats of the 2017 Women's March in Washington, D.C." seems disingenuous in an exhibition that otherwise does not shy away from language relevant to craft and its associations with "thorny" issues, including hand work by enslaved people and the impacts of colonization on indigenous crafts. By not using the name "pussyhat," the object loses its original context and meaning.

The following quote is almost hidden on an object label within a case, close to the end of the exhibit, but it eloquently wraps up the considerations of the curator: "Craft is a language of material, provenance and making. It is learning the value of things and understanding how the world is connected. Manual skill, artistic sense, curiosity, and experience are important factors for craftspeople." Even for those who are not local, this exhibit serves as a jumping-off point to think about craft in the history of our communities—where examples can be found, how it has changed over time, and how examples from today are linked to the past.

It is important to note that the exhibit is located in the Franchere Education Center at the Mabee Farm Historic Site, which is located on State Highway 5S in Rotterdam Junction, NY. Hours of the Mabee Farm differ from those at the historical society's main building in the Stockade District of Schenectady. The website (https://www.schenectadyhistorical .org) and Facebook pages (https://www.facebook.com/schenectadyhistorical and https:// www.facebook.com/mabeefarm) provide additional information and an overview of the exhibition.

Reviewed by Ashley Hopkins-Benton, Senior Historian for Social History, New York State Museum, Albany.

ALBANY INSTITUTE
OF HISTORY & ART

Remember New York State Revolutionary War Patriots

Commemorate your community's Revolutionary War Patriots with a fully funded roadside marker from the Patriot Burials™ grant program. This is your opportunity to recognize those who fought in or were involved in the struggle for American Independence.

Marker grants are available to Sons of the American Revolution (SAR) chapters. Interested in obtaining a Patriot Burials marker, but not part of the SAR? Contact us or your local SAR chapter about applying on your behalf.

FINDING CENTER
Access, Inclusion, Participation, and Engagement

MUSEUM ASSOCIATION
OF NEW YORK

April 15 - 18, 2023
Syracuse, NY

SAVE THE DATE
2023 Annual Conference

Call for Proposals closes Nov. 14, 2022

Awards of Distinction nominations close Nov. 30, 2022

Conference Scholarship applications close Dec. 2, 2022

Conference Registration opens Jan. 23, 2023

Learn more at nysmuseums.org/annualconference
#MANY2023

OLMSTED'S ELMWOOD

The Rise, Decline and Renewal of Buffalo's Parkway Neighborhood

A Model for America's Cities

CLINTON E. BROWN, FAIA AND RAMONA PANDO WHITAKER

"A well-researched and engaging journey to uncover how and why Buffalo's Elmwood District developed, persisted, and thrived for hundreds of years with the end goal of prescribing its continued renewal. This wonderful record of the architectural and cultural history of an iconic neighborhood is a must for lovers of city planning as it exposes the universal patterns and extraordinary heritage of the places that surround us."

~ Ashley Wilson, FAIA, ASID
Historic Preservation Architect, Fellow of the American Institute of Architects and former chair of its Historic Resources Committee, and Graham Gund Architect, Emeritus, National Trust for Historic Preservation

OLMSTED'S ELMWOOD

The Rise, Decline and Renewal of Buffalo's Parkway Neighborhood

By Clinton Brown, FAIA and Ramona Pando Whitaker

Publication date: November 1, 2022
Trim: 10.75" x 8.75"
Page Count: 282 pages, with Endnotes and Index
ISBNs: 978-1-942483-37-3 (softcover)
　　　　978-1-942483-38-0 (hardcover)
　　　　978-1-942483-39-7 (eBook)

http://tinyurl.com/olmstedselmwood

Available via all book wholesalers and distributors.

CITY LIGHT